The Well-Tempered Critic:

ROBERTSON DAVIES

The Well-Tempered Critic:

One Man's View of Theatre and Letters in Canada

Edited by Judith Skelton Grant

McClelland and Stewart

Grateful acknowledgement is made to the newspapers and periodicals that originally published these articles for permission to reproduce them in this book.

"Party of One: The Northern Muse" reprinted from *Holiday* magazine, now published by Travel Magazine Inc., Floral Park, New York. 11001

"A Dialogue on the State of Theatre in Canada" reproduced by permission of the Minister of Supply and Services Canada.

The Canadian Publishers
McClelland and Stewart Limited
25 Hollinger Road, Toronto
M4B 3G2

CANADIAN CATALOGUING IN PUBLICATION DATA

Davies, Robertson, 1913-
    The well-tempered critic

ISBN 0-7710-2567-X

1. Canadian literature (English) – 20th century –
History and criticism – Addresses, essays, lectures.*
2. Theater – Canada – History – 20th century –
Addresses, essays, lectures.   I. Grant, Judith
Skelton, 1941-   II. Title.

PS8507.A95A16 1981   C814'.54   C81-094257-7
PR9199.3.D3A16 1981

Printed and bound in the United States of America

Table of Contents

II LETTERS

Acknowledgements

I would like to thank Ann Saddlemyer of Victoria College for reading the "Theatre" section when it was twice its present length with an eye to suggesting what to cut and what to keep. Moira Whalon, Robertson Davies' secretary at Massey College, kindly produced several items from her files which had vanished from local libraries. The E.J. Pratt Library at Victoria College, the Metropolitan Toronto Public Library, the National Library of Canada, and the John P. Robarts Research Library at the University of Toronto were all most helpful in giving me access to the microfilms of newspapers to which Davies contributed.

J.S.G.

Introduction

Five previous books have already been drawn from Robertson Davies' forty years of journalism. Yet those volumes only hint at his output. He was editor of the *Peterborough Examiner* for twenty years, literary editor of *Saturday Night* in the early forties and again in the fifties, a columnist for the *Toronto Star* for three and a half years, and a freelance writer of several hundred articles in many other periodicals. It is not surprising that many excellent pieces remain uncollected, but it is surprising that none of the collections focuses on Davies' overriding concern as a journalist – that arts and letters should be taken seriously in Canada.

At the beginning of his career, he covered an astonishingly wide gamut. Ballet, painting, architecture, drama, opera, sculpture, history, cinema, puppets, bands, mime – all drew vigorous comment. But the two subjects that commanded much of Davies' energies for the next four decades already preponderated – theatre and literature. He brought to them academic learning, practical experience, and infectious delight. His journalism helped shape opinion and events at the time; now, it provides a fascinating record of those forty years of Canada's cultural evolution.

This volume selects some significant and typical Davies observations on Canadian theatre and letters. I have separated the two because each subject proved to have its own rhythms and patterns. Both sections are arranged chronologically.

To his articles and columns on the theatre, Davies brought wide personal experience. He had become a keen theatre-goer by the time he was in high school. At Oxford his area of specialization was drama. His fine thesis, *Shakespeare's Boy Actors*, was published in 1939. After Oxford, he joined the Old Vic Company for two seasons as assistant stage manager, research assistant, teacher of theatre history, and bit actor. He returned to Canada in 1940, and began to write the plays that first established his name. These plays received many productions in the late forties and early fifties when the Little Theatre movement resumed activity after the war. He also put a great deal of energy into the Peterborough Little Theatre, where he directed plays from 1947 to 1953. In the fifties he wrote three plays for Toronto's Crest Theatre. During the fifties, too, he was an important figure in the Stratford Festival. He served on the festival's board for its first nineteen years, documented its early productions in three books, adapted Ben Jonson's *Bartholomew Fair* and created the "Lost Scenes" from *The Merry Wives of Windsor* for its use, contributed many pieces to its annual Souvenir Program, and addressed the Stratford Drama Seminar three times. During the sixties and seventies, of course, he had turned professor, teaching courses in drama at the University of Toronto. And in the seventies he again wrote plays, once for television and twice for the stage.

As a result of this involvement, his theatre commentary naturally reflects different interests than that of a more typical critic. A consistent element in his theatre criticism is the attempt to lay bare the historical background of current productions. He frequently recalls and re-examines his own early theatrical experiences as a device for providing this richer background. Davies is a maker of notebooks, a keeper of diaries, and a compiler of scrapbooks, and this undoubtedly sharpens his memory. I have begun the "Theatre" section with a typical column from 1940, in which Davies, surveying the theatre fare available in those early war years, relates it to the music-hall tradition. The section ends with *A Stage in Our Past* (1969) which surveys theatre in Canada from the 1790s to 1914, and "Touring Fare in Canada 1920-35" (1979) which reminisces about his earliest theatre-going years. Though this last piece takes a leisurely pace, it is the recollection of a man deeply read in theatre history, highly knowledgeable in shifts in technique and style – and very conscious of the public's misconceptions about Canada's early theatre. He argues convincingly, for instance, that Canada owes a great deal to the imported theatre that dominated her stages through the opening decades of this century. He also argues vividly for the values of melodrama and stylized acting. (What he says about melodrama here fascinates as argument, but in passing I might note that when he allows his fascination with flamboyant melodrama to direct his own play-writing efforts, it tends to produce some uncomfortable moments.)

These pieces frame selections on three subjects – Little Theatre, the historical development of theatre in Canada, and the Stratford Festival. Possibly because Davies was himself deeply involved in the revival of Little Theatre as a writer and director, he refrained from direct criticism in his commentary on the movement. In fact, he was so cautious about the subject that he wrote his Little Theatre columns as his *alter ego* Samuel Marchbanks. Marchbanks, who began life in 1940 as a pseudonymous reviewer of books and the arts, had flowered into a vibrant, crusty bachelor, whose tongue-in-cheek, razor-edged columns on the Canadian scene attracted a wide readership in some ten newspapers between 1943 and 1953. Marchbanks annually "attended" the Eastern Ontario Dominion Drama Festival and the Ontario finals (when Davies' efforts were successful), and occasionally went to the national finals. But, as the samples included here reveal, Marchbanks focused not on the plays, the acting, or the direction, but rather hurled his darts at the conditions and attitudes that impeded the success of all theatrical efforts in Canada. As long as Canadians failed to take theatre seriously, housed it miserably, and accepted laughable translations of plays in the other national language, the theatre could not flourish. Marchbanks attacked the issues with wit and irony. Here he is in 1948: "Attended a play which I had written myself, and at the end of Act One two women hurried past me, making for the door. 'I don't care what happens, those pickles have got to be done tonight,' said the larger and more determined one. It is incidents such as this which keep authors from getting swelled heads."

Davies' desire that theatre become a significant part of Canadian cultural life prompted him to speculate about ways of stimulating indigenous theatre. Several of his ruminations proved prophetic. In a 1944 column he urged the CBC to train Canadian actors and playwrights. And writing in 1951 for the Dominion Drama Festival's publication *Theatre Canada*, he argued that Canada should import directors like John Gielgud and Tyrone Guthrie, there being no Canadian directors of distinction. When the Stratford Festival opened in 1953, its Canadian actors had gained much of their experience on CBC radio, and of course its first director was Tyrone Guthrie.

Davies' most comprehensive examination of the state of Canadian theatre was his 1951 submission to the Massey Royal Commission on National Development in the Arts, Letters, and Sciences. Here, in a witty dialogue he commented at length on imported culture, audience expectation, radio and amateur drama productions, theatre buildings, and drama criticism, and urged several kinds of government intervention to hasten development. In retrospect, the timing of this submission is fortunate, because it provides us with an overview of the state of Canadian theatre just before the Stratford Festival transformed the scene. His specific recommendations were not followed, but he helped expose the limitations of current theatre; by arguing for the potential value of a professional theatre company producing the classics, Davies helped prepare the ground for public funding of Stratford. In his submission he once more emphasized the value of "living tradition" in the theatre, writing from the conviction which prompted his recurrent recollections and explorations of past productions. He declared, too, that "One of the principal tasks of every good critic of the theatre is to memorialize great performances and events in its history; part of his genius is to know when these events occur, for they are not always obvious." Davies himself undertook to "memorialize" the early days of the Stratford Festival.

From its inception in 1952 he threw his energies behind the festival. As well as making the practical contributions to the theatre's success noted earlier, he was a continuous commentator and critic, reviewing Stratford's productions every year but one from 1953 through 1967. Unlike the other regular reviewers of Stratford – such as Herbert Whittaker of the Toronto *Globe and Mail*, Nathan Cohen of the *Toronto Star*, Sydney Johnson of the Montreal *Star*, Brooks Atkinson of the *New York Times*, and Walter Kerr of the *New York Herald Tribune* – Davies had not been making his living from theatre criticism. He had reviewed plays only occasionally in the early forties for *Saturday Night*. But his journalistic experience, his academic training, and his addiction to Shakespeare served him well. His best reviews set Stratford productions against the long sweep of theatre history. They share the delight of an enthusiast reliving the magic of savoured experience. Moreover, writing for *Saturday Night* and for his own paper the *Peterborough Examiner* he had immense advantages of time and space. Davies could develop and support his ideas about the play and the production at hand very fully, and draw the disparate elements of a first night experience into a cohesive review. The unity and balance of his Stratford commentary contrasts with the briefer and necessarily less leisured copy of the other reviewers.

Nonetheless, Nathan Cohen's frequently acerbic assessments of Stratford in the *Toronto Star* provide a useful perspective on Davies' own limitations as a critic. Davies was too aware of the theatrical dearth preceding Stratford, too conscious of the strides being made by this large scale professional production providing a forum and stimulus for local talent, to feel free to mount an out-and-out attack on a weak, or frankly bad, production. His decision to be supportive inhibits the flow of his energy in reviews of lacklustre productions, and robs us of the quicksilver that could have sparkled from a less-committed pen. On the other hand it is also Cohen who illuminates Davies' particular value as a critic. Cohen wrote two lengthy assessments of Stratford for *Queen's Quarterly* – one in Autumn 1955, exposing Tyrone Guthrie's limitations, and the other in Spring 1968, assessing the festival's accomplishments briefly and its deficiencies at length. By comparison, Davies' thoughtful 1951 discussion of Tyrone Guthrie's direction, his 1953 reviews, and his 1963 tribute redress the balance – clarifying what made Guthrie one of the handful of great directors of our time and more fairly assessing Guthrie's importance for Canadians in those first years of the festival. In fact, the two critics' responses are complementary: Cohen attacks everything, from the constraints imposed by the stage to deficiencies in the company's acting and the selection of plays; Davies establishes the real gains made from season to season, from the creation of an innovative stage for Shakespearean production, through improvements in acting and the gradual fulfilment of Stratford's promise to become a classical theatre.

To his writing on letters in Canada, Davies brought as much "inside" experience as he did to his theatrical commentary. He was editor of the *Peterborough Examiner* from 1942 to 1962 (and publisher for another five years), and he made the *Examiner* one of the most frequently quoted papers in Canada. From 1940 to 1942 and from 1953 to 1959, he wrote the lead book reviews for the weekly (after mid-1955 biweekly) *Saturday Night*. From 1940 to 1953 he reviewed for the *Peterborough Examiner*, at first as Samuel Marchbanks,* but from 1948 over his own initials. His column for the *Toronto Star* syndicate, *A Writer's Diary*, which appeared on Saturdays from 1959 to 1962, frequently reviewed books. In addition he did (and still does) occasional freelance reviewing. Davies also, of course, is a writer of fiction. His creation of Marchbanks in the forties was followed in the fifties by the novels of the Salterton trilogy: *Tempest-Tost, Leaven of Malice*, and *A Mixture of Frailties*, and in the seventies by the widely acclaimed Deptford trilogy: *Fifth Business, The Manticore*, and *World of Wonders*.

Davies' critical output spans an astonishing range. He "was there" and responding to almost every Canadian literary work of significance in the forties, and he continued to tackle an amazing number (considering his other activities) in succeeding decades. Fiction drew the bulk of his attention, but he also reviewed poetry, criticism, biography, reference works, and humour. Usually he felt it a waste of time to discuss a book he did not like, so his response to those he did review was typically generous. He responded to felicitous style, to effective story-telling, to bright imagination, to strong characterization, and could admire any one of these even in the absence of the others. Although he was positive, however, he did not fail to make distinctions. His reviews are witty and enjoyable in themselves, but they also picked the winners. A list of the books he regarded as significant when they first appeared reads now like the syllabus for a course in Canadian literature.

One of the features of his commentary is a series of portraits of important literary figures. Often these pieces appeared on an anniversary, or marked the death of the individual concerned. For Davies it was natural and appropriate to mark such occasions by defining the quality of their genius and celebrating their contribution to the growth of culture in Canada.

*These columns were distinct from Marchbanks' diary. The diary appeared on Saturdays and the reviews mid week.

Sometimes Davies assumed a whimsical tone. Originally titled "Cap and Bells," Samuel Marchbanks' columns often jested with matters of high seriousness. In this collection, the review written at the publication of Marchbanks' *Diary*, the stories establishing the heroic stature of several well-known Canadians, and the explanation of the thinness of Canadian poetry (written in 1947 and 1950) exemplify many light-hearted – but ultimately serious – columns on national cultural problems.

Davies' conception of the potential cultural framework of the country was for long considerably broader than that entertained by the general public. He constantly urged his readers to adopt a more challenging conception of letters. Three reviews from 1953, when he returned to *Saturday Night* as literary editor, are concentrated doses of a kind of didacticism that recurs again and again in his writing for Canadians. His technique was a mixture of shaming and exhortation. For example, he used statistics to demonstrate how far Canadians fell behind people in other Western countries as readers and buyers of books; he then persuasively extolled the delights of creating a personal library. In a second article he berated academics for producing only serious scholarly works instead of satisfying the needs of the "Intelligent General Reader." Although he appeared to be addressing academics, he was actually intent on encouraging the I.G.R. to expand his reading range. In my opinion he generally managed to achieve his ends without sacrificing readability. He is almost always genial, urbane, and genuinely pleasurable to read.

Every few years from 1950 onwards, Davies had occasion to write an overview of the state of Canadian literature. These articles now constitute an invaluable retrospective collection. I have included five of the ten he wrote. (Those omitted were written in 1953, 1958, 1959, 1960, and 1971; they are listed in the bibliography of Davies' work soon to be published in E.C.W. Press' *The Annotated Bibliography of Canada's Major Authors*.) In such pieces, Davies' realistic awareness of the relative youth of Canada's literature and of the difficulties impeding its development provided the basis for a sensible evaluation of accomplishments.

These assessments do more than remind us of stages in our past, however. In them Davies examined Canadians' distrust of the power of art and charted a gradual shift to a more receptive attitude. In 1950 he expressed the opinion that Canadians "have been to America as Scotland is to England, or as Scandinavia is to Europe – the dour, worthy, crafty men of the North who fear the joyous arts and demand of the magnificent creatures that they should be respectable and improving." Distrustful Canadians had diminished the splendours of the arts to those elements which were moral and educational. (Consider what happens to painting and music in *As for Me and My House*, for example.) By 1964 Davies saw a significant change. In his view Canada now, somewhat naively, wanted "to win distinction in the arts," but without realizing how disturbing the arts at full power would be. Yet he saw some hope lurking in the depths of the Canadian psyche. For him, Douglas LePan's description of the *coureur de bois* as "Wild Hamlet with the features of Horatio" was "profoundly true of Canadians as a people. It is psychologically impossible for any people to live forever without some communion with those deeps of the spirit which nourish other countries – even countries as comparatively young as the United States – and which reveal themselves in national mythologies. But this is what Canada has attempted to do, and now the pretence that we have no ghosts, no unconscious, is wearing thin. The features of Horatio we may bear, but the Hamlet-like division of spirit asserts itself increasingly . . ." In 1967, attitudes, in Davies' view, had shifted little. Canadians still yearned to win distinction in the arts; yet they did not welcome literary probing of local subjects. In this article he portrayed Canada as a country which historically had elected the role of the daughter who chose to stay at home with mother. Now she would like a more attractive role, had made a few tentative gestures, but had not initiated the necessary soul searching. Davies urged that our literature, which had long been wrestling with complexities of the national psyche, be read more seriously. And he predicted that this country will "for a considerable period" have "a literature of introspection, and much of it will certainly give pain to those who dislike self-analysis. But analysis it will be, if we are ever to see ourselves plainly and discover what we are." The 1975 article returned to the yearning for excellence in the arts and the unwillingness to engage fully in a vibrant culture that Davies saw as typical of the current scene. He did not yet see a widespread embrace of the arts, but he did see occasional hopeful signs.

Once he was freed in 1962 from the treadmill of regular book reviewing, Davies had time to prepare overviews of particular writers' works. I have included articles of this sort on both Leacock and Mavis Gallant, but I will focus here on Leacock because of Davies' special affection for this earlier writer. Davies gave more time to Leacock than to any other Canadian writer, referring to him frequently in editorials, columns, and reviews during the forties and fifties, and writing seven articles, a short book, and at least one speech on him by 1971. Samuel Marchbanks and the Salterton novels (one of which won the Leacock Award for Humour) clearly owe something to Leacock's work. But the precise nature of Davies' debt will be determined only by carefully examining his many analyses of Leacock and by comparing Leacock's work with Davies' early fiction. This will be a complex, fascinating exercise since Davies' reaction to Leacock is anything but straightforward. Ordinarily a yea-sayer, Davies spent a surprising amount of time on Leacock's defects, and even his praise is left-handed. Look at the negative tone of his discussion of Leacock's "greatest strength" – his gift for language – on page 259. Obviously, a research project lurks here, but it lies well beyond the province of this introduction.

The record Davies inadvertently created through his forty years of passionate involvement in theatre and writing in Canada is many-splendoured. The collection is full of quotable nuggets and pithy ruminations that will long stimulate readers and students of Canadian drama and literature. Davies himself never thought of making a collection such as this, because he felt that the pieces were too much the ephemeral products of their time. What he did not realize is that that very reflection of earlier attitudes is the stuff of literary history and that frequently his grapplings with Canadian culture produced insights of continuing relevance.

Judith Skelton Grant

I

THEATRE

Looking Backward: 1940

The theatre in Canada has been very quiet since the Depression of 1929; it might almost be said that there has been no theatre here except in Montreal and Toronto. These towns have had fairly active theatres, visited by companies from England and the United States, and residents of Eastern Canada have had to make the journey to one or the other if they wanted to do any theatre-going. Recent experiments with road companies in the States have been very encouraging, however, and actors of the first importance, such as the Lunts and Katherine Cornell, have toured with brilliant artistic and financial success. Now it appears that we are due for a revival of theatrical touring in this country, and the first attempt will shortly be made by Francis Lederer, the well-known stage and screen star, whom many readers will have seen in the excellent movie, *I Married A Nazi*. Mr. Lederer is now rehearsing a company in New York which he will bring to the Royal Alexandra Theatre in Toronto next week after which he will go to Hamilton, Kitchener, Brantford, London, Ottawa, and Montreal. This fairly comprehensive tour of Ontario may be followed by a tour of the West.

Since the demolition of the old Grand Opera House in Toronto, scene of triumphs by Irving, Ellen Terry, Mansfield, Sothern and Marlowe, Sarah Bernhardt, Mantell, and many others, the Royal Alexandra must rank as Canada's finest and most exciting theatre. It is decorated in the good old theatre tradition of red upholstery and gilt ornament, which make a theatre the most entrancing place in the world. Some theatre-goers will regret the concession to modernity which led to the removal of the pictures of Forbes-Robertson and Martin-Harvey from the foyer, the former aloof in frock-coated dignity, the latter glowering in the robes of Richard III. The Royal Alex has the true air of a theatre about it, an air which no movie house can ever hope to catch.

For his touring play Mr. Lederer has chosen a previous success of his, *Autumn Crocus*, by C.L. Anthony. It is the story of a schoolmistress whose first youth has passed, but who finds romance on a holiday in Bavaria, where she falls in love with a young inn-keeper. After a brief interlude of happiness with him she returns to England. The charm and simplicity of the play won it great popularity in London where it played for two years, and was made into a film. Francis Lederer and Fay Compton starred in the play there, and later he brought it to New York where it played for a year. Since that time it has become a favourite in many lands.

When *Autumn Crocus* first appeared the name of the author was unfamiliar. Who was C.L. Anthony? No one knew, and most people thought he must be a man, until it leaked out that the name was the pseudonym of a schoolmistress named Dodie Smith. Since her first success Miss Smith has written many plays in her own name and has become a popular and successful playwright. Her latest play, *Dear Octopus*, ran for a year in London, with John Gielgud and Dame Marie Tempest in the chief roles. It was one of the few plays to survive the crisis of September 1938.

The war has brought many British celebrities to Canada whom we should not otherwise have seen. Perhaps the most popular of these visitors is the music-hall entertainer, Gracie Fields, who is touring in Canada, giving concerts on behalf of the Navy League. Gracie is undoubtedly one of the most popular people in Great Britain; she is received everywhere like a queen. Her appearances are frequent, and she can draw a large audience anywhere. It is rumoured that her yearly earnings amount to $750,000; certainly her donations to charity are enormous. She is the last of the great music-hall singers, last of the line of Marie Kendall, Ellaline Terriss, Lily Bernard, Vesta Victoria, Florrie Forde and, of course, Marie Lloyd. The art of the music-hall singer was that of the Israelite who succeeded in making bricks without straw; with an insignificant song these amazing folk would enchant a large audience. Vesta Victoria became the darling of London singing "Daddy Wouldn't Buy Me A Bow-Wow"; Gracie Fields does the same thing with "Sally, Pride of Our Alley."

Years ago when Gracie Fields was not so well known as she is now, a musician played me some of her gramophone records as an example of a really untrained voice which was nevertheless perfectly placed and produced. If she had had the opportunity and the inclination there seems to be no doubt that Gracie could have made a career for herself in opera. At the same time my friend predicted that she would soon shout her voice away, and when I heard her recently it certainly lacked the brilliance and clarity which it used to have. But the spirited rendition of "We'll hang old Hitler from the highest branch/Of the tallest aspidistra in the world," does not tend to rest or preserve the voice.

In that reference to the aspidistra we have a key to the success of the music hall. Audience and performers were perfectly agreed that certain things were, in themselves, excruciatingly funny. Poached eggs, spinach, cheese, kippered herrings, and prunes were funny foods, and eggplant and aspidistras were funny plants. It was only necessary to include in a song as many of these funny articles as possible and its success was assured. In the music hall it would never do to hang Hitler from a tree, for that would savour of brutality; no, an aspidistra is the official funny plant, so up on an aspidistra he goes, amid gales of laughter. It is a simple formula for humour, but its effectiveness lies in its simplicity. When we hear Gracie Fields we cannot help regretting that the day of the music hall is almost done and that we have nothing half so good to put in its place.

"Cap and Bells," *Peterborough Examiner*, 10 September 1940

Why Not A Canadian Drama?: 1944

It is now more than ten years since there was any living theatre in the smaller cities of Canada, and although the Little Theatre tried to make up the loss, the war brought its activities to an end. Doubtless the Little Theatre will be revived when peace comes once again, but it can never be a satisfactory substitute for the genuine article – what, for purposes of contrast, we may call the Big Theatre. For the present we are without theatrical entertainment except in Toronto, Montreal, and occasionally Vancouver; yet the success of the Army Show and the Navy Show is clear proof that the people of Canada like the theatre and will support it handsomely when they have a chance to do so. Can nothing be done to foster and develop this strong natural taste? In the opinion of the present writer something could be done which might eventually give us a Canadian theatre and which would soon give us a body of Canadian drama.

It could be done through the CBC, by developing and encouraging good radio plays. A radio play is gelded drama, true enough. It is impossible to see the actors, and thus two-thirds of the pleasure of the play is gone, but we are assured that television is on its way, and when it comes we may expect new developments in drama which will take advantage of its special capabilities. But in spite of its handicaps radio drama can be first rate in its way, and an author who realizes its limitations can write very interesting plays for broadcasting. *The Fall of the City*, by Archibald MacLeish is an example of what we may call Greek drama for the microphone; *The Dark Valley* by W.H. Auden is a brilliant example of drama for radio on a theme which could not be used either for the stage or the screen; in Tyrone Guthrie's three plays for radio, *Squirrel's Cage*, *Matrimonial News*, and *The Flowers Are Not For You To Pick*, the author shows how successfully radio can take us into the mind of a dramatic character; almost any radio play by Norman Corwin shows us what can happen when imagination is brought to broadcasting; and in Great Britain the BBC has been successful in presenting dramatizations of great novels – *War and Peace* was one of the best – in several episodes. We have had nothing comparable in Canada, although we have a national broadcasting corporation possessing great powers. Why not?

The CBC may reply that the talent for such work does not exist in Canada. Possibly that is so, but we are convinced that there is more talent in Canada than the CBC knows about; indeed, many people are not convinced that the CBC knows original talent when it sees it. It certainly knows an imitation of American talent, and it has given us many such imitations, but it steers clear of originality. There are writers for the radio in Canada, some of whom are good and some of whom are bad. There are also people who can act – that is to say, speak – acceptably over the air. But the best is not being made of this talent. I hear all the Canadian radio drama that I can coax into my home through my receiving set, and most of it is dull and wretched stuff. But some of it is so good that it is a very great pity that it is not encouraged and stimulated to be better. There have been broadcasts of Russian drama and of Eric Linklater's war dialogues from Montreal which showed promise; but they were under-rehearsed, under-directed and under-studied. On Christmas Day in 1941 there was a broadcast of a Nativity Play from Vancouver which was, without reservation, as good as anything which has ever been heard here from the United States, and certainly as good as anything I have ever heard done by the BBC; and why – because it was thoroughly rehearsed, sensitively directed, and adequately studied.

Already I can hear the mutters of "too highbrow," from those who are convinced that Canada is inhabited exclusively by low-brows and uncritical folk who are content with radio rubbish which would not be good enough for the States or for England. These mutterers we have always with us; they are the curse of the country. And they are quite wrong. The Canadian people are not stupid, and they do not prefer vulgar, shoddy, and second-rate work to distinguished, meaty, and first-rate work in the field of entertainment. If you doubt that, recall that Toronto a fortnight ago gave enthusiastic support to ten days of ballet; is the rest of Canada more stupid than Toronto?

I am going to give the new general manager of the

CBC – whoever he may be – some good advice which he probably will not take. Let him establish in Montreal, Toronto, Winnipeg, and Vancouver four companies of radio actors, each with a good director and a good technician; let each of these companies broadcast a play over a network every fortnight; in that way listeners would be given two plays a week. Make the companies work hard on their productions – ten rehearsals of two hours each is not too much to prepare a good radio drama – and urge them to use their imaginations to the full. Let them give us classical plays, dramatizations of novels, and new radio plays by Canadian authors whenever they can get good scripts. And let these companies be as little as possible infected with the superciliousness, over-caution, and intellectual aridity which seems to afflict professional radio people. Such a policy, continued for three years, would surely lay the foundation for a truly Canadian drama.

Peterborough Examiner, 15 March 1944

Samuel Marchbanks Ruminates On Actors and Playgoers: 1948

TUESDAY: Of late I have been much in the company of some professional Canadian actors who were engaged in the production of a play. Most Canadians still think of actors as gay, carefree souls and not quite respectable by our grisly national standard. (In Canada anyone is respectable who does no obvious harm to his fellow man, and who takes care to be very solemn, and disapproving towards those who are not solemn.) But my experience of Canadian actors is that they are intense and earnest folk who work very hard and spend the time when they should be asleep chewing the rag about a national theatre for Canada. For this reason I think that it is wrong to call pieces which are written for the theatre in Canada "plays," for that word suggests lightness, fantasy, and ease of accomplishment. Canada will only respect her theatre when plays are called "works." Canada has a high regard for anything that involves toil. Therefore I think that in future I shall describe all my plays as "works," and if they ever reach the apotheosis of print I shall take care to call them *The Complete Works of Marchbanks*. Let triflers talk of plays; Canada wants to be given the works.

SATURDAY: Attended a play which I had written myself, and at the end of Act One two women hurried past me, making for the door. "I don't care what happens, those pickles have got to be done tonight," said the larger and more determined one. It is incidents such as this which keep authors from getting swelled heads. And indeed at this time of year pickles are the prime concern of every really womanly woman. The subtle alchemy which transmutes a mess of tomatoes and celery (which looks like something the police have swept up after a disastrous bus collision) into chili sauce, cannot be understood by men; nor can the coarse male hand compound mustard pickles which do not scorch the epigastrium of the eater, and give him a breath like the monsoon of the spicy East. There are indisputably some jobs which women do better than men, and making pickles is one of them. Women cannot make wine – Sir James Fraser tells why in *The Golden Bough* – but they are priestesses of the pungent mystery of the pickle, and the twenty-fifth of September is their Picklemas.

From "Diary Of Picklemas," *Peterborough Examiner*, 18 September 1948

Samuel Marchbanks' Diary of a Drama Festival: 1949

MONDAY: Made my way to Toronto today to attend the Dominion Drama Festival, and engaged a room in the Big Pub. The whole building, when I arrived, appeared to be in the throes of a convulsion, which turned out to be the Progressive Conservative Convention. In the drugstore in the basement I absent-mindedly picked up a child's air rifle which was offered for sale and (not knowing that it was loaded) shot a delegate in the back, just as he was drinking a much-needed bromo-seltzer at the soda counter. It turned out that he was a supporter of Kelso Roberts. By some very pretty footwork I managed to leave the scene of my crime before I was found out, but soon the news was all through the convention that a Roberts man had been shot by an unknown assailant, and immediately the rubbish bins were full of Roberts buttons, and Frost buttons were in heavy demand. My action, I fully believe, cost Mr. Roberts the leadership. . . . All night long the war drums could be heard beating on every floor of the hotel, and from time to time herds of enthusiasts galloped past my door, baying for "Good Ol' Les," but whether Les Frost or Les Blackwell I could not tell.

TUESDAY: As the Dominion Drama Festival is a national affair, it is bilingual, and today I saw a play in French. When this happens, a synopsis of the play is printed for dullards like me, but these synopses are of very little assistance, being written, I suppose, by a Frenchman whose knowledge of English is about on a par with my knowledge of French. They generally run something like this: "Alphamet, the lover of Pheenaminte, is eager to break off his intrigue with Flanelette, ward of the miser Planchette, whose earlier affair with a woman of the town, Clitore, has been discovered by the wily notary Bidet. To achieve his end he disguises himself as a country cousin, Merde, and seeks the assistance of the maid, Vespasienne, who is in reality the disguised Comtesse de Blancmange. Meanwhile the miser has altered his will, leaving everything to the poet Garotte, whose love for the beautiful Parapluie is made known to her supposed father (but in reality her ward) Derrière, bringing the whole merry business to an end with a sextuple marriage and the birth of the triplets, Un, Deux, and Trois."

WEDNESDAY: Saw *The Glass Menagerie* this evening, very well acted, but it did not move me to tears or laughter because, I think, I am temperamentally unsympathetic to such pieces. The plot was about a group of people who were in terrible fixes of one sort or another, with no hope of getting themselves straightened out. Now when I encounter such situations in real life my instinct is to run, for I know that if I remain among such people I shall not be able to help them, and they will only succeed in involving me in their troubles, and dragging me down to their own hopeless level. One of the bitterest realizations which life offers us is the knowledge that there are some people who are doomed, either through ill luck or their own unsatisfactory characters, to be always in trouble; it is necessary to be kind to such people, of course, but it is dangerous to try to straighten them out, for their genius for misfortune is far greater than my genius for assistance. When I see them on the stage I do not have to take a humane attitude towards them, and I reflect that it would have been far better if they had all committed suicide before the curtain went up.

THURSDAY: Much of the excitement of drama festivals is caused by the fact that somebody is always in a difficult spot. Every time the curtain goes up on a new performance the whole audience knows that the actors have spent several hours wrestling with an unfamiliar stage, a group of union stage hands whose attitude towards their work is contemplative and mystical, and such disagreeable facts as their own neglect to bring objects which are vital to the play. In this condition of nervous frenzy they appear before the most critical audience in Canada, and it is nothing short of astounding that they give the excellent performances they do. And always, in the front row of the balcony, is the figure of the Adjudicator, like Tiberius watching the Christians wrestling with the lions.

FRIDAY: A beautiful day, and as the festival audience went into the theatre I heard several people say that they wished that in fine weather all performances could be given outdoors. I disagree. Outdoor theatres are, except in the most unusual circumstances, unsatisfactory. For one thing, groups of people in costumes, with their faces brilliantly painted, look rather foolish in an outdoor setting; for another, Nature is rather a sordid old girl, and her dirty greenery, her dusty grass, her noisy birds, and her sudden changes of temperature are unfriendly to theatrical performances. The theatre is an artificial place, and is better kept in an artificial setting. The worst theatre in the world is the outdoor theatre at Niagara Falls; directly behind the stage one sees this continent's largest waterfall; no actor can be heard above it, and no actor looks like anything but a fretful pygmy in front of it.

SATURDAY: The last day of the festival, and the day when I and a large group of friends submitted ourselves to the Adjudicator's scalpel. When all was over we returned to the Big Pub, thinking that we would make merry in the quiet, inoffensive way of our kind. But no sooner had we settled ourselves in a room and opened a bottle or two of raspberry vinegar than there came a knock at the door, and a large man with the unmistakable boots of a detective forced himself upon us. He was the House Dick, and he urged us not to make a noise, although we had not yet had a chance to make any. He even suggested that we disperse, so we pretended to do so, and cunningly slunk off to another room. But lo! we had no sooner settled ourselves again than the House Dick leapt out of a clothes closet, his face contorted with rage, and gave chase again, as we rushed to yet another room. But this time we managed to eat a few ginger cookies and drink some tap water undisturbed. . . . Why is it, I wonder, that Progressive Conservatives are permitted to turn the Big Pub into a fun fair, when half a dozen innocents from the drama festival dare not gather in one room? There is an ugly hint of favouritism about this.

"Diary of a Hunted Man," *Peterborough Examiner*, 7 May 1949

Samuel Marchbanks Writes a Letter to Apollo Fishorn: 1950

Dear Mr. Fishorn:

You want to be a Canadian playwright, and ask me for advice as to how to set about it. Well, Fishorn, the first thing you had better acquaint yourself with is the physical conditions of the Canadian theatre. Every great drama, as you know, has been shaped by its playhouse. The Greek drama gained grandeur from its marble outdoor theatres; the Elizabethan drama was given fluidity by the extreme adaptability of the Elizabethan playhouse stage; French classical drama took its formal tone from its exquisite, candle-lit theatres. You see what I mean.

Now what is the Canadian playhouse? Nine times out of ten, Fishorn, it is a school hall, smelling of chalk and kids, and decorated in the Early Concrete style. The stage is a small, raised room at one end. And I mean room. If you step into the wings suddenly you will fracture your nose against the wall. There is no place for storing scenery, no place for the actors to dress, and the lighting is designed to warm the stage but not to illuminate it.

Write your plays, then, for such a stage. Do not demand any processions of elephants, or dances by the maidens of the caliph's harem. Keep away from sunsets and storms at sea. Place as many scenes as you can in cellars and kindred spots. And don't have more than three characters on the stage at one time, or the weakest of them is sure to be nudged into the audience.

Farewell, and good luck to you.

S. MARCHBANKS

From "The Marchbanks Correspondence,"
Peterborough Examiner, 4 March 1950

Samuel Marchbanks Writes Another Letter to Apollo Fishorn: 1950

Dear Mr. Fishorn:

I am ashamed that a young Canadian playwright such as yourself should write to me complaining that he cannot think of a theme for a major work. If you intend to get your manuscript in for the London Little Theatre's prize of $1,000, you had better hurry; the closing day is December 31.

Out of pity for you, I suggest the following theme: the steps by which the barbarous medieval treatment of insane persons was supplanted by our modern comparatively humane methods. That would make a fine chronicle play. And don't forget that the Quakers were the first people to establish a hospital in which the insane were treated as human beings with personal preferences and rights. It is a matter of history that Quakers spent many hours finding out from their patients what they liked to eat, instead of giving them dirty skilly in dippers. And there is one of your best scenes, roughly like this:

(Scene: A cell in a Quaker hospital. Mad Bess is happily banging her head against the wall. Enter a Quaker.)

QUAKE: Peace be upon you, woman. Prithee give over. Thee will injure thee's brainpan.

MAD B: Yahoo! Cockyolly, cockyolly!

QUAKE: Tell me, prithee, dost thee like marmalade or jam on thee's breakfast toast?

MAD B: They say the owl was a baker's daughter.

QUAKE: Very like, dear sister. But speaking of breakfast toast —

MAD B: Come, my coach. Good night ladies, good night.

QUAKE: It may be as thee says. But in the morning, dost thee like jam or marmalade on thee's breakfast toast?

(Enter Elizabeth Fry, the great Quaker humanitarian.)

ELIZ. FRY: How fares the work, brother?

QUAKE: But tardily, sister. This dear sister here cannot say whether she wants jam or marmalade on her breakfast toast.

ELIZ. FRY: Come sister, I am Elizabeth Fry. Tell me what thee wants on thee's toast.

MAD B: Oh, you're one of the Frys, are you? Then bring me a great, big, delicious, steaming, vitamin-packed cup of Cadbury's cocoa!

(Confusion; Elizabeth Fry and Quaker look pained, and Mad Bess strikes the wall again with her head; the wall breaks through; she escapes.)

There; you see how impressive it could be? Shame on you for despairing.

S. MARCHBANKS.

From "The Marchbanks Correspondence,"
Peterborough Examiner, 16 December 1950

Directors for Canadian Theatres: 1951

There are many people, well qualified to form an opinion, who feel that the Canadian theatre is advancing with discouraging slowness; I, on the contrary, think that it is going ahead at a brisk pace. We have an encouraging number of good actors, some capable managers, and some excellent designers. But one necessary ingredient of a good theatre, professional or amateur, which we lack and which we seem to have no immediate hope of acquiring, is a body of first-rate directors. There are a few, but they are scattered and their influence is comparatively small. Where are the others to come from?

Let us not pretend that any reasonably competent person with ideas about plays can become a director. Qualities of intellect and personality are demanded which are rare, and sacrifices are demanded which few people care to make. It cannot be said, in the language of civic enthusiasm, that a director must give "leadership." He must do much more than that. His acceptance of responsibility for the artistic guidance of the play involves a surprising variety of tasks. He must enter into a relationship with his actors which is friendly, but which must stop short of familiarity. He must be sympathetic, but not to the point where he is inhibited from uttering necessary criticisms. He must value all his workers highly, but none so highly that he cannot do without them. He must, in short, accept all the disabilities which go with being the boss of the show.

It has been my good fortune to work under several admirable directors, and a few thoroughly bad ones. The two best, in my experience, have been John Gielgud and Tyrone Guthrie. The thing which impressed me most forcibly about both of them was their readiness to admit that they had made a mistake in direction. But I must immediately qualify that comment by saying that neither of them made very many mistakes. They came to rehearsal with their homework thoroughly prepared; they knew the play upon which they were working line by line, and they knew what effects they wanted to create upon the stage. They did not come to rehearsal with prompt-books filled with plans; I cannot recall ever having seen either of them at rehearsal with a book in his hand; they experimented with moves and groupings until, sometimes, as many as half a dozen variations had been tried and discarded. But this experimentation was not the result of indecision; it was, on the contrary, a search for the best possible way of creating an effect which they had determined to make. And once that best way was found it was never changed.

Both men were remarkable for the atmosphere which they created at rehearsals. Mr. Gielgud's atmosphere was pleasant, but extremely businesslike; with the utmost courtesy he cut short those discussions which so easily arise in rehearsal, and which can consume so much time. Courtesy was a very powerful element in his rehearsals, and it did much to produce an atmosphere in which creative work could be done. I have said that he was businesslike; it was also plain at all times that his business was the creation of beauty, and that there was always time for anything which contributed to that end.

Mr. Guthrie's method was superficially different, but basically the same. He is a man of uncommon wit and charm, and he sometimes says penetrating and apparently cruel things to actors. But his sharp words are directed against the actor's work, and not his spirit, and I have never seen him discourage or shame anybody. He creates, in astonishing measure, enthusiasm, and even originality in his actors. Perhaps it is more correct to say that he makes it possible for shy people – and many excellent actors are shy – to bring out ideas and technical experiments which they would conceal from a less discerning and discriminating eye. He is celebrated, among other things, for his superb handling of crowds. It was always his method to treat each member of a crowd, however numerous, as an individual, and to encourage him to create a character. He has an endless enthusiasm for detail, but he never allows his plays to be swamped under detail.

Characteristic of both men was a great store of knowledge of history, of manners and customs through the ages, and a richly imaginative conception of the uses to which this knowledge might be put in the service of the stage. They were particularly knowledgeable in all matters relating to rank and social distinction, and the behaviour suitable and unsuitable in aristocratic or formal societies. We may choose to pretend nowadays that such differentiations between man and man no longer exist, but we cannot hope to see very deeply into classical plays, or to present them effectively upon the stage, without such knowledge. A good director must not be too much the prisoner of his own era in matters of thought.

But neither Gielgud nor Guthrie, though on the best of terms with their actors and technicians, were ever "one of the boys." They did not hold themselves aloof, but it was plain that their work and their gifts set them apart. They accepted that apartness as a condition of their lives and their work.

It is here that the amateur director, especially, is in a difficult position. He fears aloofness, and it is possible that his fellow workers would keenly resent aloofness on his part. And in the professional theatre, as it exists in Canada, the situation is not greatly different. The director lacks the moral authority over his company which is absolutely essential if he is to get the best work out of them. He is, all too unmistakably, "one of the boys."

I cannot pretend to have found a solution for this problem. It takes more than the desire and a lot of hard work to make a good director. But where the gift exists, it is not always possible for it to function. One reason for this, I feel, is that in our Little Theatres we have fallen victim to a delusion, rooted in our devotion to democracy, that nothing is well done unless it is done by popular consent. The theatre, professional and amateur, is democratic in the sense that nobody is compelled to enter it against his will. But we should realize that, once inside, a theatre does not have to be run like a township council in order to be artistically good. Art is not democratic in all its workings, and if we want good work in the theatre we must consent to do what we are told by the people who know best. Unless we accept this principle, we shall not increase our number of good directors, for a director must be a benevolent tyrant.

He pays for the obedience which is accorded to him by sacrificing some of the good fellowship which is one of the most delightful by-products of the theatrical life. He pays also in the exhaustion which is inseparable from being the arbiter and lightning-rod of a group of people who are engaged in an act of artistic creation. He pays in the opprobrium which – quite rightly – attaches to any failure for which he is responsible. But if he is really a good director, the sacrifices which he makes, and the sacrifices which are made to him by his fellow workers, are all worth while. For without good directors there cannot be, under the conditions of the modern theatre, any really good theatrical work.

Theatre Canada, 1 (January-February 1951)

A Dialogue on the State of Theatre in Canada: 1951*

I have revived the characters of LOVEWIT and TRUEMAN who, in a pamphlet on the condition of the English theatre in 1699, have already shown themselves admirable assistants in this sort of work.

(LOVEWIT is seated in his study. To him, TRUEMAN in haste.)

TRUEMAN: Good morning, Lovewit; I am lucky to find you at home. You have heard the news?

LOVEWIT: That we two are to prepare a memorandum on the state of the theatre in Canada for the Royal Commission? It came to me by the morning post. What a chance to speak our minds!

TRUEMAN: My dear fellow, you must contain yourself. A memorandum to a body of such solemnity and dignity will be no place for your jokes and your flights of exaggeration.

LOVEWIT: What, honest Trueman? Do you suggest that His Majesty's Commissioners are so far outside the bounds of common humanity that they cannot relish a joke now and then?

TRUEMAN: I did not say so. But I have seen some of the petitions and memoranda which have been presented to them already, and they are, as the schoolboy said of the works of Matthew Arnold, "no place to go for a laugh." Indeed, I wonder if we can come up to the standard of sobriety which they have set.

LOVEWIT: Why, my dear fellow, it will be the easiest thing in the world. We will put down what we want to say in some form congenial to ourselves – as it may be, a dialogue – and when it is done we will send it to a bureaucrat or a public relations counsel to be translated into the proper style, for this language of official documents is not one which any artist can master.

TRUEMAN: No literary artist would dare to touch it, for fear some

*Many ideas in this submission were honed in a long discussion Davies had with Michel Saint-Denis, then co-director of the Old Vic Theatre School.

of it would stick, like pitch, and ruin him. We must have plenty of tabulation of points, labelled (a), (b), and (c). And we must make a pretty show of numbers, and even Roman numerals – But no; numerals look unbusinesslike, and our age wants its artists to be as businesslike as possible.

LOVEWIT: And rightly so. But to be businesslike, and to make a parade of the apparatus of business are different things. We will be businesslike, and the press agent shall make the parade.

TRUEMAN: I know a needy, pragmatical fellow who, for a trifle of money, will supply us with a rare show of statistics to prove anything we choose to say, and these shall provide us with appendices to drag at the tail of our memorandum, and give it weight.

LOVEWIT: And I know an astrologer who has foresworn the casting of horoscopes and now gives all his time to making pie-charts for business houses.

TRUEMAN: Oh rare! The press agent, the pedant, and the astrologer shall give our memorandum the modish air of a modern state paper. But if it is to have any sense in it, Lovewit, we must provide it.

LOVEWIT: You are right. And to talk sense about the theatre demands a high degree of self control, for it is the Temple of the Passions, and too often its devotees allow the passions to escape from the temple and invade their conversation.

TRUEMAN: Let us resolve, here and now, to be as sensible as we can in what we say about the Canadian theatre.

LOVEWIT: To avoid special pleading –

TRUEMAN: Ay, and to avoid also that pitfall of those who talk of the theatre – I mean what George Jean Nathan so aptly calls "ersatz profundity."

LOVEWIT: Agreed! And yet never to forget that the theatre is an art, or a compost of many arts, and that it must be treated at all times with love. For he who makes the theatre his harlot, or his little-regarded companion of the evening, or his school-mistress, will never know her or enjoy her fairest favours. They know her best who love and serve her best.

TRUEMAN: I suppose, for a beginning, we must answer those who question whether the theatre exists at all in Canada, in any form which deserves careful consideration. Yet it seems to me that it exists here, as it does everywhere in the world, in those centres of population which are big enough to support it. For whatever the enthusiasts may say, not everyone wants the theatre, and of those who want it, not all want it on the same level.

LOVEWIT: True, for the moving-pictures supply the wants of thousands of people who would seek their entertainment in the theatre if no movies existed. But the theatre they would demand, and get, would be the theatre of windy melodrama and domestic comedy. In some countries the theatre can, and does, compete with the movies in providing this sort of fare, but it cannot be said to do so in Canada. The failure of many a Canadian travelling company, jaunting from town to town by car, and putting on its show with borrowed furniture, under the auspices of some local service club, is due to this alone: it is doing badly what the movies do much better. And when Canadian actors who have engaged in such pursuits say that Canadians are indifferent to the theatre, they delude themselves. The fact is that Canadians are indifferent to bad theatre.

TRUEMAN: I am glad to hear you say so. For it appears to me that Canadians are as responsive to first-rate work as any other people. A Canadian audience may sometimes be naive; it may be a little behind the times when confronted with the latest confection from New York or London. Sometimes we are a little provincial. But we are by no means stupid.

LOVEWIT: I agree. And I may tell you, Trueman, that I have myself been an actor in London, and I have known London audiences to be naive, old-fashioned, and provincial when confronted with something they did not understand. And need we suppose that a New York audience is any different? Their treatment of some fine plays certainly does not suggest it. I am with you: Canadians are as quick as anyone to recognize and applaud what is first rate. Their reception of fine foreign artists has shown it.

TRUEMAN: It must be said, however, that they have not yet put the stamp of unmistakable approval upon any theatre artist of their own who has not first gained some recognition abroad.

LOVEWIT: There are two answers to that. Perhaps they have not yet found an artist of the theatre so plainly of the first rank that they choose to acclaim him. And also it is almost out of the question at present for a Canadian theatre artist to be seen in all parts of the country and thus to gain national acceptance. Monsieur Gratien Gelinas hopes to try the experiment soon. If he succeeds as well in English as he has done in French, he will be the man.

TRUEMAN: True: but it is not our task to prophesy. The artists of *Les Compagnons de St. Laurent* are also working on a very high level, but while they act in French their fame will be confined to Quebec and to that very small part of the English population which knows French well enough to follow a play with pleasure – a proportion, I may say, which is even smaller than it professes itself to be. But in the English-speaking theatre who have we?

LOVEWIT: There is no one. And it is impossible to say how much the fame of Fridolin and *Les Compagnons* owes to the fact that their audience is a compact one compared with the audience which English-speaking actors face. No one doubts their ability, but it must be allowed that they are fortunate in not having to establish their celebrity in all ten provinces.

TRUEMAN: We are agreed, then, that Canadians who care for the theatre at all are warmly responsive to first-rate theatre. And let us be generous in our definition of first-rate theatre: a classic thoroughly understood and finely presented, a display of virtuoso acting in a play of modest merit, a fine piece of ensemble work in a play of Chekhov or Ibsen, a farce played with skill and gusto – any of these may, in its degree, provide that special pleasure, that sense of exhilaration and fulfilment which first-rate theatre can give. For make no mistake, friend Lovewit, the theatre is a vigorous, living, and in a certain sense, a coarse art; it is vulgar in the true sense of the word. I am always suspicious of theatre-lovers who insist that they can only endure the finest plays performed to perfection. There are many kinds of excellence in the theatre, but all are recognizable by the completeness of the special effect which they produce upon the audience, and by the unmistakable deep satisfaction which they give.

LOVEWIT: Do you think that this completeness of effect is often achieved in the theatre in Canada?

TRUEMAN: Sometimes, certainly, in the performances of the professional companies which visit our big cities.

LOVEWIT: Ah, but they come to us from England or from the United States; we cannot count them.

TRUEMAN: No, but we must not overlook them, for they provide examples for our native actors, and in the theatre, as in all arts, example is of the utmost value to those who would reach a high level of achievement themselves. The pity is that they come so seldom, and visit so few of our cities; for this reason we lack the constant inspiration of theatrical work on the highest level. It is an economic problem, of course. When the Old Vic visits New York it cannot come to Canada without losing money. When Gielgud brings us *Love for Love* he does so at a money sacrifice, and the unfamiliarity of the play keeps people out of the theatre.

LOVEWIT: There you touch upon a point which we must not neglect. We have said that there is an audience in Canada for any sort of first-rate theatre. But there is one class of theatrical work which must be excepted, and that is the performance of unfamiliar classics. You spoke of *Love for Love*; our Canadian education is so poor in quality that virtually no Canadian who is not a university graduate in English has ever heard of its author, much less felt any anxiety to see his works on the stage. There are great realms of drama closed to us for this reason alone. In England, and to a very much lesser degree in the United States, it is possible to see plays performed which are out of the common run. But we Canadians are an illiterate people in this respect, and we fear the unknown as only the ignorant and the intellectually lazy can fear it. This is a matter, my dear Trueman, in which our country desperately needs reform.

TRUEMAN: You will start no quarrel with me on that score, and I am as good a Canadian as yourself. I think it may fairly be said that except for two or three comedies of Shakespeare, *She Stoops to Conquer* and Sheridan's *Rivals* and *School For Scandal*, and two or three Ibsen bogies, a classic is rarely performed in the English-speaking theatre in this country.

LOVEWIT: An Australian told me recently that before he was eighteen he had seen twenty plays of Shakespeare performed, more or less ably, by the company which Alan Wilkie maintained in that country. This experience has enriched his life in a fashion inexplicable to most of our countrymen. Have you ever asked a group of Canadian schoolteachers, professionally engaged in teaching Shakespeare, how many Shakespearean plays they have seen on the stage?

TRUEMAN: I confess that I have shrunk from such depressing investigation.

LOVEWIT: Their answers would sadden your heart and chill your blood, I promise you. What can they know about Shakespearean drama if they have never experienced it in its proper form? Who attempts to explain the works of Beethoven if he has never heard an orchestra play them?

TRUEMAN: You need not confine your pity to schoolteachers alone. I think it very likely that a majority of Canadians of good education – as education goes here – and good financial estate, have never seen a Shakespearean play performed.

LOVEWIT: As far as the classics of the theatre are concerned, we are a nation of ignoramuses, and the oft-advanced excuse that because we do not know what we are missing we are none the worse for it, seems to me to be a disgraceful evasion.

TRUEMAN: That brings us back to what I said a short time ago: I think that one reason why we slight the classics is that we lack the example and the tradition which is wanted by those who tackle them.

LOVEWIT: Tradition! You have hit it!

TRUEMAN: Do not mistake me. A weight of tradition may be as great a handicap as none at all.

LOVEWIT: But a genuine, living tradition is constantly renewing itself, and the theatre, perhaps more than the other arts, relies upon a living tradition. The theatre has its relics and its apostolic succession, you know, and among actors reverence for the great ones of the theatre's past is a living and potent force.

TRUEMAN: Your phrase "apostolic succession" catches my fancy. Will you not clarify what you mean?

LOVEWIT: With pleasure, if you will allow me a personal reminiscence. When I was a young and unimportant actor at the Old Vic I had several conversations with Ben Webster, who was himself of a great theatrical family; he told me how, when he and May Whitty, his wife, were touring on this continent on the fifth of Sir Henry Irving's visits, they helped to cheer the last hours of an old member of the company, Henry Howe, who died when they were in Cincinnati; "Evergreen" Howe was born in 1812 of a Quaker family, and when he wanted to go on the stage he asked advice of Edmund Kean. Webster told me of Kean's surprised "Why, cocky, you're a Quaker!" When Howe said that none the less he wished to act, Kean thrust his face into the boy's and rasped, "Well, cully, can you starve?" . . . I tell you this story because, as I sat in awed admiration at the feet of Ben Webster, a man with roots deep in the theatre's past, I seemed, through his kindly acceptance of me, to reach back into the past, through Evergreen Howe, to Kean himself. That is tradition, Trueman. I do not pretend that it made me a better actor, but it gave me a sense of the wonder and nearness of the great past which made it impossible for me ever to give the theatre less than my best, whatever that best might be. And that is the thing which our Canadian actors cannot get, although I know how powerfully many of them desire it. They want the living tradition, and as yet there is no one to give it to them.

TRUEMAN: Acting, as a profession, is still in its infancy in Canada. We might hope for the establishment of a native tradition if there were not strong forces working against it. But to earn a sufficient income as an actor in Canada is possible only to a score or so of people. The remainder must work as radio actors in order to live.

LOVEWIT: And in saying that you explain many of their deficiencies. Radio acting makes no demands upon the body; an actor whose body is untrained will never make his mark upon the stage except in a limited range of roles for which he is perfectly suited. He will be lucky if he rises above mediocrity even in those. Acting in the classics, or in a modern play which is not realistic in manner, is impossible for him, for he does not know his business.

TRUEMAN: I suspect that you do not consider radio acting as real acting.

LOVEWIT: Radio, unaided by the stage, has not produced a single actor of the first rank. The microphone imposes too many limitations. Emotions must be expressed in such a manner as to agree with the machine, for the machine is the final arbiter. The speech of even the best radio actors is unsuitable for the stage, without radical change. And what passes for sincerity in radio has nothing to do with the larger sincerity which is demanded of an actor who must fill a theatre with sound. Yet this is the work by which most of our actors have to live.

TRUEMAN: Do you consider that in general it makes bad actors of them?

LOVEWIT: Not of the wise ones. The encouraging fact is that many of these young men and women take great pains to learn to act well on the stage. They train their bodies and their voices. And when they have the chance they act in a way which gladdens the heart.

TRUEMAN: Do you refer to their performances in the summer theatres?

LOVEWIT: Yes, and anywhere that they have a chance to work under conditions which are in any way conducive to real artistic effort. I have seen them in classical plays, in commercial plays and in musical comedies and revues. They are not numerous, but there are enough of them to give us a theatre if they could live by it.

TRUEMAN: Ah, but as soon as they had reached a certain level of excellence they would get offers from the States and we would lose them.

LOVEWIT: We would lose a few of them. But there are others—some of them among the best—who would stay here. For patriotism in the arts is no less common than it is in other spheres. If they had a chance at a respectable livelihood and an honourable way of life, they would stay, and they could give us a truly fine theatre.

TRUEMAN: While such people exist it cannot be said that we are without the means to create a theatre. But so far we have said nothing of the theatre which exists widely everywhere in Canada, and flourishes triumphantly in some parts of it.

LOVEWIT: Our amateur theatre? Yes; if it flourished on such a scale, proportionately, in the United States, news of the prodigy would have been spread to the uttermost ends of the earth. For where else in the world will you find a national amateur theatre movement comparable with our Dominion Drama Festival?

TRUEMAN: It is one of Canada's cultural glories, but Canada characteristically does not know it. The Dominion government is indifferent to it, and hundreds of thousands of citizens either know nothing of it, or are profoundly misinformed about it. It receives no penny from the public purse. And yet it engages the attention of much of the ablest artistic talent of the country, and it provides, in its final yearly festival, a week of drama which has won the sincere admiration of extremely able professional men of the theatre, who are brought here to judge it. I cannot think of any other country in the world where a comparable effort would be so persistently snubbed by the government. Even on the lowest level, its publicity value to the country is enormous. The libel that Canada hates the arts is more strongly supported by the resolute official slighting of the Dominion Drama Festival than in any other single matter.

LOVEWIT: Do not grow too heated, my dear fellow. It may be a blessing in disguise. The artist who is slighted by his government is at least not under his government's thumb. But more of this later. The curious fact, in my estimation, is that in Canada the amateurs are so much better off than the professionals.

TRUEMAN: It is a fact that some of the large amateur societies own fine theatres and have a good deal of money to spend on presenting their public performances. Such a group as the Little Theatre of London, Ontario, which owns a handsome, full-sized theatre, supports a studio for experimental work, gives assistance to promising young people, and employs several persons to attend to its business all the year round, is a brilliant exception. The average amateur theatre group works in a hired hall, pays its way from year to year, and in the course of time acquires a wardrobe and some scenery. If, at the end of a season, it has paid its bills and still has enough in hand to finance some of the preparatory work for the season to come, it has done well. And in addition to these groups of average success, there are struggling groups which often cannot make ends meet.

LOVEWIT: Lack of merit?

TRUEMAN: Very often, but in some cases it is because they present unpopular plays which they think should be seen. In large cities there are also groups of poor people who, as they act for poor audiences, never have quite enough money. But a few of them do work of artistic value, for all that.

LOVEWIT: When you speak of "artistic value" in an amateur performance do you mean the same thing as when you use that phrase of a professional performance?

TRUEMAN: Such a phrase cannot have a constant value, like a bar of gold of a fixed weight. But you are right to take me up in that way. When speaking of the amateur theatre one must beware of sophisticating one's standards.

LOVEWIT: You agree with me, then, that the amateur theatre must be judged by the same standards as the professional?

TRUEMAN: I agree that the best amateur work must be judged by the same standards as the best professional work, for it has earned that compliment. When judging the work of amateurs who plainly are not the best one must use one's common sense, and some measure of charity. Do not forget, Lovewit, that I am a Canadian playwright, and I have seen my plays acted by professionals, good amateurs, and bad amateurs; if I had judged them all by the same standard I should not be here to collaborate with you now upon this memorandum, for I should have slain the bad amateurs and chopped them into messes before the astonished eyes of their friends and relatives. When one has said that they, too, are God's creatures one has said absolutely all that can be said in their defence.

LOVEWIT: You speak as if there were no bad professionals.

TRUEMAN: A bad professional will bedaub your play with his own egotistical nonsense, but he will leave something of its original substance. But your bad amateur will ravish it and dance upon its corpse without any comprehension that he is doing it a disservice. But let us talk no more of bad amateurs. My gorge rises.

LOVEWIT: Speak then of the good amateurs. Do you think that they ever surpass the professionals?

TRUEMAN: I will not say that they cannot do so: I say only that I have never personally seen them do so. I have seen here in Canada some fine, sensitive work by amateur actors, but it has always seemed to be lacking in the qualities which fine professional work possesses. The tragic purgation by pity and terror;

48

the comic glory of laughter; these have never been present in their full and unmistakable power.

LOVEWIT: Are you not a little unreasonable? These amateurs must earn their bread by other work; how can they have the same energy to give to acting that professionals have, who do nothing else?

TRUEMAN: You do not deceive me, Lovewit; you are joking. Of course what you say is half the explanation. But the real fact is that the amateurs lack the imaginative power which the professionals bring to their work. I have seen very capable amateurs; they have some technique of body and voice, and they have a certain amount of flair. But they have not the copious imaginative power which in the gifted professional actor illuminates everything he does and, in his great moments, raises acting from a craft to an art.

LOVEWIT: Yet there is truth in what I said. The actor does no work during the day, and why? Is it because he is idle? No: it is because a creative or interpretive artist needs long periods of leisure in which to prepare for the work which he is going to do. Foolish people envy him this leisure. They think how lucky he is to be paid for three hours' work a day. Yet if he is to work at the necessary pitch of intensity during those three hours, he needs the whole day free to prepare for it. It is in this respect that the amateur is at a permanent disadvantage. However seriously he may take his acting, he cannot give all of what is best in him to it. And thus he remains an amateur. Yet for all this it must be said that the best Canadian amateurs are very good indeed.

TRUEMAN: So good that if there were a professional theatre here in which an honourable livelihood could be made, many of them would be in it, and might achieve heights of which they have not dreamed.

LOVEWIT: Do you think so? I too have seen a good deal of amateur work here, and the point which has depressed me about it is its old-fashioned quality.

TRUEMAN: You mean that it lingers still in the realistic, understated mode which was popular in the 1920s? That is true.

LOVEWIT: The best actors of today have adopted a more robust style, and have left understatement to the movies, the radio, and the amateurs. How thrilling the robust style can be, even in a movie, has been amply illustrated by Sir Laurence Olivier in *Henry V* and *Hamlet*. But amateurs are desperately afraid of what they call "ham." Now if they only knew it, "ham" is one thing they can never be, for "ham" is robust acting from which intelligence has been removed. If they are never robust, how can they be hams, stifle their intelligence as they may?

TRUEMAN: Very often our amateurs remind me of Roy Campbell's comment on some South African novelists:

> *You praise the firm restraint with which*
>   *they write —*
> *I'm with you there, of course:*
> *They use the snaffle and the curb all right,*
> *But where's the bloody horse?*

They make a fetish of restraint when what they need is to cut loose.

LOVEWIT: Aha, but there you touch on what I believe to be a vital point. One can only cut loose in an act of artistic creation if one is in it up to the neck. The amateur theatre, at its best, still continues to have strong social implications. Qualities which have little to do with good acting — fairness to others, teamplay, and the like — are given an exaggerated value there. For social reasons the good actor must not soar too far beyond the level of the mediocre actor. And although we must respect the ideas which lie behind such behaviour, they have nothing to do with great art.

TRUEMAN: Precisely so, for art is undemocratic and unsocial in much of its working. Nothing so cruelly and irrevocably separates man from man as the existence of unmistakable artistic talent in one and the lack of it in another. And no one is more ruthless in his subjection of others to his needs than the great artist who is engaged in an act of creation. In the amateur theatre these facts must be kept in restraint as much as possible or the amateur theatre would cease to exist. But in the professional theatre they are the ordinary facts of existence; every professional accepts them, and they do not, in themselves, cause any friction. Though actors are, in the main, unusually genial and charitable towards one another in their private relationships, they recognize when they are at work that the superior and the inferior artist do not stand upon an equal footing. The amateur theatre is too close to private life for that.

LOVEWIT: It is really very simple. It is the economic factor which puts everything in perspective. The professional has his value and all his colleagues know it. The amateur has no unmistakable means of determining his artistic worth.

TRUEMAN: Yet if we say these things in our memorandum will not the Commissioners think that actors are mercenary dogs who judge a man only by the fee he commands?

LOVEWIT: We may trust them to understand the matter in the way we mean it. After all, it is true in every kind of professional work that the big rewards – be they money, or honour, or public acclaim – go usually to the man whose talents give him the best claim to them.

TRUEMAN: There is always one way in which the first-rate amateur can rid himself of his disabilities.

LOVEWIT: You mean that he can become a professional?

TRUEMAN: Yes, and it may be said that the amateur who does so is in little danger of falling prey to that cynicism about his work which wrecks the careers of many professionals who have gone on the stage at the earliest opportunity. Two theatres which have exercised an incalculable influence on modern drama began as amateur theatres: I mean the Moscow Art Theatre, and the Abbey Theatre of Dublin. They were born of a great love of the theatre; when the time came to break with the disadvantages of amateurism they faced that risk bravely. But during their years of professional greatness they never lost the fresh approach and the devotion of the good amateur. And it may be said that the Theatre Guild of New York had its beginning in the amateur Provincetown Players. Our Dominion Drama Festival proves to us every year that there is the raw material of a professional theatre in Canada which might rise to very great heights.

LOVEWIT: Well, let us suppose that such a devoted group of amateurs as began the Moscow Art Theatre were to try its luck in Canada; could it exist in one of our big cities?

TRUEMAN: It might, if it had adequate financial backing. Don't forget that Constantin Stanislavsky was a man of wealth. In my opinion, it would take three years for such a group to reach a point where it could pay its own way. Most of the theatrical ventures which I have had a chance to watch in Canada have died from a combination of two diseases: they were not good enough, and they were not wisely financed. The two diseases are interlocking, for lack of money leads to bad work, and bad work keeps money out of the theatre.

LOVEWIT: Just a moment; I am an Old Vic man, as you know. Lilian Baylis was never discouraged by lack of money.

TRUEMAN: Lilian Baylis was a financial genius; she also owned a theatre and thus had one large tangible asset; and she worked in a country and a city where the theatre counts its lovers in millions. The Canadian companies of which I speak are in a different position. If I were forming a Canadian theatre company, the second man I would engage would be the best business manager I could find. And I would not seek to establish a company in one place; I would travel.

LOVEWIT: But have you not heard the moans of those who have travelled already? Where is there for them to play? In school auditoriums, which have no space for scenery, no adequate lighting, and stages which might better be described as niches in the wall. There are also town halls, skating rinks, and armouries. Theatres are few, and many of them are barn-like edifices, impossible to fill and as uncomfortable, in their way, as the school auditoriums.

TRUEMAN: But if the theatre in Canada is to wait upon the establishment of well-founded playhouses in every small city and large town it will wait until the crack of Doom. For—get this through your head, Master Lovewit—the theatre is not first a thing of bricks and mortar, but of players and playwrights, and if first things are to come first the inconveniences of the existing halls must be met and overcome.

LOVEWIT: Pray do not hector me, my dear friend, for I present difficulties only to draw you out.

TRUEMAN: Your pardon, honest Lovewit. But when I hear it suggested that a play cannot be done well without a perfect theatre—meaning some version of the peep-show theatre of the past 200 years—I cannot contain my choler.

LOVEWIT: Arena staging might be tried. Fine things have been done in that manner.

TRUEMAN: Yes, and there is our old friend the fit-up – the portable stage equipment. And the depressingly educational appearance of school auditoriums could be relieved by an imaginative portable false proscenium. For a great step is taken towards stage illusion by any means which conceals from the audience that it is in the assembly hall of the Podunk Collegiate and Vocational School, where it has succumbed to boredom so often in the past.

LOVEWIT: I really do not see why a well-equipped and artistically respectable company should not travel in a circuit, as the players did in eighteenth-century England. Indeed, when one considers the success of Community Concerts in Canada, one wonders if circuits might not be financed on a similar subscription plan. They would have to take in many small places, to cut the cost of travel, but that would be desirable.

TRUEMAN: An advantage of such a plan would be that, as with Community Concerts, the audience and the money would be assured, and the company would be able to judge its expenses with its eye trained upon its income. So long as it kept the confidence of its audience, it would have little to fear.

LOVEWIT: And it would keep the confidence of its audience so long as it could provide first-rate theatrical entertainment.

TRUEMAN: That is the nub of the whole matter, for as we cannot repeat too often, more theatrical ventures are killed by their own lack of merit in a year than are killed by the neglect or malignity of the public in ten. I said that the second man I would hire, if I were charged with the task of establishing such a venture, would be a first-rate business man. The first man, and the keystone of my arch, would be a first-rate artistic director.

LOVEWIT: You would be hard set to find him.

TRUEMAN: Men of capacity are hard to find in all walks of life. He would have to be a man of fine taste, yet with a keen sense of what his audiences could be persuaded to like. He would have to keep not only his actors, but his directors, designers and technical people up to the mark. He would have to listen at all times to his business manager, and he would have to possess a good knowledge of business himself. He would have to provide, like Stanislavsky or Lilian Baylis, inspiration, instruction, succour, rebuke, and a focus of faith for all who worked with him, and he would have to provide the public with a figurehead whom they could trust and admire.

LOVEWIT: You ask for a paragon.

TRUEMAN: No; merely for a man big enough for a big job. Such people are not common, nor are they cast in one mould. Can you think of three people more apparently different than Stanislavsky, W.B. Yeats, and Lilian Baylis? And our leader here, whoever he may be, will be like all of them, and yet not like any of them.

LOVEWIT: Come, Trueman, we agreed to stick to common sense. You are talking as though our Canadian theatre would be the work of some single remarkable figure.

TRUEMAN: Perhaps I am wrong, but I do not think so. Such a leader would collect about him the admirable single talents which exist in our country now, but which have no focus. If I write a play, to whom can I turn for an opinion which will content me? And you, Lovewit, who direct and act with a certain taste and discretion – is there anyone for whom you are ready to give your utmost, and whose banner you would follow through good times and bad? Canada has plenty of theatrical talent which is very nearly first rate, and which would be so if it could find a catalyst – a messiah – call him what you will.

LOVEWIT: If we send a memorandum to the Commissioners saying that we want a messiah they may take us for madmen –

TRUEMAN: I doubt that. The Chairman of the Commission is a notable patron of the drama, and the other Commissioners, being persons of cultivation and noble spirit, must love it too. Let us say that we need a messiah by all means, and I am sure that they would unite in the Song of Simeon if he were to appear.

LOVEWIT: Trueman, restrain your Celtic emotion! Any suggestion that the Commissioners are ready to sing a *Nunc Dimittis* will undo us utterly! To imply that a Commission is ready to depart, even in peace, is inexcusable impertinence! What they want from us, I venture to say, is concrete suggestion. What, in

54

short, can the Government of Canada do about the theatre in Canada?

TRUEMAN: It could do several things. It could give reputable travelling companies, composed of Canadians, a special favourable rate on the Canadian National Railways, by making some suitable arrangement with the railway authorities. The haulage of a company and a quantity of scenery is a formidable consideration for any theatrical venture.

LOVEWIT: That would be a practical benefit certainly.

TRUEMAN: And it might induce provincial governments, at a dominion-provincial conference, to relieve reputable Canadian companies of the burdensome amusements tax which the provinces now levy.

LOVEWIT: True, for it seems unjust that the native theatre should be expected to tack onto every ticket of admission an extra charge which is not used for the furtherance of the theatre or any of the arts. If there is a case for such an impost upon any form of entertainment—which I am disposed to doubt, for it is discriminatory, and I shrewdly suspect that it has its root in a puritanical dislike of merrymaking in general—there is surely none upon the Canadian theatre, which deserves well of its country and its country's governors.

TRUEMAN: Well, there we have two benefits which might be conferred.

LOVEWIT: Both, it may be said, are negative; they let the theatre companies off certain expenses. They do not plainly give them anything.

TRUEMAN: And that, in my opinion, is as it should be. For you may as well know, Lovewit, that I oppose giving artists money from the public purse except under the most unusual circumstances: lessen their burdens, but give them no cash.

LOVEWIT: For the reason, I suppose, that I spoke of earlier: the artist who gets nothing from his government is not under his government's thumb.

TRUEMAN: Precisely. If the theatre is to have a patron today it must be the government, for the government now takes the means of patronage from private persons. But government patronage, unless it is of the negative, unobtrusive sort which I have mentioned, or unless it operates under special safeguards, can become severely repressive in its influence. Let us suppose that some governmental scheme for a National Theatre were set at work in this country within the next five years: at every election economies are promised and the National Theatre would come under fire. That would beget a spirit of nervous tension and servility among the artists and administrators of the National Theatre which would make first-rate work impossible.

LOVEWIT: Alas, yes! And can you not imagine some Member of Parliament complaining bitterly in the Commons every time the National Theatre performed a play about people whose morals were not identical with those of his constituents? Or if he saw an actor from the National Theatre whose dress displeased him, or who wore his hair at a length deemed unbecoming in a servant of the state?

TRUEMAN: Our elected representatives are already heavily burdened with public business: let us not lay upon them the responsibility of overseeing a theatre, as well.

LOVEWIT: There may come a day when a Canadian theatrical company has unmistakably earned the right to be called a National Theatre. By that time it will have its traditions, its method of work, its individual style, and its faithful and appreciative public. If the nation chooses to offer support to it, it can accept upon honourable terms, and insist that it be allowed to know its own business better than the noble tribunes of the people. For although I am a democrat, Trueman, I do not believe that people who know nothing about the arts should be allowed to make life miserable for those who do.

TRUEMAN: Because I am a democrat, I thoroughly agree with you. And I agree, too, that a National Theatre cannot be brought into being simply by the expenditure of public money. It must grow. Set up a National Theatre, and remove it from money anxieties by a state grant, and in ten years it will have become a pension scheme for the artistically worn out, the incompetent, and the faddists.

LOVEWIT: Either that, or a new playground for the professional do-gooders. Never forget those well-meaning enemies of art. They are the people who will not allow the theatre to be its own justification. The theatre is educational and recreative. But it is not so primarily. It is first of all an art, and it is as a form of art that it stands or falls. Let people get their hands on it who regard it as means of spreading some sort of education dear to themselves, or who think that it is a social medicine, and you will kill it as dead as a doornail. But let the theatre develop freely and gloriously as an art, let it present classics and good modern plays, let it ravish the souls of its audiences with tragedy and comedy and melodrama, and it will educate and recreate them more truly and lastingly than the zealots think possible. The car of Thespis must not be turned into a travelling canteen, dispensing thin gruel to the intellectually under-privileged.

TRUEMAN: Yes, if the theatre in Canada is to develop into anything of worth it cannot afford shortcuts. It must take the long way, in order that it may have time to learn not only its own business, but the special tastes and needs of our people. It is superficially attractive to think of a National Theatre created by government fiat, but I fear the consequences. In our country officialism is splendidly developed; the art of the theatre, though promising, is no match for it. Officialism and public interference might well prove too overpowering, and the result would be a National Theatre continually engaged in a losing fight with essentially inartistic influences.

LOVEWIT: By the bye, my dear friend, we must be careful of our use of that word "artistic" in our memorandum. Through no fault of its own it has acquired overtones of preciousness.

TRUEMAN: Yes, we must make it clear that we employ the word "artist" in its true sense of "maker." The artist is he who creates. And he must be as little as possible hampered by people whose work is not to create but to complicate, obfuscate, worry, and destroy.

LOVEWIT: We are agreed then, that the Canadian theatre should thoroughly learn its job before there is any talk of a National Theatre? Even though its way may be hard?

TRUEMAN: Most certainly. Nor must we forget that to many people the words National Theatre mean a building, probably in Ottawa. Now unless such a building is a centre from which travelling companies go on tours through the length and breadth of Canada, it is a foolish extravagance. A theatre is not a thing of bricks and mortar. If a djinn from the Arabian Nights were to whisk the Shakespeare Memorial Theatre from Stratford and set it down in Ottawa, with all its equipment, we would still be without a National Theatre. But if we can develop even one company, acting in a tent or in school halls, which can move Canadians to tears and laughter with the great plays of the past, and with great plays of the present (including perhaps a few of their own), we have the heart of a National Theatre.

LOVEWIT: The emergence of such a company would be an interesting phenomenon; I have sometimes wondered if criticism would have any considerable part in shaping and polishing it.

TRUEMAN: Informed criticism could do much, but informed criticism is an uncommon thing in the periodicals of our country. If a critic is to be of any use to an artist, he must understand and love the art he criticizes, and he must be deeply versed in its literature and its tradition, as well. He must know at least as much about the art as one of its practitioners. The hack critic, the mere reviewer, the reporter given leave to editorialize, is of no positive value and can be a real danger if he is himself a maligned or frustrated man.

LOVEWIT: Our attitude towards criticism is too deeply affected, I fear, by that of the United States. There a critic is too often employed merely to give his opinion on a matter which he has not studied deeply, because he is a wit or can pass for a wit. This style of criticism is dangerous at its best, and when imitated by men of meagre gifts it is execrable.

TRUEMAN: A fine critic is himself something of an artist, and he may, in some cases, encourage an art or even bring forth new developments in it. One of the principal tasks of every good critic of the theatre is to memorialize great performances and events in its history; part of his genius is to know when these events occur, for they are not always obvious. But it is to be feared that most critics serve the theatre as a flea serves a dog – as an irritating parasite which may at times bring the dog into derision.

LOVEWIT: Do you speak as a playwright whose work has, at times, been scorned?

TRUEMAN: It may be that I do, but that does little to lessen the truth of what I have said. To have one's work condemned is unpleasant but not insupportable; to have one's work condemned irresponsibly is gall and wormwood. I think that the newspapers and periodicals have a duty in this matter which many of them neglect. But a growing theatre will make them repair their neglect.

LOVEWIT: I suppose the case of the Canadian playwright must be considered in any complete review of the Canadian theatre. I am told that a great many people in Canada write plays, and yet comparatively few Canadian plays are shown upon the stage. Are the majority so bad?

TRUEMAN: Because I am a Canadian playwright myself I must be careful how I answer you. Only a few of these manuscripts have come my way, and the thing which astonished me about them was not that many were bad, but that several were near to being very good. People whose judgement I trust, who have acted as judges in playwriting competitions, have said the same thing to me often, and they have better cause to know the facts than I. But in order to write a play one must be not only a person with some degree of literary skill, but a theatre craftsman as well. One must know not only how people talk, but how to make them talk in such a way as to complete a piece of action in two and a half hours without too much padding, or too much jumping about in the plot. One must consider the actors, and give them opportunities to show their own special skills as distinguished from your own. One must know how to build up a speech to a climax, and then how to get down from the climax without tumbling. One must not introduce characters who do not help to carry forward the story, for actors cost money and must not be wasted. And above all, one must beware of the wrong kind of subtlety, for the delicate shades which give distinction to a novel have no place in a play: the subtlety of the playwright lies in quite another direction—not less than the novelist's, but different.

LOVEWIT: Aha, you touch upon something which I have often thought, and you must forgive me if I interrupt. It has occurred to me many times that the radio has a weakening effect upon many admirable Canadian writers who occasionally write plays. Radio drama being – let us not mince words – an enfeebled echo of the real thing, encourages the sort of subtlety of which you speak. When a speech can be whispered into a microphone with such immediacy of effect that the listener may almost fancy himself sitting in the larynx, if not in the heart, of the speaker, the writer is tempted to try effects which are quite lost when transferred to the stage. But because unthinking people admire what they regard as subtlety, and condemn breadth of effect, these ineffective devices are attempted again and again.

TRUEMAN: It is this very thing which makes it so hard to put a good stage piece on the radio. A broad effect in radio is merely confusing. Alas for those who beat the drum on behalf of radio drama, the mind's eye is imperfectly hitched to the mind's ear. Hence the Procrustean "adaptation" which is necessary to crush a play into an hour's length, and make it endurable to one sense alone.

LOVEWIT: Not all Canadian playwrights, of course, suffer from the baneful influence of radio writing, but some of the most potentially brilliant of them do so.

TRUEMAN: You interrupted me in my discourse upon the things which a playwright must know. He must be able to tell a story, with a certain richness of embellishment which it is the fashion of the day to mistake for thought, entirely in dialogue and action, usually without shifting his scene from a single place. He must –

LOVEWIT: My dear fellow, please do not tell me any more of the things that he must be able to do. We do not propose, after all, to write a treatise on the playwright's craft.

TRUEMAN: Very well, let us say merely that it *is* a craft and that it must be learned. The best way to learn is to write a play and see it through rehearsals and in performance. But as it costs quite a lot of money to give a play a production even in the amateur theatre, this cannot happen very often. The next best way is to see a lot of plays, and to learn from them. That can only be done where a theatre exists. I am quite sure that a robust Canadian theatre would bring forth a large body of Canadian plays, some of them good enough for export.

LOVEWIT: Hm. Do you think that people abroad would be interested in Canadian plays?

TRUEMAN: Lovewit, you disgust me! Is not the theatre of the civilized world interested in plays by and about Russians, Norwegians, Frenchmen, Swedes, Hungarians, Italians, Belgians, and even –God bless us! –Irishmen and Scotchmen? Are Canadians so cut off from the charity of God and the indulgence of mankind that they alone are of no interest to their fellow-beings? Take my word for it, if the plays are good enough, the world will like them.

LOVEWIT: Hm. I am reminded of the story of a gifted young woman who asked a celebrated orchestral conductor if her sex would prevent her from getting a place in a first-rate orchestra. No, said he; you will manage it if you are able to play twice as well as any of the men. Canadian plays will have to be very good indeed to break through the prejudice which exists against them, on the ground of their origin.

TRUEMAN: I will confess to you that the agent who hawks my plays in England keeps mum about the fact that I am a Canadian. He says that it would work against him. Nobody thinks that there is anything odd about an Englishman or an American writing a play, but apparently it is still considered unpropitious for a play to come from Canada. Still, I think that the prejudice will be overcome and that we shall see Canadian plays performed abroad –when we have the playwrights capable of bringing that about.

LOVEWIT: It seems to me unlikely that we shall have plays which will command the attention of the outside world until we have a national drama which has roused and stirred us on our own soil.

TRUEMAN: Agreed. Nevertheless, I like to look forward to that day, whenever it may be. For I like to think that Canada will have a proud place among the nations, and I fear that her integrity, her good sense, her honest dealing, and her indisputable political genius will not suffice to gain it for her. Think: do you know of any nation that the world has considered truly great which has not had one or many manifestations of great art? Canada will not become great by a continued display of her virtues for virtues are – let us face it – dull. It must have art if it is to be great, and it has more real vitality, in my opinion, in the art of the theatre than in any other save music. And I think its theatre is potentially just as good as its music and perhaps better.

LOVEWIT: I agree, but art cannot be compelled. It will not flourish here simply because we wish it.

TRUEMAN: But we can remove some of the hindrances which lie in the way. I agree with you that the offer of prizes for plays, and establishment of scholarships for talented writers and actors is not the government's responsibility, but the government might change its ideas about taxation as it affects writers; if royalties were treated as capital gains, which they are, rather than as profits, which they are not, it would help the writer to improve his position when he has a stroke of good fortune. A writer, surely, deserves well of the state. He exploits nothing but his own talent; he does not impoverish the land; whatever he creates he creates out of nothing which anybody else wants. And yet his creations give pleasure, and in special cases they may reflect honour upon his native land. I do not suppose that the Ministers of Finance and National Revenue are conscious of the existence of authors in any real sense. Yet to the author who, after years of work, a stroke of good fortune brings a considerable sum of money, it sometimes appears that these gentlemen are simply waiting to swoop upon him and despoil him. Canadian authors who are worth their salt do not want subsidies and handouts, but they would like a chance to build up a sufficient estate to permit them to live by writing alone, and to take the time necessary to do their best work.

LOVEWIT: Very well; let us turn from the authors to the actors. Should promising artists of the theatre be given state scholarships in order to study abroad?

TRUEMAN: I would rather make it possible for them to study at home. The establishment, now, of a National Theatre would be a great mistake; we do not know enough to ensure the success of such an undertaking. But the time is ripe for the establishment of a Theatre Centre, where all the arts of the theatre could be studied and practised under expert supervision, and where our excellent amateurs could find the polishing they need to make them good professionals, as well as the inspiration to carry them beyond their present limited artistic vision. Government assistance in establishing such a centre would be public money well spent.

LOVEWIT: A centre? A school, you mean?

TRUEMAN: No, a practical theatrical studio, not a drama school. I would strongly recommend a centre based upon the Old Vic Theatre Centre in London; Sweden has copied it, and we could find no better model. Furthermore, I have the assurance of its director, Monsieur Michel Saint-Denis, that he is willing and indeed eager to help in the establishment of such a centre here. What better model than the Old Vic Centre? What better adviser than the director of that centre and one of the ablest men of the theatre in the world today? If anything is to be done, Saint-Denis is your man; and it isn't every day that people of his quality offer to help a struggling art in a new country.

LOVEWIT: How is such a Theatre Centre financed?

TRUEMAN: By fees from each student, and by a government grant which, in the case of the Old Vic Centre, is £5,000 a year. Call it $25,000 a year for Canada, and a trifle for what it would do.

LOVEWIT: And who would head such a centre?

TRUEMAN: It would have to be a man with some experience of such a place, and I am sure that Monsieur Saint-Denis would help us to find him.

LOVEWIT: And he would be our messiah?

TRUEMAN: Perhaps: or our John the Baptist. Or even a thoroughly competent minor prophet would be a blessing. And when such a centre, and its students, were sufficiently strong we might think about a National Theatre. If the government wants to help us, let them help us in this way: let them make it possible for us to *learn*. But as you see I am mistrustful of any sort of direct state patronage of the arts when the artists are not in a strong enough position to make conditions.

LOVEWIT: France, to name only one country, has had national patronage of the theatre for nearly three centuries.

TRUEMAN: Which means that such patronage began in an age when it was in effect personal patronage by persons deeply concerned about the theatre. Our modern bureaucracies are not rich in such enlightened patrons, and our succeeding ministries are almost antiseptically free from them. The *Comédie-Fran-*

çaise was a product of the spirit of its time, and it had its roots in a strong popular theatre. When we have a strong popular theatre here, it will be time for us to think about a National Theatre. We live in an age of ever-increasing socialism, as you know, and it is good socialist practice to take over a going concern.

LOVEWIT: You are not to be shaken, then, in your belief that Canada does not need a National Theatre?

TRUEMAN: Have I been talking all this while in vain? Of course I believe that Canada needs a National Theatre! But I want Canada to have a strong National Theatre, directed by competent artists of the theatre, and so highly esteemed by our country and by the civilized world that it can, literally, run its own show and be under no obligation to cringe whenever a contumelious parliamentarian knits his brows! I want Canada to have a National Theatre which will be in competition with other Canadian theatres of the first rank. I want Canada to have a National Theatre which is one of the proudest possessions of the state, and not a drag upon the public purse! For the theatre is one of the arts which can maintain high standards and still pay its way; it is a truly popular art, and the people will support it when it is unmistakably of the first quality. I want a National Theatre in Canada as soon as we have developed a fine native theatre which has learned to support itself by its own efforts, asking from the government a very little money and a few favours as assurances of goodwill. I want, in short, a National Theatre with its roots in the country, nourished by experience, craftsmanship, and a noble ideal of what a theatre should be!

LOVEWIT: Honest Trueman! Give me thy hand! I have but dissembled my agreement in order to provoke this splendid rage in thee! Pardon this tear! 'Tis but an ebullition of joy!

TRUEMAN: Enough for one morning. Come, let us to the cocktail lounge where we may drain a bumper to the future!

(Exeunt arm in arm.)

From *A Selection of Essays Prepared For The Royal Commission on National Development In The Arts, Letters, and Sciences* (Ottawa, 1951)

The Festival Idea: 1952

A few weeks ago we commented in these columns on the enterprise of the people of Stratford, Ontario, who have been investigating the possibility of holding an annual Shakespeare festival in their city. Since that time they have taken the advice of Mr. Tyrone Guthrie, who is internationally known as a theatre director, and whose association with the Edinburgh Festival has contributed greatly to the success of that venture. What Mr. Guthrie said about Stratford has significance for Canada as a whole.

He warned against any festival which was organized solely as a money-maker. Such advice must be unwelcome in the ears of many Canadians who feel, quite honestly and sincerely, that the chief aim of a festival is to attract tourists and charm money out of their pockets. But a festival, as Mr. Guthrie pointed out, may have another and greater purpose; it may be an expression of what is finest in the life and aspiration of a country. That is what the Edinburgh Festival has become. If it were organized solely to make money, it could be done comparatively cheaply by arranging some Highland games and some parades of Highland regiments; instead, it recruits the finest musical and dramatic ability in the world, and that costs vast sums of money. The Edinburgh Festival makes money, certainly, because it brings money to the Edinburgh hotelkeepers and shopkeepers, but the festival itself is not organized with the making of money as its chief aim. What the Edinburgh Festival does do is to direct the attention of the whole civilized world towards Scotland, and to raise Scottish prestige everywhere.

In the world of art Canada has no prestige whatever; in the eyes of the world we are a nation of wealthy, law-abiding, hard-working, lucky savages. If we want prestige other than the kind which comes from having the best dollar in the world (and it may be that we do not) we must gain it by showing the world that we can do something which cannot be duplicated elsewhere. If Stratford wishes to have a Shakespeare festival it must not be an imitation of the festival at Stratford in England; it must be something different and something first rate in its own way. The organization of such a festival, says Mr. Guthrie, will cost a great deal of money, and we are certain he is right. But it would present Canada to the world in an entirely new and flattering light, he continues, and we believe that, also.

The advice that Stratford has received is valid for the rest of Canada, as well. This is now a rich and important country, and the seedy amateurism which has afflicted the arts here for so long is not good enough for our new place in the world. A majority of Canadians, having no interest in the arts, and no suspicion that the arts are important, do not recognize this situation as yet, but that is not a matter of consequence; a majority of Canadians have never yet recognized the importance of any great forward movement in our country's history until a minority of alert and perceptive people had completed it. If any development in the festival line is to take place in Canada it can only succeed on the highest level; it must not be organized to make money, but to be the best thing of its kind in the world; if it makes money, well and good, but its first task is to be good, and to bring honour to Canada.

Peterborough Examiner, 26 July 1952

66

Are Canadians Dull?: 1953

Last week the English magazine *Truth* published an anonymous article which said that Canadians, supposedly citizens of an important world power, were very dull people – dull in comparison with New Zealanders, Australians, and, of course, the people of the British Isles. Some Canadians have resented this; others have agreed with it. At the risk of seeming dull, we suggest that the truth lies in the middle ground. Some of us are terribly dull; others are not dull. We think that the livelier sort of Canadian is rather more numerous than the dull Canadian, but there are moments when it is touch and go.

Consider, for instance, some comment on the Stratford Festival which appeared on June 30 in Stratford's own paper, the *Beacon-Herald*. It regrets that the festival will open with Shakespeare's *Richard III*, and its reasons are best given in its own words:

> Having in mind that this summer's Shakespearean Festival must win strong approval and support if it is to become a permanent enterprise, the thought will not down that an unfortunate choice was made when *King Richard III* was selected as the spearhead stage offering. It is definitely the most unwholesome of all Shakespeare's tragedies, and its only character of any real dramatic interest is that of Richard himself – a physically repulsive hypocrite, liar and murderer, without one redeeming feature. No modern-day criminal has yet matched in foulness this detestable villain, whose evil hypocrisies, falsehoods and cold-blooded murders are an unbroken string from beginning to end. He occupies the stage much of the time, and there is nothing to applaud unless the audience enjoys a monstrous menu of blood-letting, with women, and even children the victims of the rottenest recorded character in the history of the British Throne and of English "nobility."

Frankly, this column regrets that a deplorable chapter in

history – one which is better forgotten at any time – is being made the centre-piece of a supposedly "cultural" crusade. That this hideous blot on Royalty should be featured so brazenly in this Coronation Year of 1953 seems incredibly poor judgement. Can we turn so easily from acclaiming the glories of the Monarchy of Queen Elizabeth the Second to applaud the murderous King Richard the Third? It is surely a pretty tall order!

If the *Beacon-Herald* wants "wholesomeness" it must not turn to Shakespeare, and particularly not to his histories. What could the festival have offered? *King John* was a bad egg; definitely not wholesome. *Richard II* is about a naughty king who was made to abdicate by a self-seeking thug – not wholesome, especially in Coronation Year. The two parts of *Henry IV* and *Henry V*, are about the thug who deposed Richard, and his son, a tavern tough and a faithless friend; tut tut – worse than crime comics. Besides, they contain that old reprobate Falstaff, who could never have got a job on the *Beacon-Herald*. *Henry VI* is full of wars and treachery and takes a poor view of Joan of Arc; markedly unwholesome. And that leaves us with *Henry VIII* which, as the *Beacon-Herald* knows, is chiefly about a parson who went into politics, and came to a bad end; we must preserve respect for the clergy, at all costs. No, with all the goodwill in the world, we cannot find a single wholesome play among Shakespeare's histories. As for the tragedies – well, we wouldn't expect the *Beacon-Herald* to tell its readers what goes on in *those* regrettable pieces.

In fact, wholesomeness is not a Shakespearean characteristic. Poetic, certainly; but who cares about that? Keenly perceptive and intuitive about people, of course; but the whole staff of the *Beacon-Herald* may say the same of itself. But not wholesome. Too many murders.

Murders which succeed, too. Not like the murder which the *Beacon-Herald* is trying to commit upon the infant body of its local festival; that murder somehow has not succeeded. We suspect that the *Beacon-Herald*'s dagger is too dull. Perhaps the staff should see *Richard III* after all, and watch the deft manner in which he polishes off those little princes. Clever fellow, Shakespeare.

Peterborough Examiner, 3 July 1953

68

Stratford: 1953
Richard III / All's Well That Ends Well

It is already widely acknowledged that the people of Stratford, Ontario, have done a remarkable thing in organizing a Shakespearean festival, and launching it successfully on the best professional level, and all within the space of about fourteen months. This was a stupendous undertaking and it has been carried out with a combination of audacity and faith which commands our highest admiration. But having seen the plays at Stratford, and having thought about the festival for a while, I am moved to say that I think that they have done very much more than this, and their venture is one of historic importance not only in Canada but wherever the theatre is taken seriously – that is to say, in every civilized country in the world.

They have built a theatre for their festival which is designed on a new principle – or rather on a principle so old that it comes freshly to modern audiences. Nothing like it has been built for commercial theatrical work within the past 300 years; nothing exactly like it has ever been built before. It has often been described as a tent, but it is no more a tent than the Music Shed at Tanglewood is a shed. It is a large concrete amphitheatre which is roofed with canvas, and hung on the inside with maroon and blue drapery. Inside, it is like a large deep-dish pie from which all but one large slice has been removed; this slice, projecting into the centre of the amphitheatre, is the stage area. Upon this stage is an erection of columns, a large balcony, and two staircases; the stage may be reached from its own four doors, from the aisles of the theatre, from a trapdoor and from two entrances which rise from its cellars. All spectators can see and hear, and nobody is as far from the stage as he would be in the second balcony of a theatre of nineteenth-century design.

This building, designed from plans evolved by Tyrone Guthrie and Tanya Moiseiwitsch, is a reminder to us that a theatre is not necessarily an auditorium with a raised room at one end into which the audience is permitted to peep, like eavesdroppers or Peeping Toms, but is, in the old sense "a place for viewing," and a place where things happen. It is a reminder also that a theatre is always, in part, a temple, devoted to the service of gods whom we too often forget; these gods are Pity, Terror, Tenderness, and Mirth.

Having built such a theatre, the Stratford Festival has committed itself to the production of great plays, for lesser plays could not stand up to the demands it makes. It has committed itself to the production of Shakespeare in a new way. It is not, contrary to some opinions which have been expressed, the Elizabethan way, though it has a kinship with that method. Nor is it Greek, though it has Greek components. It is a new way.

This new way of producing Shakespeare has elements which can be traced to several different sources, and those who delight in looking for "influences" may do so. But these factors have been brought together and given coherence and a new emphasis by Dr. Tyrone Guthrie. The Stratford Festival cannot be fully understood without taking account of who and what he is, and what he has done in the past. At fifty-three he is the most influential man of the theatre alive; for at least twenty years he has been evolving a philosophy of the theatre and an approach to classical drama which is strongly individual without being in any way eccentric or faddy. In order to clarify the principal elements in his work it may be convenient to consider briefly three productions of his which throw those elements into sharp relief.

The first of these was a production of *A Midsummer Night's Dream* at the Old Vic in 1937. This was Shakespeare seen through Victorian eyes. To suit the character of the theatre, which was built in 1816, the play was conceived as a lavish Victorian production, in which fairies in ballet dress flew through the air, in which the mortals were dressed in the elaborate spangled costumes of the Victorian tinsel theatrical portraits, in which the scenery was painted in the high romantic style, and in which all of Mendelssohn's music was used to accompany the action. This was Guthrie in his brilliantly inventive vein, using every element of the conventional theatre with consummate skill.

The second of these important productions was *Hamlet* in modern dress, at the Old Vic in 1938. Alec Guinness played

Hamlet, but the striking feature of the production was that, for once, Hamlet did not monopolize the attention. It was a play of ensemble, in which elements which are usually subsumed in the extreme emphasis on Hamlet himself were given their full value. It was also modern dress as it had not been seen before; the clothing, though modern in a Ruritanian style, was far enough removed from gents' natty suitings and modistes' up-to-the-minute *demi-toilettes* to have romance and timeliness. This was Guthrie as an illuminator of the classics – as a man who sees freshly and whole what has been rubbed and smudged by time.

The third production was at the Edinburgh Festival, and it was of Sir David Lindsay's strange old blunderbuss of a play *The Three Estates*. Performed on a platform in the Assembly Hall of the Church of Scotland, it was a boiling down of a play which originally took a whole day for its presentation. Music, pageantry, invention, and every theatrical device was used to show what was great and lasting in a forgotten work. But most surprising of all was the style of fluid, constantly moving, richly expressive acting which had been drawn out of the players. This was Guthrie's new style of production, or rather the fulfilment of what he had been heading towards for several years. Since that production in 1948, Guthrie has been producing plays in several parts of the world, with the finest actors in the world and with some who were little more than amateurs. But his development of this style has continued and has shown itself successful with plays of tremendous significance, such as *Oedipus Rex* (with the Habima Players in Tel Aviv), and with delicate trifles such as Alan Ramsay's *The Gentle Shepherd*, done by candle-light in a pretty eighteenth-century assembly room in Edinburgh.

In the performances of *Richard III* and *All's Well That Ends Well* in Stratford we have this style of production, I think, at its best in a theatre specifically designed to hold it. This, surely, is the theatre of the future.

As Tyrone Guthrie's work has received a great deal of un-critical adulation, it has also received a great deal of unintelligent blame. To look at it through eyes still dimmed by the nineteenth century (and if I may say so, I think that at least one of Mr. Brooks Atkinson's eyes was thus dimmed when he wrote of the Stratford productions in the *New York Times*) is to miss the point. Guthrie is not one of those producers who despises star actors; he values them because their superior abilities have brought them to stardom; but he always looks at a play as a whole, and while a star actor usually dominates one of his productions, the star does not swallow the play. This is not because Guthrie lessens the brilliance of his stars; it is because he gives every part in the play a sufficient importance to balance it against the star performance. He does not mistake ensemble-playing for a pseudo-democratic levelling of talents; he is determined, rather, to reveal the last crumb of talent that exists in any cast, from star to super.

Artistically, Guthrie is in a curious and difficult position. He is less an interpreter than he is a creator, and in the theatre, as in music, this sometimes brings about odd and not always happy effects. When Dr. Johnson commented upon the appearance of the bear which eats up Antigonus in *The Winter's Tale* he called it "a naughty superfluity"; his greatest admirers will not deny the appearance of naughty superfluities in some of Guthrie's productions. One may regret them, but it is silly to harp on them. A man of genius is not to be accountable to professors and schoolmasters for all his errors of judgement, when these are outweighed immeasurably by stroke after stroke of magnificent insight and lightning-like illumination of great plays. Good taste is, after all, a thing that almost any dolt can learn; the effects of genius are not so easily mastered. Guthrie's offences are principally against bourgeois convention, but his own attitude towards his work and the plays which he produces is a truly aristocratic one, and he cares little for commonplace opinion. He is as much an innovator and liberator of the theatre as Harley Granville-Barker, but as he works through plays rather than through books his innovations and illuminations come with the full impact of theatrical force upon his audience.

His attitude towards his work is, without an atom of pretentiousness or fake profundity, a religious one, and he approaches it with a dedication and nobility of purpose so complete that it may escape a superficial observer. He serves a high cause and he serves it humbly. It is from this deeply important element in his character that the strongly ritualistic character of the productions at Stratford arises.

Ritual in the performance of a bloody melodrama like *Richard III*? In a wryly tender comedy like *All's Well*? Yes. Watch the performances; under the acting, sometimes naturalistic and sometimes flamboyant, there is a firm ritualistic pattern. For what is ritual but conventions of gesture, movement, and dance performed within a prescribed area in order to evoke the essence of something much greater than themselves? When Lady Anne moves around the bier of Edward of Lancaster, pursued by Richard of Gloucester; when the watchful soldiers close in upon the condemned Hastings; when the ghosts of his victims cluster around the sleeping Richard; when Helena dances with her suitors at the French court; when the soldiers take cover to surprise Parolles; when Helena, triumphant in yellow, takes the centre of the stage as a victorious wife – what are these and a hundred other moments in these productions but ritual? And ritual, moreover, to which we respond with eager emotion. Ritual is man's way of evoking what is too great for realistic portrayal; ritual in these productions brings us a high sense of the wonder, the beauty, the horror, the tenderness, the merriment, and the overwhelming complexity and glory of life – in fact, it brings to us what is truly romance. Not, it need scarcely be said, the ersatz romance of Hollywood, but the true, superlative romance which is inherent in the Shakespearean vision of life. And, in this wonderful theatre, we have ourselves helped to evoke this greatness, for we are made more than spectators; we are a part of it. Is it any wonder that, when the plays are over, we are shaken and yet uplifted? We have moved through ritual to romance.

What does this mean for Canada, and for our Canadian theatre? It means that this country now finds itself in the forefront of a development of the theatrical art which has its roots deep in what is best in the classic theatre, and which sweeps aside much of the accumulation of rubbish which has cluttered the theatre we inherited from the nineteenth century. This new movement is not all-embracing; it does not exclude or render out-of-date all other theatres. This is not, for instance, the theatre of Ibsen, Chekhov, Pirandello, or Shaw. It might, in skilled hands, be the theatre of Congreve and his contemporaries, and of Sheridan and Goldsmith. But this is one of the great theatres of the future, and here in Canada we have a splendid temple built for it alone.

This cannot help but have its effect on work everywhere in the country. For one thing, many of our best Canadian actors are working at Stratford, and working as they have never worked before. We may be proud of them, for they are, in the main, very good actors. We may be especially proud of the way they speak, for in this country where slovenly and ugly speech is part of our national pose of mediocrity, we produce actors who speak a splendid, vigorous English, and in Miss Eleanor Stuart we have one actress whose speech is a model of unaffected beauty. Are these actors, who have tasted the wine of true theatre, ever again to be satisfied with the sour slops of under-rehearsed, under-dressed, under-mounted, underpaid, and frequently ill-considered and ill-financed theatrical projects? The answer is for them to give, but I cannot feel that it will be an affirmative one.

The Stratford Festival has done far more than provide us with two splendid productions of Shakespearean plays. It has given to those people in Canada most able to absorb such impressions a new vision of the theatre, and a new realization of what our Canadian actors can do when they are given a chance. It might also give a new inspiration to our playwrights, for stages on the Stratford pattern cry for modern plays conceived on more aspiring lines than our conventional stages can command. The Stratford Festival is an artistic bombshell, exploded just at the time when Canadian theatre is most ready for a break with the dead past and a leap into the future.

"Through Ritual To Romance," *Saturday Night*, 1 August 1953

Stratford: 1954
Measure for Measure / The Taming of the Shrew

Nothing succeeds like success; the high mark which the first Stratford Festival reached in 1953 created an enthusiasm which showed itself in the rush for tickets this year. And, in artistic ventures, nothing creates so much apprehension as success, for the high mark must be reached again, and if possible it must be exceeded. For a dozen reasons, not all of which are kindly in their origin, people everywhere in Canada want to know whether this second festival is as good as the one last year. In my opinion it is better in some ways and not so good in others, and if you will be patient with me I shall try to explain what I mean in some detail. But let me say immediately that I think that the balance is safely on the credit side.

The festival is better because the amenities of the theatre have been improved and the audience is better used than it was under the improvised conditions of 1953. It is better because money has been forthcoming to give it a comfortable, but by no means extreme, degree of financial security; the venture could still be ruined, but it no longer balances on the edge of a knife. It is better because everybody knows his job better than in 1953 and there is an air of professional certainty about the whole venture which was lacking at the beginning.

The shock of surprise which the opening last year gave to us all is necessarily missing; we hoped then for something good, but we were not prepared for the new theatre, the splendour of the productions, for an excellent *Richard III* and a superbly illuminating *All's Well That Ends Well*; that surprise can never be repeated. This year we expected great things. We have had a *Measure for Measure* which was not up to expectation, on the first night at any rate; we have had *The Taming of the Shrew* in a spectacular, stunning experimental production; at the time of writing *Oedipus* is still to come but, as I have been permitted to see some rehearsals, perhaps I may say that I confidently expect it to be the crown of the festival, and conceivably a production of historic importance.

Shakespearean commentators have had little to say about *Measure for Measure*; the indefatigable Victorians and the painstaking Germans found it baffling and not to their taste, and our modern critics are not much better off. They are fond of saying that the psychology of the play is involved and obscure and undoubtedly this is true; the puzzle is even greater if we make our psychological approach through the conventional morality of the world as we know it. But if we bear in mind that Shakespeare apparently considered this play as a comedy, some of our perplexity dissolves.

None of Shakespeare's plays can be considered "realistic" in the sense that they are representations of everyday life. They are all – comedies, tragedies, and histories – artificial constructions. Because they are the work of a great poet they are filled with truth – but it is poetic truth and not photographic truth. If we ever permit ourselves to believe that Shakespeare thought his plays "like life" we are certain to go wrong in our opinions about them; they are not "like life," but *about* life, which is a different thing, giving the poet far greater scope. The author who writes about life is set free from innumerable considerations of probability and possibility which must concern the author who tries to write "like life." Yet the man who writes about life may achieve a degree of poetic truth quite outside the range of the man who is "realistic." Whatever "realism" of this photographic sort there is in Shakespeare is incidental. He chose to write in artificial forms, which filled human needs.

This is not as high-falutin as it may at first appear. The cabinet maker who builds a table or a chair is also working in an artificial form designed to fill a human need. We do not reproach him because his table does not remind us of a tree, even though we know it was made from a tree, and even though we admire the way he has shown off the grain of the wood. Let us not make the mistake, therefore, of reproaching Shakespeare because his plays do not remind us of life in the raw; they are, like the table, intended to serve and delight us in ways which the raw material could not do.

The most important job of the director of a Shakespearean play

76

is to discover the poetic truth which lies in it, and to make sure that this is revealed as fully as possible by his actors and the designer. The external things – the way the actors are deployed on the stage, the way in which they speak and present themselves, what they wear and the dressings of the stage – these are important but they are not of first importance. Only when the poetic truth of a great play is revealed to the audience does it carry full conviction, and give full satisfaction. We experienced such conviction and satisfaction last year in the production of *All's Well*. For the duration of the play we lived in a world where the poet's concept was more important to us than the logic and the morality of everyday life. By such logic and morality both *All's Well* and *Measure for Measure* are ridiculous. Yet last year's comedy captured us, and this year's comedy did not. Why?

No fault can be found with the externals of the Stratford production. Colour and design had been skilfully used to create the atmosphere of a city in which dark and dreadful things could happen. The actors moved about the stage in a way which showed that Cecil Clarke, the director, has a strong pictorial sense and plenty of ingenuity. In every external matter this play was fully successful. Why then, did the heart beat so feebly in this handsome body? Why were we never persuaded to substitute the logic of the play for the logic of daily life?

A critic is on dangerous ground when he dogmatizes on such a matter. A hundred things can go wrong with a production, and even those who have been at every rehearsal cannot account for them; let me beware, then. But it is not my task to give prizes and rebukes, like a schoolmaster, but to bring what appreciation I may have to this play, and to make what guesses I can about the malady which prevented it, on the first night, from making its full effect. First of all, I felt that the actors were like an ill-assorted orchestra; Mr. Mason's admirable harpsichord was not well-suited to Mr. Bochner's splendid French horn, and Miss Hyland's silver flute was never really in touch with either of them; Mr. Harron fiddled away like a solitary virtuoso, and Mr. Campbell was playing his splendid bassoon as though he had mistaken it for an oboe. All were admirable in their way but they wanted pulling together by, let us say, Dr. Boyd Neel.

Keen interest was shown, understandably, in the work of James

Mason. I sat near enough to get the full impact of Mr. Mason's performance, and I thought it a fine one – but on a scale much too small for the rest of the players. He acted with great feeling, and his moment of remorse at the end of the play moved me – but I question whether it moved people who sat three rows behind me, because they could not see clearly enough what he was doing, nor could they hear his sobs. No one can persuade me that this is the biggest acting of which Mr. Mason is capable. He is a tall, strong man, with a sufficient, though not a large, voice. I hope that by the time this appears he is reaching the back rows, for I am certain he could do it. And when he does it, he will thrill them. But like the rest of the cast, he has not been made to work hard enough along the right imaginative lines.

The most thoroughly satisfactory performance was that of Lloyd Bochner, who gave us very nearly a complete realization of this fantastical Duke of dark corners, whose perverse sense of the duties of an absolute ruler puts this extraordinary plot in motion. But how can Mr. Bochner complete his fine study without more help, more "playing-in," by the other actors?

Miss Frances Hyland is an actress of great spirit, but she does not carry quite enough guns for Isabella, who is a creature less of airy spirit than of passion. In consequence she was a little too sharp and censorious in some of the bitter denunciations which Shakespeare has given to his heroine, and she lacks the physical opulence which would make Angelo risk his life and career for her embrace. Frankly, I thought Miss Hyland gave Isabella too much brain, and not enough heart. This is Shakespeare's sexiest play, and sex is not a matter of the head.

It was this brooding atmosphere of sex and intrigue which we missed in the play, and which is the heart of it. The first night performance was cool and dry when we wanted it to be hot and steamy. Even that excellent comedian, Mr. Douglas Campbell, played the bawd, Pompey, without really suggesting the grossness of his trade, or the nasty brutality of it.

The poetic truth of *Measure for Measure* demands more blood and guts, and not so much cool calculation as this production offered. Sex and intrigue and passion are wanted, in generous measure, if we are to accept the logic of the play and set aside the logic of everyday. Given these elements in greater measure this would emerge as the very great play it is, and as a comedy in the richest and fullest sense. As it was, we were never quite swept away by it.

Let us turn to *The Taming of the Shrew*, a favourite warhorse of the director, Tyrone Guthrie. This was a great success, and a rip-roaring success, though I do not think it was an unqualified success. It was a staggering assault upon the funny-bone, but it had not enough to say to the heart. Should *The Shrew* speak to the heart? Of course it should, for it is a very great play, and one of the best farces in our language or any language.

One moment, professor, before apoplexy grips you! I know, as well as you, that it is a coarse old grab-bag of tricks and dirty jokes, reputedly unworthy of your Swan of Avon. I know all the hard words that critics and commentators have thrown at it, to show what refined fellows they are, and how far their minds soar above such vulgar buffoonery. But tell me, professor, have you any idea how hard it is to write buffoonery on this level? Try it, some time when you have a spare half hour. *The Shrew* is a work of genius, and has held the stage for that reason, just as *Hamlet* has done.

The rowdy old play is the sex war turned into drama. Petruchio is every man's dream of himself – the triumphant woman-tamer. And Katharina contains more of every woman's dream than most women are ready to admit. Nor must we lose sight of the fact that at the end of the play, if we understand Katharina's last speech fully, the sex war ends in a draw. But until the end is reached the sexual ambitions of all of us are royally goosed by the Swan.

As played at Stratford, the Padua of the play might be any-where, though the hunting costumes of the Induction, and the Spanish-American fancy dress of the conclusion suggest that it is a combination of Canada and California, at about the turn of the present century. The director has revealed the timeless, and thus contemporaneous quality of *The Shrew*, as he did last year with *All's Well*. Christopher Sly looks like one of Walter Trier's won-derful hobos, and the strolling players who entertain him suggest the Marks Players who used to tour rural Canada. Horses are no novelty in this play, but the red limousine in which the True Vin-centio appears is a brilliant invention. The play is a wild romp; the mirth of the audience is Bacchic. And the rich comic acting of at least ten of our Canadian players is a notable rebuke to the accusa-tion that we, as a nation, cannot be funny.

As for the principals, William Needles is wonderfully endearing as the woman-tamer whose courage occasionally fails him; Barbara Chilcott is a shrew of fiery, Latin temper, most beautiful when most utterly dishevelled, and of a winning grace when tamed. It is of the highest importance to the Canadian theatre that here we have two leading players who can carry this tremendous production on their backs.

But about the heart? About the poetic reality of *The Shrew*? Well, there were moments when we wished that the pace would relax, and that some tenderness might assert itself. It did so, fleetingly, in Robert Christie's wonderful creation of an air-borne, enchanted Pedant. But in recollection the production seems to have been a little more raucous and driving than was necessary, and the players were so busy treading the quaint maze of the wanton Guthrie that they imparted to us a sense of strain, rather than the complete comic release we sought. But a few performances will set that right.

The production of *Measure for Measure* does not quite reach the top rank of achievement, but it is very well worth a visit. *The Shrew* is an exciting experience in the theatre. As for *Oedipus Rex* —well, I can hardly wait.

"Stratford: Second Year An Air of Certainty," *Saturday Night*, 17 July 1954

Stratford: 1954
Oedipus Rex

It was made clear to us last year that the festival at Stratford, Ontario, did not aim at being a careful imitation of the Shakespeare festival at Stratford-on-Avon; there was enough that was new and refreshing in the Canadian effort to quiet any suspicion of that. However, it was called a Shakespeare festival and the two plays presented were by Shakespeare, and it would have been logical to make Shakespeare the stock-in-trade of the festival for all time. But in this second year one of the three plays offered is Sophocles' *Oedipus Rex*, and because it is the finest presentation to be seen at Stratford in 1954 it has probably decided that the festival will never be exclusively Shakespearean again. There may well be years in which all the plays presented will be by Shakespeare; we hope it will be so. But it is good to know that Stratford has claimed the freedom to move into other realms of classic drama when it pleases. The importance of this step cannot be fully appreciated now, but we may hope that in ten years the Stratford Festival will have given its supporters the opportunity of seeing a large number of the world's greatest plays, performed by Canadian players within reach of a large Canadian public.

The performance of *Oedipus* this year is a triumph for all who are concerned in it. There will be plenty of dispute about it, as there must be about any considerable artistic achievement. Some people are certain not to like it, and they will be able to bring strong arguments to bear against it. But I doubt if anyone will be able to maintain successfully that it is not complete and magnificent within the limits which it has set for itself, or that these limits are not in themselves nobly conceived.

Before any profitable discussion of the production is possible, it is necessary to say something about the play itself, and as I cannot pretend to have any original opinions about it I shall be as concise as I can. The story of the play is well known: the city of Thebes suffers under a plague, and the citizens appeal to their adored king, Oedipus, for help; he learns from the Delphic Oracle that the plague is a punishment from the gods because Thebes harbours an unclean thing, and the prophet Tiresias tells him that he is himself the reason for the curse; Oedipus searches for the truth about his own parentage, and learns that he has, without knowing it, slain his father and married his mother Jocasta, and is thus irredeemably defiled; Jocasta commits suicide, Oedipus blinds himself and leaves Thebes, and his brother-in-law Creon is left to rule in his place.

Taken at its face value this is nothing more than another tale of the cruel sport of the gods with man, and we are not in our day particularly susceptible to such stories. Why, then, has the story of Oedipus so strong a hold on the imagination of man? Even in the Middle Ages, when Greek legends were little heeded, the story of Oedipus was known, and there were attempts to link it with the mythical history of Judas. In our own day Sigmund Freud has given us an answer.

Freudian psychology, supported by an impressive weight of clinical evidence, maintains that the crime of Oedipus is the crime that every man desires in his inmost heart – that the infant in the cradle yearns passionately to get rid of his father, and be all in all to his mother; as infancy gives place to childhood this desire is thrust down into the almost inaccessible depths of the mind, but its power, and the guilt that it engenders, is a potent element in the structure of man's mind. In Oedipus every man recognizes himself.

In the drama of Oedipus, then, we are confronted less with a play which we value for its exciting story, or its poetry, than with a ritual which evokes – as all true ritual does – emotions which lie in the depths of the soul. And the emotional release which the play brings us is the consequence of meeting some portion of our inmost spirit in a form which we can recognize.

The Stratford production is ritualistic and is carried through by means which give the impression of simplicity, although they conceal much superb artifice. As was the custom in the Greek theatre, all the actors wear masks, revealing the nature of the roles they play in a single, set expression. The face of Oedipus is of gold, and is marked by pride; Creon's is of bronze, and its expression is watchful; the prophet Tiresias is like some dreadful bird, in which the furies of the spirit have reduced the flesh to bony ruin; Jocasta's face is silver, and she seems a Moon to the Sun of her husband. The faces of the Old Men of the Chorus are gnarled and twisted by age and wisdom into startling presentations of compassion and resignation. The robes of all the characters are simple and beautiful. The principal actors wear the thick-soled shoes of the Greek tragic stage, to give them the height of men and women above the common run, and they walk with the measured step which such shoes make necessary. The physical presentation of the play is of great beauty, and the fear which I felt beforehand that the delicate pillars of the Stratford theatre would not make a fitting background for this monumental tragedy proved to be wholly groundless. An impressive proportion of the credit for the success of this production must be given to the designer, Tanya Moiseiwitsch.

The chief glory for the success of *Oedipus*, however, must go to the director, Tyrone Guthrie, who has carried it through with grandeur and simplicity. The actors move in patterns which are ritualistic without ever becoming rigid; the restless search for novelty which almost went too far in *The Taming of the Shrew* is never felt for an instant in *Oedipus*. The towering heights of the tragedy are approached by the most direct paths and are magnificently surmounted. The production gives us that sense of fulfilment which is the last and finest gift of a noble play, nobly brought to life.

Having said this, some words of criticism will not be misunderstood. The translation used was that of W.B. Yeats. It is marked by the sparse dignity of its prose dialogue, and the poetic grandeur of its choruses. But as a translation for use in a production on this scale it has serious shortcomings. The Greek of Sophocles, and of all the Greek dramatists, was richly poetic and elevated; they had no fear of highly-coloured words and fine phrases. Yeats' prose dialogue gives us no feeling of this, and there are occasional Irishisms in it which would sound better from Irish than from Canadian tongues. And Yeats has given us magnificent poems in place of the choruses, written in splendidly moving iambics – but he has not given us all of the choruses, by any means, for he has lopped and docked them in some cases to less than half their length. The Yeats translation gives the impression of a version prepared to be done under very simple circumstances; conditions at Stratford are not simple, and we grudged the loss of so much beauty.

The Chorus of Theban Elders was admirable, and one is tempted to say that it was, collectively, the best actor in the play. They spoke their choruses, not "beautifully," as verse choirs too often do, but with passion, and intelligence, and compassion. We forgave them for not singing, as a Greek Chorus should, they spoke so well. We forgave them – until, magically, they broke into song in a simple, but eloquent and beautiful, setting of the invocation to Mount Cithaeron. Then we regretted deeply the fact that all the choruses had not been given suitable settings by Cedric Thorpe Davie. This is not to wish that *Oedipus* had been turned into an opera; it was, rather, to wish that Stratford had mastered the Habima Players' way of moving easily from speech into song, when song heightens without interrupting the drama.

The role of King Oedipus was played by James Mason with fine understanding and dignity, and at the finish of the first performance the audience rose to do him honour – a great tribute. But the fact cannot be concealed that Mr. Mason lacks the range and power of voice for this or any other great tragic role. Every visitor to Stratford is conscious that Mr. Mason has not been content to rest upon his great movie popularity; he has sought to act great parts in a large, legitimate theatre, and this shows a love of his art which commands our respect. But in so doing he has laid himself open to the criticism which awaits great artistic feats, and it is impossible to say that he has the voice of a tragedian, or anything approaching it, as yet. He gave us much of Oedipus, and what he gave us was of fine quality, but he could not give us all. Yet, if he chose to submit himself to very stern discipline, he might emerge as a tragic actor of the first rank.

As Jocasta, Miss Eleanor Stuart seemed anxious to avoid anything savouring of a sentimental appeal, and she overshot her mark, being a little too vehement; she had power and nobility, but the Desired and Feared Mother must also have feminine tenderness.

As Tiresias, the blind, bird-inspired prophet, Donald Davis gave a wonderful picture of a being of more than mortal knowledge, and of less than mortal physical powers. This was a figure which struck strange alarm into the heart. As Creon, the inflexible brother of Jocasta, Robert Goodier made fine use of his splendid voice, and reminded us that Creon was a man of cold and bitter spirit in his subsequent treatment of the children of Oedipus. (Why, by the way, was he called Crayon?) The Messenger from Corinth, as played by Douglas Campbell, had a splendid warmth and humanity, not in the least overdone but in powerful contrast to the exalted ruling house of Thebes. The great Messenger's speech was admirably given by Douglas Rain, and Eric House, as the ancient Priest of Zeus played, as he always does, truly and affectingly. Without divorcing him from the splendid Chorus, which he led, a special word of commendation must be said for the fine speech of William Hutt.

A.E. Housman said that he knew true poetry when he heard it by the prickling of the hair on his scalp; I, too, know this feeling, and time and again during the Stratford *Oedipus* I felt this sensation of mingled terror and delight. Can there be higher praise?

"Simplicity and Artifice Combine at Stratford," *Saturday Night*, 31 July 1954

Canada's Great Playwright: 1956

From May 23 to 29 a variety of celebrations are taking place in the city of Oslo, in Norway, to celebrate the genius of Henrik Ibsen; the fiftieth anniversary of his death fell on May 23 of this year. But then, any time is a good time to remember a great man.

And what a very great man Ibsen was! Although some of his enthusiastic admirers, notably Bernard Shaw, exaggerated his importance as a social reformer, it is true that he let a lot of fresh air into the nineteenth century, and attacked a lot of ideas which still linger, though in a somewhat broken form, in many modern societies. Much of what Ibsen attacked is still to be seen everywhere about us. Indeed, what Ibsen depicted in society is so commonly met with in Canada still, that we have long thought of him as Canada's particular playwright. He cannot have been very conscious of us while he lived, but unquestionably he would find much that is familiar if he were suddenly to be manifested in Canada today.

For instance, the municipal struggle which is at the centre of *An Enemy of the People* is a very familiar one in this country of polluted waterways. And though reformers may pretend that the plight of Nora in *A Doll's House* is a thing of the past, we could throw stones from our window and hit a dozen Noras, and so could any editor in Ontario. General Gabler's daughter is known to scores of us. The theme of *Brand* is certainly well understood in Canada, and though we may not see the typical Canadian in the extravagances of *Peer Gynt* he is certainly there; how many people in this thriving land are in Peer's predicament, when at last the Button Moulder gets them! And *The Wild Duck*, that poignant and uproarious play of disappointed idealism – in how many Canadian lives is this drama not played out?

Oh yes, Henrik Ibsen knew Canadians. It is not enough to say that he knew people, and that the universality of the great artist was his. He knew Canadians, and for a long time to come he is likely to remain our greatest playwright.

Peterborough Examiner, 24 May 1956

Stratford: 1961
Coriolanus / Henry VIII / Love's Labour's Lost

This is a season of unfamiliar plays at Stratford. When was *Coriolanus* last seen in Canada? I have no record that it was ever done here. *Love's Labour's Lost* is no more familiar. *Henry VIII*, if I am not much mistaken, was last given a professional showing here by Beerbohm Tree. This is a daring season, and the most daring choice is the tragedy, *Coriolanus*.

The plot is simple. Caius Marcius, a great Roman general, defeats the Corioli, and is given their name as his own (just as we now give our generals titles relating to their victories, like Viscount Montgomery of Alamein). His friends make a familiar mistake; they insist that a great soldier must necessarily be a great statesman, and make him Consul. The people of Rome, learning how much he despises them, insist upon their ancient power, and banish him. Bitterly hurt, and mad with pride, he joins their enemies and advances upon Rome. He is about to destroy the city, but yields to the pleading of his mother, and spares it. His allies, seeing this as an act of treachery, kill him.

What makes this play a difficult one is the bitterness with which Coriolanus speaks of the Roman mob. Shakespeare was no democrat; his hero is fiercely proud, imperious, and sure of his own worth and that of his patrician caste; the mob are ninnies, easily persuaded to any sentimentality or stupidity; they are toys in the hands of their tribunes who are themselves base men. Through the mouth of Coriolanus Shakespeare lets us know what he really thought of the Common Man.

The character of Coriolanus is not immediately attractive. The deeply democratic hate his pride; the subtle despise his stupidity. But we are won by his lion-like courage and his readiness to speak his mind without fear or foresight. In time of trouble, every nation longs for a Coriolanus to fight its battles. Shakespeare has given us a matchless portrait of a kind of hero who is to be found at every period of history, and he shows us not only the hero, but the force which has made him heroic – in this case, his noble, dominating, son-consuming mother, Volumnia. Coriolanus has a wife, a child, and the triple crown of victory, but he is still his mother's boy, the instrument of a woman's dauntless will.

The Stratford *Coriolanus* is a mighty constellation of stars. Michael Langham has directed it with clarity of outline and a subtlety of detail, so that we are aware from the beginning of the inevitable tragic outcome of the situation, but always hopeful that it may be averted. This is stardom in the realm of direction, where the stars of the modern theatre are few indeed.

Tanya Moiseiwitsch has dressed the play in the costumes of 1798, which gives us the Classical Revival splendours of Revolutionary France, and makes it infinitely easier to know who's who than if some version of pre-Christian Roman costume were used. The stage picture is always beautiful and arresting, and the suggestion of gradually increasing cold, so that the play ends in winter, assists the impression of darkening and hostile fortune. This is stardom in design, supporting and augmenting, but never overwhelming, the play.

As Coriolanus, Paul Scofield gives us an exhibition of what is surely the rarest quality among actors today – heroic acting, without distracting personal mannerism, splendid in physique and voice, and with a finely controlled romantic flourish. He is first in a cast which is strong throughout. As the Roman lioness Volumnia, Miss Eleanor Stuart shows an equal quality of classic, unmannered performance; she is wholly credible as the mother of such a man. It is rarely that family relationship in a play is so easy to accept. This is one of Shakespeare's few great parts for an older actress and Miss Stuart plays it superbly.

Douglas Campbell gives us a new phase of his talent as the elderly, wise patrician Menenius, whose hopeless task it is to counsel Coriolanus towards moderation. This is quite the best thing Mr. Campbell has shown us at Stratford, and suggests that the actor's maturity may far outshine his youth. It is Menenius who makes the patricians likable in this play, in which they otherwise appear as larger models of our own still-remembered and still-hated Family Compact.

John Colicos plays the defeated general Tullus Aufidius with splendid passion. Where the Romans are restrained, he is exuberant; where they are crafty, he is trusting; their spirit is uncompromisingly Roman and marble – his, Greek and golden. His performance, so good in itself, also sets off the qualities of the tragic hero.

At this point it is not possible to praise others by name. All were admirable parts of a splendid whole. *Coriolanus* is one of Stratford's finest productions in its history.

A number of critics have found great fault with the 1798 costuming of this play; from what they have written it is clear that they are unaware of the curious sympathy between Revolutionary France and Republican Rome, which showed itself not only in philosophical and political belief, but in clothing, furniture, and even in the names that were given to children. It would be interesting to know how many of the critics who attended the first night had ever seen *Coriolanus* before; my guess would be, not more than one-third. Several confessed that they had never read it. The critical intellect is a strange and wonderful organism.

Henry VIII is a play of magnificent parts; the King himself, Queen Katharine, Wolsey, Buckingham, and Cranmer all demand actors of high abilities if the interest of the drama is to be sustained, for only the King holds his place through the whole. Buckingham vanishes early; Wolsey is through by the end of Act Three; Katharine is finished with Act Four. Cranmer is not seen until the middle of the action. The coming and going of these people admirably reflects the vicissitudes of life, but it presents the director with great problems, and only the most fortunate casting can help him to solve them.

In this production Douglas Campbell gave us a great Henry. This was the outwardly bluff, intellectually subtle Tudor, the man whose training had been theological and who leaned on churchmen as the men he knew best. The gormandizing woman-chaser of legend was nowhere to be seen. Mr. Campbell held the play together as Henry should, but does not always succeed in doing.

Douglas Rain can act much of Wolsey, but not all of him. Mr. Rain can show us anything that is intellectual, but he has no turn for sensuality; the butcher's son in Wolsey quite escaped him. Consequently we were much moved by his fall, but not shocked by his worldliness; his was the Wolsey who founded colleges, not the Wolsey who outshone the monarch in display.

Miss Reid is an undoubted star actress; when she is on the stage, we cannot look at anyone else. She is splendid in anger and in self-defence; her performance in the scene of Queen Katharine's trial was superb. But Miss Reid dearly loves a death scene, and long before Queen Katharine had expired, we uncharitably wished her elsewhere. She has obviously been doing some good work on her voice.

Mr. Creley, an excellent actor, was miscast as the great Duke of Buckingham. He is too capable to fail utterly in any part; he could play the Hound of the Baskervilles and make a pretty good fist of it; but he is not a haughty, wronged nobleman.

As Mr. Creley is not pathetic, Mr. Gerussi is not saintly. If Cranmer is not gentle, mystical, and devout he is not right; Mr. Gerussi's indomitable spirit cannot subdue itself to Cranmer. His great passage of prophecy at the end of the play sounded like a call to battle. Again, he is too good an actor to fail, but this is not a part in which he can wholly succeed.

It was disturbing to see the missing bits of some of these portrayals in other actors. Max Helpmann, as Gardiner, gave us some of the butcher-prelate that belonged to Wolsey; Eric Christmas, as the Chancellor, the saintliness lacking in Cranmer; William Needles, as Campeius, had the nobility we wanted in Buckingham. Yet we can readily understand why the director, George McCowan, did not cast them for these parts, and they gave weight and impulse to the play where they were.

The play is a director's headache, and Mr. McCowan solved his problems pretty well, except for some bad failures of pace and rhythm which will grow worse if they are not dealt with at once. Twelve minutes could be cut off the running-time if some passages of ineffective dumb-show were removed, and if those who are called upon to die would be spryer in answering their Maker's call. Nor was the fun of certain scenes of the best quality; the humour in the lines does very well, without so much running about and sitting on lunchboxes.

Nevertheless this is a superior production of a play which is not often seen and which conveys, in finely dramatic form, the hurly-burly of an exciting passage of history. And the King, for once, is not outshone by his court.

Love's Labour's Lost is a Shakespearean play which has slept for almost 300 years; from the time of its first performances until this century it has had comparatively few performances, and commentators have been apt to patronize it. It is really only within the last thirty years that it has been rediscovered as a buoyant, witty, fragile comedy that demands uttermost skill from actors and directors, but which has a matchless charm when it is perfectly done.

On the surface, the play appears to be made up of topical allusions that have lost their topicality, strained word-play, and satire of something called "The School of Night" about which professors haver in their dusty caverns. But under this surface is an exquisitely romantic idea, treated by Shakespeare in his first youthful confidence as a high-bred joke. Miss the idea, miss the high breeding, and you have missed the play.

Michael Langham, the director, has missed nothing. Tanya Moiseiwitsch, the designer, has dressed it in a style deriving from Watteau which suits it to perfection. John Cook has provided, in the final songs of this play, the best, most sensitive work he has done for the festival.

Of the actors it is not possible to speak with such enthusiasm. John Colicos, as the witty Berowne, has everything the part calls for – ebullience, a high-bred style, and a splendid variety of voice. But Miss Zoe Caldwell is not an adequate partner for him as Rosaline; she seems to mistake that lady for Katharina, in a somewhat rowdy production of *The Taming of the Shrew*. Miss Joy Parker, who plays the Princess of France, might have been a happier choice for this role; she makes her effects firmly, but without vehemence, and thoroughly understands that a witty battle is not a fight over a lost sixpence. Of the other two gentlemen in this realm of the comedy Peter Donat is excellent and very funny as Longaville, but Gary Krawford asks for sympathy as Dumain, and this little-boy-lost style of playing is not in the Shakespearean vein. Miss Mary Anderson is good as Maria, and Miss Michael Learned as Katharine brings so much beauty to the stage that we overlook the fact she consistently underacts in comparison with the others.

The funny-men are more completely successful. As the pedant Holofernes, Jack Creley shows us that the academic life has not really changed much in 350 years, in its lower reaches. William Needles as that mildest of curates, Nathaniel, is a great delight, and adds another fine stroke to his definitive study of the Shakespearean Ninny. (It was cruel of him to make up as the Prime Minister.) Mervyn Blake completes this trio as a very funny policeman who, at need, can become a one-man band.

Again, below the courtly level, Eric Christmas is first rate as the Sancho Panza character Costard, and Kate Reid is wonderfully rustic as a dairy maid. Douglas Rain has not thoroughly shaken down into the difficult role of Boyet, the elderly gentleman usher; doubtless in a week or two he will be more elfin and less fairylike. Master Murray Scott tackles the part of Moth, which is one of the problems of this play, for we have not the Elizabethan boy-actors to call on, who were trained from their earliest days to this sort of work; Master Scott sings charmingly, which is, after all, his main purpose in the play.

This brings us to Paul Scofield, who plays Don Adriano de Armado, the fantastical Spaniard. *Love's Labour's Lost* appeared in 1595; Don Quixote made his first appearance in 1605 and it is unreasonable to suppose that the one had any influence on the other; yet we could swear that Shakespeare and Cervantes were writing about the same man. The gravity, courtesy, splendid lunacy, and essential sweetness and nobility of the two creations is from the same storehouse of inspiration. Mr. Scofield gives us a great Don Adriano; he is never funny in the sense that he does ridiculous things to make us laugh; he is funny in the much finer sense of being imbued with the Spirit of Comedy; he is a reflection of a smile on the face of God. Mr. Scofield is the leader of those associated with this production who have found the path to the very heart of the play.

The production is swift and sure, moving through gaiety, tomfoolery, and romance to a conclusion of autumnal beauty.

Thus concludes this appreciation of the first performances of the ninth festival at Stratford. If the productions have not met every demand of every critic, it may truly be said that you will not see these plays so well done again in a hurry. And to measure everything against perfection is to assume that one knows what perfection is, and that is a big claim, even for so shameless a creature as a critic.

Peterborough Examiner, 24 June 1961

Stratford: 1962
Cyrano de Bergerac

On Monday night last, *Cyrano de Bergerac* opened at the Stratford Festival to applause and shouts of acclaim such as have not been heard since the first night of *Richard III* in 1953. It was a great night for the star, Christopher Plummer, for the designers, Tanya Moiseiwitsch and Desmond Heeley, and for the director, Michael Langham.

It was apparent before the play began that the audience wanted the play to succeed with more than ordinary goodwill. Mr. Plummer had been unfortunate in *Macbeth*; not only is he a very good actor – he is also a very popular one, and his friends wanted him to make the unequivocal hit in Cyrano that had been denied him in the greater role. Even the playing of "God Save the Queen" by the orchestra brought a round of applause, for the musical director, Lou Applebaum, had arranged it in a seventeenth-century style congruous with the play. Success was in the air.

The performance bore out the wishes of everybody on the stage or in the house. It went with splendid verve; there were no dull patches, during which the attention might stray; there was plenty of laughter, and the scenes of pathos drew plentiful tears. It was just such a production, indeed, as this extraordinary play deserves, and rarely gets. Canada has not seen a professional *Cyrano* since José Ferrer's production in 1946; the Stratford offering provokes comparison, and in the words of another romantic old play, "it is a far, far, better thing."

There are elements in this play which have never, in the sixty-five years of its life, been satisfactorily transferred to the English stage. Rostand wrote *Cyrano* in French rhymed verse, which has resisted several very able translators. The wit, the butterfly grace, and the sheer beauty of sound which makes the play so delightful in French, cannot be rendered in any comparable degree in English. Some of the great speeches – the splendid rhapsody on Cyrano's nose, the scornful rejection of patronage, and the conclu-

94

sion of the play in which Cyrano soars on the very wings of romance – suffer heavily in translation. So does all the love-making, which has more sound than sense. But in spite of this serious handicap the play remains, in English as in French, the last and greatest example of a splendid school of romantic drama that had its beginning with Victor Hugo. Only a curmudgeon could fail to warm to it; only a very young playgoer takes it with complete seriousness.

One of the critic's disagreeable tasks is to find what fault he can, so let us get that unpleasant business over. Some of the Cadets of Gascony in this production lack the high-bred manners they ought to have; when these same gentlemen introduce themselves in a song, we wonder for a moment whether we have not wandered into an old-fashioned musical comedy; Cyrano himself, on two or three occasions, chooses to be funny when we would like him to be tender. Perhaps he loves; he never adores.

But balance against these defects the splendour of the spectacle, the masterly handling of the crowds, the very high level of performance achieved by the entire cast, and the fine conception of the play as a whole to which everybody, from Cyrano himself to the tiniest crowd player contributes, and the Stratford *Cyrano* emerges as a triumph.

Now to the actors. Christopher Plummer is a brilliant Cyrano, bringing wit, physical grace, a remarkable voice, and a thrilling quality of grotesquerie to the role upon which all else depends. This is among the finest exhibitions of the art of the classical actor that Stratford has given us in its distinguished ten years of production. He has a beautiful, elegant Roxane in Miss Toby Robins. The part is a difficult one, because almost its sole purpose is to be admired – and that is harder than those who have never been overloaded with admiration can possibly conceive. She almost persuades us, also, that Roxane is a woman of distinguished mind, which again is hard to manage without sacrificing romantic quality. These two leading players have gallant, unobtrusive assistance from Peter Donat in the utterly awful role of Christian; his task is that of representing male beauty, without any special intelligence; to do this with dignity requires an actor of quality, and Mr. Donat rises manfully to the occasion.

Douglas Rain, one of Stratford's best players, resists all temptations to be sentimental in the role of Ragueneau, the pastry cook with a mind above his trade. In the pathos and dignity he brings to his part, he is a lesser Cyrano. John Colicos is an admirable De Guiche; this actor knows the secret of playing villains – he believes in villainy; as a result he emerges as a real person, and not as an inexplicably naughty child. William Hutt and Eric Christmas show us authentic figures from seventeenth-century prints; the pictorial quality in acting is of great importance in bringing such a play as this one to life. Nor must we forget Bruno Gerussi, not only as the drunken poet Ligniere, but as a wonderful peasant figure who appears to sing a song of Gascony at the siege of Arras. Once again Stratford shows its strength in persuading actors of distinguished abilities to give glowing life to small roles.

The most touching moment is an exchange between the star, and Miss Mary Savidge as Sister Marthe; anyone who is not moved by it is impervious to great acting.

The company brings all its forces to this production and succeeds brilliantly. The performances scheduled between now and the end of September cannot possibly suffice; why not revive it next year?

Peterborough Examiner, 23 June 1962

Tyrone Power and Dr. Thomas Guthrie in Canada: 1963

Tyrone Guthrie was asked to advise on the planning of the Shakespeare festival at Stratford in Canada during its earliest stages, and from the moment he arrived in that small city, in 1952, he was known as "Doctor" Guthrie. He had been given an LL.D. by St. Andrew's University in Scotland, as a recognition of his work in the theatre, and he valued the academic distinction. At Stratford we still speak of him as Dr. Guthrie more often than as Sir Tyrone. We remember that doctor is Latin for teacher, and Dr. Guthrie was a teacher to every one of us, from the president of the Board of Governors to the humblest assistant.

He taught us on the grand scale and by the best method. Much has been written, in sentimental vein, about the "miracle" at Stratford. If a miracle is an arbitrary reversal of natural order, there was no miracle: but if a miracle is an instance of the spirit's triumph over material difficulties, the Stratford Festival was indeed a miracle. Its story has been told elsewhere; Dr. Guthrie's contribution to it is what concerns us here.

He was a leader with the power to rally and unite a group of able but disorganized followers. His greatest gift was not specifically theatrical; it was that power to discern what was best in each one of a group of widely differing people, and to use them in a common cause, which is characteristic of great leaders in politics and the church – indeed, wherever great efforts must be made. In Canada we had good actors, good technicians, people of vision, people of strong patriotic feeling, people with financial acumen, but we had nobody to unite them, or to urge them on when every dictate of common sense – O, the inadequacies of common sense! – told them to fall back. That was what Dr. Guthrie could do, and our gratitude towards him is still that of brave troops towards a great commander.

Let no one suppose that I underestimate his powers as an artist; I shall speak of those in time. But it was his power as a leader that pulled us through, gave us a faith in our own abilities, and a standard of judgement which still sustains us.

His ancestry unites two strains which admirably symbolize what he is. On his mother's side he is descended from Tyrone Power, the early-nineteenth-century Irish actor whose gifts and charm won him a high place before his untimely death. A first meeting with Tyrone Guthrie shows what he owes to the hero of *Teddy The Tiler*. But on his father's side we encounter an even more remarkable great-grandfather – Dr. Thomas Guthrie, the Scottish preacher and philanthropist, a thundering orator, fighter for total abstinence, and organizer of the Ragged School movement to give elementary instruction to the children of the poor. This great-grandfather was as much a charmer as the great actor. "You must be accustomed to people getting very seriously and truly attached to you at first sight," wrote John Ruskin to this earlier Dr. Guthrie; the words apply as truly to the Dr. Guthrie we know at Stratford.

Everybody who was interested in having a festival became seriously and truly attached to him on short acquaintance. He paid us the high compliment of treating us as equals, not in theatrical experience, but in courage and intelligence. He assumed that we did not want to play at theatre, hoping that social ambition, or national pride, or the tourist industry might be served thereby. He assumed that we were for the festival plan through thick and thin, and that we were not frightened when the "thin" dwindled to a barely perceptible tenuity. He assumed that we wanted the best, and that nothing else would do. He told us what wanting the best would cost.

It was not the outlay of money that struck awe into our hearts, fearful though that was. As organization and rehearsals developed it was the cost in courage, in abandoned preconceptions, in humbled pride that went beyond anything we had foreseen.

There was all the business of setting up our theatre in a tent, for instance; this was dear to Dr. Guthrie's heart, and I had heard him put forward his tent plan at a Christmas party as early as 1945; but to many people the tent suggested impermanence, squalid makeshift and – our North American bugaboo of bugaboos – discomfort. Now that the tent is a thing of the past, most of us remember it with affection; before the tent proved itself there were many to whom it seemed more doleful than the tents of Kedar to the Psalmist.

The platform stage, without scenery, caused comparatively little misgiving, for some of us had seen what Dr. Guthrie had done on a less versatile platform stage in Edinburgh. It was a revolutionary idea, as so many returns to the past are, but we were prepared for revolution and shocks to others. It was the shocks to ourselves that robbed us of breath.

There were shocks for the thrifty; whatever was cheap was false economy. Shocks for the actors; cherished "technique" was condemned as stagey tricks. Shocks for the press; rehearsals were behind locked doors. Shocks for the scholars; Shakespeare had fewer rights than a mediocre living playwright. Shocks for the innocents who thought that a theatre company would have lots of time to play and chatter at parties.

There were repeated brutal shocks for everybody who thought that the best results could be brought forth from anything but the best and most self-sacrificing efforts. And all of these shocks were given with a moral rigour which descended straight from Dr. Thomas Guthrie, the Scottish preacher and philanthropist.

The shocks would have been much less severe if Dr. Guthrie had been content to play his part, in theatre jargon, "straight." We are accustomed to Scottish theologians and spellbinders in Canada. But we needed time to grow accustomed to the sudden metamorphoses of Dr. Thomas Guthrie into Tyrone Power, hopping about the theatre with his shirt-tail out, cursing the actors in language that might have dismayed a longshoreman, flitting through the streets on a bicycle, licking an ice-cream cone, launching into high-ranging flights of verbal fantasy that delighted his hearers, and devising farouche practical jokes to disquiet the solemn. Those who had not known the Doctor before were confused by his protean, shot-silk personality.

This mercurial spirit is common among artists. In Doctor Guthrie, however, the disparity between the leader, who put steel into the backbones of everybody connected with the festival, and the director, who put the plays on the stage, was greater than had been expected. At rehearsal he was temperamental but pliant, doing what only the great director can do; he created an atmosphere in which other artists could work at the top of their form.

The selfish spirit which is one of the bugbears of theatre work was rebuked by his magnanimity.

He was the only director in the 1953 season; the plays were *Richard III*, with Sir Alec Guinness in the title role, and *All's Well That Ends Well*, in which Irene Worth played Helena. *Richard* was an able production in the rapid, pageant-like style which has for a quarter of a century been the fashionable way of staging the Shakespeare histories. It is a style of which Tyrone Guthrie was one of the originators, and of which he has long been a master. The excitement of the first night was more than theatrical; not a production alone, but the success of a desperately hazardous venture, was to be decided. After the first five minutes many of us felt a merciful lightening of the spirits; by the end of the performance we were just as heavily committed to the unknown, our debts were just as alarming, our future still uncertain, but we knew that we had assisted at a performance which, without being great, was in the first class and for which no apology need ever be made to anyone.

The following night a spirit suggesting greatness enfolded our tent. *All's Well* is a play unfamiliar to most audiences – one of the "difficult" comedies. We saw it in that Ruritanian costume which passes as modern dress on the stage, and which gave it the external appearance of a comedy by Molnar. Unexpected beauty and fresh humour were made plain by this reasonably familiar style of dress; the problem which so often troubles audiences at Shakespearean plays – the social level of the characters and their relationship to one another – was thus made clear. With this clarification came a searching of the depths of the fable of the complex, bittersweet play, and an illumination of an enigmatic classic. The only fly in the ointment was that some of the clarity was achieved by serious cuts in the text.

In 1954 Dr. Guthrie was again the artistic director of the festival, and of the three plays offered he directed two, *The Taming of the Shrew* and *Oedipus Rex*. The farce was not a happy venture; Dr. Guthrie had done it better in 1939 and the festival presented a greatly superior production of it in 1962, directed by Michael Langham. It was dressed in the costume of 1900, and the milieu seemed to be Californian. Under the whirlwind of action lay a perverse concept which recalled the Restoration version of the play, named *Sauney the Scot*.

Oedipus was a magnificent evocation of the spirit of one of the great classics of world drama. Without antiquarian pretensions, the play was produced with masked actors wearing the *kothornos* and moving ritualistically through the action, which was necessarily slow and stately. It was nobly spoken, though the Yeats version of the play, to which some haphazard additions and alterations had been made, did not meet with entire approval. James Mason, who played Oedipus in 1954, was impressive but a little over-parted; when the play was repeated in 1955 Douglas Campbell showed himself more nearly equal to the role.

By 1955 Dr. Guthrie had resigned as our artistic director, despite our pleadings. It was not good for the festival, said he, to be made too much in his image. This was the kind of wisdom he could give, and the value of which we could not perceive, but we bowed to his will, and we know now how wisely magnanimous he was. In this season, however, he directed *The Merchant of Venice*, and gave us an exquisite rendering of a play which seemed to be irrecoverably shopworn. He restored it as a fairytale from those depths of the spirit where poets are the explorers.

In 1957 Dr. Guthrie returned to Stratford to produce *Twelfth Night* and drew us even further into the world of great Shakespearean comedy. Here again it was his delicate releasing of those enchantments which lie at the heart of these plays, and which are so often unseen by players and scholars alike, that assured us that we were in the presence of two masters, the poet and his finely attuned interpreter.

In the theatre it has long been the custom to speak of the production of an old play as a "revival." The word has a special meaning when applied to Dr. Guthrie's productions of *The Merchant of Venice* and *Twelfth Night*; they lived again, and enriched the sensibility of any in the audience who were in the least responsive to poetry. And how many are those, in any audience? Let the cynic hold his peace, for who can say how many they are, or what life may be changed by a matinee encounter with poetic beauty?

Drama Survey, 3 (1963)

Stratford: 1964
Richard II / Le Bourgeois Gentilhomme / King Lear

Stuart Burge has gone directly to the heart of *Richard II*, producing it not as the tragedy of a man unfit to be a king – although this was included – but as a play about power. Some of the first-night audience were puzzled and a little disappointed that the king did not dominate, as he often does in productions which are cut ruthlessly in order to allow him to do so; but Stratford is an ensemble company which contains some actors who would be stars elsewhere, and William Hutt is too fine an artist to play against the ensemble. In consequence we saw a true chronicle, the hero of which was neither Richard nor Bolingbroke, but England, and the theme of which was not a king's fate, but kingship.

Mr. Hutt refuses to play Richard as the weak poet familiar in some contemporary productions; he shows him as a man whose strength, though real, is fitful; this king is ill-balanced, and his fits of groundless optimism are more alarming than his descents into despair. His belief in his Divine Right is strong, but his belief in Divinity is shaky. Facing the terrible resolution of Leo Ciceri's Bolingbroke, this Richard is ruined by his own fatal capacity to see several sides of a question, many of them irrelevant to a man whose first duty is to rule.

Mr. Burge has directed for character first, and pageantry second. The pace of production is a beat slower than is usual at Stratford, and this is reason for gratitude; we can hear, and what we hear is well-spoken; there is time for characterization in depth, which gives us a chance to be deeply involved, and to know the great nobles by more than their outward appearance; especially, we have time to get the relationships straight, in a play where family rivalry is at the root of the plot. Power is everything, and Mr. Burge has made even the "caterpillars of the commonwealth" more intent on that than on sensual enjoyment.

In this connection it is necessary to make one strong adverse criticism of a fine production. The role of John of Gaunt was shallowly and conventionally played, as a dull old party with some poetic notions about England. Unless this man is shown to be the waning power in the kingdom, greatest of the league of dreadful uncles who broke Richard's character before he grew to be a man, neither Richard's character nor Bolingbroke's can be completely realized, nor can the fierce allegiances of the nobles be fully understood.

Because the play is an ensemble, let us omit the customary bouquets for individual players. With the exception already noted, the cast was admirable and played together like a fine orchestra. Stratford proposes to give us all the cycle of chronicles which follow *Richard II*, and it has made a distinguished beginning. Let us hope we shall see more of Mr. Burge's work in the special chronicle genre.

Molière in English is not everybody's *tisane*, but the dissenters must remember that Stratford has already given its public some first-rate Molière in French. Nor is *Le Bourgeois Gentilhomme* the most characteristic of Molière's plays; it is an entertainment with music, a farce-comedy, a romp. The Stratford company gave it a piquant Gallic flavour without fake Gallicisms, and for this we must undoubtedly thank Jean Gascon, the director.

Nevertheless, we may find fault with Douglas Rain's performance of Monsieur Jourdain; he is not a bourgeois of aspiring mind trying to behave like a nobleman; he is too clearly an actor of physical grace and acute intellect trying to behave like a clod. Jourdain is a nice-minded man, and a romantic; here we see him as a proletarian, too sullen and suspicious ever to have fallen prey to the insidious Dorante. But in the framework of this mistaken conception, Mr. Rain is very funny, and he is surrounded by a company who can be extravagant without falling into grotesquerie; the solid technique, the high professional competence of the Stratford ensemble shows to great advantage in this trifle by perhaps the most competent professional actor who ever wrote for the stage.

Special compliments must be paid to Helen Burns, who wears a farce in her face, and expresses bewilderment with an almost imperceptible declension of the jaw; to Diana Maddox, who is a delightful *bourgeoise*, and to Messrs. Blake, House, Christmas, and

Gerussi, who are as fine a group of oddities as you are ever likely to see on one stage.

It was not kind to cast Len Cariou for a part which requires romantic style, and it was almost malignant to mar Gabriel Charpentier's otherwise delightfully witty music with four actors whose singing can only be described as disciplined groaning in unison.

The translation cannot give us the sturdy elegance of the original, but it is decidedly the best that exists, and it has some wonderful turns of phrase. We may perhaps wonder why Jourdain is absent from so much of the Turkish ceremony which is, after all, for his benefit; but this apart, the "Turkish foolery" for which Louis XIV called is a splendid *jeu d'esprit*, and should not be missed by anyone who relishes brilliant farce.

The real problem of *Le Bourgeois Gentilhomme* is that it is a play about social distinctions. How is this to be made comprehensible and valid to an audience whose notions of social status are plutocratic, rather than aristocratic? Jean Gascon has solved the problem by fantasticating the play so that, while Molière is not best served, we are given a performance we can understand.

By the time this reaches print, it will be known everywhere that *King Lear* crowns the festival, and is indeed the highest achievement of its existence. Stratford has now succeeded splendidly in the greatest of tragedies; there is no fiercer test. Here again we see a great ensemble, in which each performs, with high artistry, to the uttermost of his abilities. John Colicos' magnificent Lear plays out his fate in worthy company.

Michael Langham's concept is nobly tragic; there is no whiff of sentimentality, no avoidance of cruelty, no concealment of the fact that Lear is a monster of self-will who, as Regan says, "hath ever but slenderly known himself." His tragedy is that of a man whose lack of self-recognition makes a hell on earth for himself and all around him. Given this Lear, we understand his "pelican daughters"; why would they be otherwise? Given this Lear we can have a Cordelia with blood in her veins and fire in her eye. Given this monomaniac splendour, we understand the stubborn loyalty of Kent, and the daring of the Fool.

Self-recognition is the theme, and Lear and Gloucester both

have to endure to the uttermost before it is attained. This production carries the theme further still. Edgar, who first appears as a carefree, drunken youth, must find his way through poverty and madness to his own true centre. The play batters us with its warning; failure to win some degree of wholeness poisons the greatest life; the infection spreads to those around, and creeps from generation to generation.

No star casting can alone suffice to make this clear. But star quality is wanted for Lear, and John Colicos has it; without notable advantages of voice or feature he has a magnetism which springs from a very rare combination – intellectual power and the ability to make it manifest by bodily means. This *Lear* is in itself enough to make Stratford this year a place of pilgrimage. On the four hundredth anniversary of Shakespeare's birth his greatest tragedy – and with due respect to the noble Greeks, they never reached this height – is greatly understood and greatly acted. Langham and Colicos give us the play as Shakespeare meant it – not as the tragedy of a mythic Lear, but as the Tragedy of Man.

One cavil cannot be avoided: the electric storm has the fault of all such canned noise – it can do no more than a machine can compass, and it has, even at its loudest, a contained and tamed sound. A few cannonballs, artistically dropped, would have spoken with greater truth; wooden thunder is not Jove's, but it is far better than recordings, tapes, and similar electronic rubbish.

The standards of stage decoration and costume are as high as ever. Desmond Heeley's *Richard* is rich, and his controlled use of heraldry, erring neither on the side of dowdy accuracy nor mere decoration, is admirable. Watching Mr. Heeley's work deepen has been one of the pleasures of the festival for some time. So also with Robert Prevost, who has never been happier than in *Le Bourgeois Gentilhomme*. Leslie Hurry's designs for *Lear* are brilliantly in the key of the whole conception; this is a primal world, but never a squalid one; suppression of detail has made these people seem to dwell in a land of mythology – as indeed they do, for *Lear* is part of the mythology of man's soul.

Never before has the company played so well together and never have they reached and possessed such heights. Is this new confidence found at Chichester? Not entirely. It is the outcome of work conditioned by high artistic purpose, and seasoned by years of practice. Stratford this year is at the top of its form.

A word to the three first-night audiences: ladies and gentlemen, need you really cough so much? There are other bodily noises of which you are capable, which would undoubtedly give you ease, but decency demands that you suppress them. Why not extend this suppression to your hawkings, gaggings, and nauseating effluxions of phlegmy wastes? Hold in, or stay at home.

"Stratford's Festival of Man," *Saturday Night*, August 1964

Stratford: 1965
The Rise and Fall of the City of Mahagonny

The Stratford Festival established itself with astonishing speed as an important centre of classic theatre. There are encouraging signs that it now aspires to an honourable position in the world of opera. It would be foolish to say that eminence in classic theatre is easier to achieve than in opera, but it must be admitted that opera presents special and formidable difficulties.

This year the festival offers two operatic works at the beautifully refurbished Avon Theatre. They are Mozart's *The Marriage of Figaro* and *The Rise and Fall of the City of Mahagonny* by Kurt Weill and Bertolt Brecht. *Figaro* was seen last year, and is now revived with a strengthened cast; it is a charming production of one of the great operas of the world repertoire, and we need say no more about it. But *Mahagonny* is a novelty.

A novelty, let it be said, to North America; this is its first production here, though Weill won a great reputation during the latter part of his career with such superior musical shows as *Knickerbocker Holiday, Lady in the Dark, One Touch of Venus*, and *Lost in the Stars*. But though *Mahagonny* was written in 1928, and was a controversial work in Europe, Stratford has shown it first on this continent. There are rumours that it will appear (not by this company) in New York next season. When Broadway follows Canada, that is news.

Whatever novelty or shock value the work may once have had has disappeared, but it is able to survive vigorously on the more enduring qualities of theatrical strength, brilliant music, and a pungent historical flavour which has been added to it by time.

The work has its roots in the disillusion of Germany during the twenties – an era of inflation, cynicism, and desperate opportunism. The plot is simple. Three crooks, Fatty the Bookkeeper, Trinity Moses, and Mrs. Begbick, having come to the end of their tether in the wilderness of Alabama, decide to found a new city called Mahagonny – which means "City of Nets." The city will have but one purpose, which is to make them rich, and no law save Do As You Please. So the squalid shakedown begins, the harlots and crooks stream in, and Mahagonny becomes a paradise of gluttony, lechery, and avarice.

The only dissenters from the general philosophy are Jenny, a harlot, and Jim Mahoney, who loves her. They are intolerable to the greedy bosses, and are dealt with; Jenny embraces the Mahagonny philosophy, and Jim is electrocuted at the order of a corrupt court.

This does not sound especially stimulating, but it is so. The piece is theatrically vivid; the music is melodically rich and occasionally reaches splendid emotional heights. The unrelieved cynicism of the plot is in Brecht's heavily Germanic style; this writer, so much admired today, never credited his audience with ordinary common sense, and persistently hit them over the head with the most obvious elements in his plots. But there is a pleasure even in this kind of pounding. The cynicism of *Mahagonny* is as simple-minded as the optimism of Pollyanna, and our pleasure in it springs from its theatricality rather than its philosophy.

The Stratford production gives the opera every possible assistance. Jean Gascon has directed it with brilliant resource; there is not a languid moment in the action, and he has – wonder of wonders – made singers act much better than singers usually do. Louis Applebaum finds all the drama in Weill's music, and sometimes passages of tenderness which could easily have been lost. The orchestra on the first night was too loud, but that is a trouble that can be set right. Brian Jackson's setting is ingenious, but does not clutter the stage, as ingenious settings have been known to do.

Of the singers, the three crooks are admirable. Jean Bonhomme as Fatty combines menace with humour, and Yoland Guerard as Trinity Moses, sets a tone of menace from which all the rest of the cast take their cue; his brutality really frightens, but not so much as his dreadful macabre farce in the scene where The God Game is played. This is an actor of remarkable star quality. Muriel Greenspoon as Mrs. Begbick has fine authority, and a voice that tops the orchestra without effort. This trio raises the opera to distinguished heights.

Not so much can be said of the lovers. Martha Schlamme, so effective in concert performance, lacks the stage authority for the role of Jenny; when she has the stage alone, she is admirable, but she cannot pull her weight in the ensembles. Thomas O'Leary, as Jim, has a pleasant tenor voice, but it is lyric in quality, as is his personality. He is simply not tough enough.

These criticisms, however, are not to be taken as meaning that the opera is not a success. As an ensemble it is very strong, and can carry the occasional weaknesses of some of the performers. Further it is a sign of a new spirit in opera at Stratford.

For a time, Stratford opera meant Gilbert and Sullivan, somewhat tentatively revivified, and well acted and sung. But whatever our devotion to Gilbert and Sullivan, it is not enough for a company with serious operatic ambitions. Such works as *Mahagonny*, which are not grand opera in the nineteenth-century sense of vast musical melodrama, with a chorus and a ballet, demanding an orchestra of seventy or more, exist in large numbers, and it is time we had the chance to see them adequately performed in Canada.

The Toronto season next September will offer us Stravinsky's *Mavra*, Strauss' *Salome*, and Puccini's *Turandot*, as well as three popular works from the repertoire of thirty or more operas that dominate the stages of Europe and this continent. But if we are to have fine productions of smaller works, which are more sophisticated in plot and more adventurous in music than the favourites of the nineteenth century, we must look to Stratford to give them to us. Stratford has begun this work with a flourish, and we are eager for more.

"Opera at Stratford," *Peterborough Examiner*, 6 July 1965

Stratford: 1965
The Cherry Orchard

Let us suppose that an examining board of critics were set up to determine the position of the Stratford Festival company as a classical theatre. What marks might it hope for in the searching group of examinations that such a board would impose, each one taking the form of work in a classical theatrical mode, and 100 being the impossible attainment – perfection?

I make no great pretence to answer for such a board, but I suspect that the marks might run something like this:

Shakespeare: for a series of thirty productions, topped
by a splendid *King Lear* last year and a fine *Henry IV*
(both parts) this year 90
Greek Drama: two attempts at *Oedipus* 70
Restoration Drama: a production of *The Country Wife*,
good but somewhat heavy 62
Molière: a production of *Le Bourgeois Gentilhomme*
in translation 78
Romantic Melodrama: a production of *Cyrano de Bergerac*
in translation 78
European Classics: one bash at Kleist's *The Broken Jug* ... 33
Chekhov: one production of *The Cherry Orchard* 87

The examinee has not yet attempted the examinations in Ibsen and Old Comedy (Sheridan and Goldsmith).

We shall not, like the Ontario Department of Education, average the marks. The showing is admirable in two of the three most searching examinations.

The plays of Chekhov are among the most difficult to present satisfactorily in all of world drama. The slightness of their dialogue and the seeming naturalness of their manner present extraordinary pitfalls, for these are truly "dramas of things unsaid." Lives crumble while the characters are chattering, often vapidly, around the matter which is uppermost in their minds. Poetic beauty of the tenderest and most poignant kind is evoked while the harshest facts of life are demonstrated before us: such gritty truths as that men cannot reap where they have not sown, that you cannot make a silk purse of a sow's ear, that people who most need love are often least capable of inspiring it.

Chekhov is devastatingly frank about the shortcomings of mankind, and nobly compassionate in depicting them. He was, by training and temperament, a physician, and when, on the stage, the patient is dying, he never pretends otherwise.

In *The Cherry Orchard*, which many people think the greatest of his plays, the plot is simple. An aristocratic Russian family has come to the end of its tether; folly, superficiality, procrastination, and debt have brought them to the point where their country estate, distinguished for its beautiful cherry orchard, must be sold; it is sold to the son of one of their serfs, now a thriving man of business; he will cut down the cherry orchard, and build summer cottages on the land.

This simple plot takes in the end of one way of life, and the beginning of another. We are invited to watch this happen, and to feel for the dispossessed, while recognizing that there is nothing unjust or avoidable about it.

Here is a task of the greatest delicacy for actors and director. The characters must be life-size, but no more; in their fate we see an aspect of life which all of us, to some degree and from some aspect, have known. And yet the irony, the pathos, and the wild comedy of life arise from a fine performance of this play, and we leave the theatre enriched and enlarged.

In the Stratford production which opened on Monday last there were few false notes, and the first compliments must go to the director, John Hirsch, a Canadian man of the theatre in whom this country has a great possession; let us take care that he is adequately rewarded in appreciation and understanding. There was never the slightest break in the sensitivity with which the play was set forth, and the beauty of the play was evoked naturally from it, not imposed upon it from without. We must have more Chekhov at Stratford from Mr. Hirsch, and some productions of Ibsen, too.

The cast was in almost every respect admirable, and if I begin by picking a few flaws, it is a critic's business to be hard to please. As Dunyasha, the maidservant with ideas above her station,

Martha Henry gave us no hint of the peasant girl she really was; her foolishness was of an urban kind. As Anya, the schoolgirl who is infatuated with her lover's "advanced" ideas, Susan Ringwood gave us all the joy of youth, but lacked something of the shallowness and unconscious cruelty of youth. It was, by the way, unfortunate that she pronounced "Mama" as "Momma" every time she uttered it: the effect was proletarian, in an aristocratic role.

In a distinguished company, however, these performances could not unbalance the ensemble. Bruno Gerussi as the Russian peasant who fancies himself above his origins; William Needles as one of those men upon whom Fate has played a tasteless joke; Mary Savidge as the brave, consciously "amusing" governess, almost crazed with loneliness; Mervyn Blake as a Russian landowner straight out of Gogol, and gaily unaware of his fossildom; Hugh Webster as the prudish, unworldly student, determined to reform the world but incapable of keeping track of his galoshes; and Powys Thomas as the old serf, Firs, who is feudally absorbed in the existence of his masters and his home; every one of these portraits is drawn with great skill and artistic discretion, and the ensemble playing is such as to leave us with the conviction that we have, for two hours, lived in a complete world.

This brings us to Frances Hyland's moving performance as Varya, one of Chekhov's sorry spinsters, burdened by moral and financial responsibilities that have been flung off by somebody she loves, and herself starved for the tenderness which would save her from a shrewish, miserly middle age. Miss Hyland's tears when her last hope of marriage is taken from her bring to the production one of its two or three most piercing moments of insight into the pathos of life.

To Douglas Campbell falls the part of Lopahin, the son of a serf who buys the estate on which his father was a slave. This is quite the finest thing this brilliant but woefully uneven actor has done at Stratford. It is the sensitivity, the native nobility, the fineness of spirit which he reveals in the part that gives this play much of its greatness. He is a peasant, a hard-headed man of business, a "man of the future," but he is also a Russian, distraught and frightened by the dissolution of his country as he has known it.

Thus we come to Kate Reid, as Madame Ranevskaya, the owner of the cherry orchard, and William Hutt as her brother

Gaev: in these characters Chekhov shows us both what was wrong and what was right with the Russia of 1904. They are incapable of understanding anything of the slightest importance; they are almost pathologically incapable of action, even when Lopahin tells them what to do and offers to do it for them. They are selfish. But they are also charming, sensitive, elegant in their approach to life, and possessed of a distinguished, aristocratic gaiety, which they can communicate to other people. They illuminate and lift the lives of those around them and this is their real strength. They are the sort of people Lopahin would like to be, if it could be managed without sacrificing his intelligence.

Miss Reid and Mr. Hutt give us almost everything that is contained in these characters, leaving only a measure of aristocratic distinction to be desired; these people would surely have revealed a little more of their superior station in the tone and nuance of their voices? After all, Ranevskaya is a great charmer, and Gaev wins everybody's love, in spite of being not much better than an idiot. But to make up for this lack, both these splendid players give us emotional riches that make the play a great experience. Their delight at being home in Act One, and their desolation—which she meets with courage and he with utter collapse—in Act Four, are among the finest things Stratford has given us since 1953.

Here, then, is a fine performance of a great play, which extends the range of what is possible at Stratford vastly, for this poetic realism suits the open stage very well, and Brian Jackson has made a convincing 1904 Russia out of comparatively simple elements. This production is a collector's piece, and you should take pains not to miss it.

"The Cherry Orchard at Stratford," *Peterborough Examiner*, 31 July 1965

Stratford: 1966
Twelfth Night / Henry V / Henry VI

This year's production of *Twelfth Night* has, of course, to withstand comparison with the 1957 production by Tyrone Guthrie which so sensitively brought forth the poetic, bittersweet beauty of the play. Let it be said at once that the new *Twelfth Night* takes its stand on elegance, wit, and a gentle mockery of the concept of romantic love, and succeeds admirably. But the poetry is not scamped, and at least one performance – that of Martha Henry as Viola – erases memories of Siobhan McKenna principally because of Miss Henry's superior poetic fervour.

Twelfth Night is Shakespeare at the height of his power as a writer of comedy. The director has gone beneath the surface of the play, to reveal it as a great myth about love. The twins Viola and Sebastian are a unity; together they are Eros, the very spirit of love, and in some respect every major character in the comedy is under the sway of love – even Malvolio, who is a victim of self-love. Only Feste, the Clown, is not a lover, and he moves through the play like a Chorus, illuminating it with two of Shakespeare's most beautiful love songs. The result is a fantasy that must be handled by director and actors with a firm but gentle touch if it is not to degenerate into two plays – an improbable romance, and a rather cruel farce; the touch at Stratford this year is appropriately strong yet gentle.

All the characters are shown as very young, except for Feste, who is old and wise, and the movement of the action is swift. Sometimes it may be a little too swift, but this will adjust itself as the season continues; some of Malvolio's scenes were rushed, probably to avoid the common tendency to extend them unwisely. The love of the separated twins was given unusual emphasis, and this brought an exquisite poignancy to the final scene of recognition.

All of the cast was admirable, and to name individual performances of merit would be to name all. But because they were out of the common in their realization of their roles it is fitting to name Miss Henry's tender but never weak Viola, Douglas Rain's gallant and intelligent Sir Toby, and Leo Ciceri's tortured, absurd, youthful Malvolio.

As always when Malvolio is finely performed, the scene in which the madman is tormented was uglier than all the stabbings and beheadings in history; those might have been moved by necessity, but that was an exhibition of the sheer, wanton, bloody-mindedness of mankind.

To conclude with a few general reflections about *Henry V* and *Henry VI** as well as *Twelfth Night*, it may be asked why, in *Henry V*, some excellent real offstage noise was mingled with some bad canned sound effects? When the instrumental music in all three plays was so good, why was the singing so bad? Why do stage designers continue under the delusion that bishops attend royal councils in full Mass vestments? Why, in *Henry VI*, is Hume presented as a courtier when the text of the play specifically says he is a priest?

To turn to positive matters, some skilled editing of the texts had been done, to clarify meanings which might otherwise escape modern ears. It was good to hear the name of God restored in *Twelfth Night* in those speeches of Malvolio's where it has been turned by a non-Shakespearean hand to "Jove"; this restores Malvolio's character as "a kind of Puritan." One wishes that this skilled editorial hand had been set to work to provide program notes for *Henry V* and *Henry VI*, for these were far below festival standard. The festival is a unity, from the courtesy of the theatre management through to the last detail of costume, and Stratford has taught us to expect the best in every detail.

Some surprise has been expressed at the comparatively restrained reception of *Henry V*; it is not hard to understand. The play was directed with heavy emphasis on the horror of war and the burdens of leadership. These are familiar themes, and in our day they have been extensively explored on the stage, on the screen, and in a mountain of books. We are keenly aware of these elements in politics.

What we are not reminded of so frequently is the reality of

*Davies had reviewed *Henry V* on June 9 and *Henry VI* on June 10 in the *Peterborough Examiner*.

heroism and as this is the foremost theme of *Henry V* it was interesting but not heart-warming that it was left out. It is foolish to blame the apathy of the first-night audience; it was, like any other audience, composed of people of every sort, and it would have cheered if it had been invited to cheer. But it was invited to be silent and reflective, and so it was. In the theatre, as in the nursery, you must not expect to eat your cake and have it too.

Henry VI, which went directly for excitement and the ferocity of politics, was a great popular success, and deservedly so. This play is very rarely presented and ought not to be missed. *Twelfth Night*, always a popular comedy, is brilliantly directed and acted; you will not see a better presentation of it in a hurry. So the festival seems to add up to two smashing successes, and one experiment which hit its mark, but unfortunately it was the wrong mark.

It is all very well to talk of "presenting Shakespeare in the light of our own time," as if we had some special claim on seriousness and understanding; but Shakespeare had his own lights, and it is wise to assume that when he wrote about patriotism, he meant what he said.

"Twelfth Night," *Peterborough Examiner*, 11 June 1966

116

Stratford: 1967
Richard III / The Government Inspector / The Merry Wives of Windsor

Inevitably, this year's production of *Richard III* provokes comparisons with that which opened the brave festival venture fifteen years ago. As soon as the lights came up and we saw the well-fleshed figure of Alan Bates sitting at the foot of the central pillar, we thought of Alec Guinness seated above on the balustrade. When Mr. Bates' plummy, persuasive voice began the opening soliloquy we seemed, distantly, to hear the precise, warning voice of Guinness. When Mr. Bates moved, and showed himself a vigorous man, marred by a hump and withered arm, we recalled the figure of Guinness, ravaged with unimaginable sickness. But the ghost of Guinness soon vanished and left the stage to Mr. Bates.

Comparisons, though interesting, are by no means derogatory to the new Richard. Whereas Guinness was a figure of chilling, aristocratic menace, Mr. Bates is a genial, exuberant Richard, so plausible that we are not surprised when warriors, women, and children all fall under his spell. He delights in evil, and we share his pleasure. Watching *Richard III* ought to be a moral holiday for the audience, and that is precisely what Mr. Bates and the director, John Hirsch, provide for us.

But comparison cannot be wholly banished. The first *Richard* was one of Tyrone Guthrie's riots of heraldry; the Boar, the Rose in Sun, the Falcon and Fetterlock, the Swan, were seen everywhere. The current production is like stained glass windows animated; touches of rich colours – a dirty crimson in particular – are set in a dusky background. This is the Wars of the Roses as they might be seen in the window of a great cathedral. This effect, and the anonymity of all the fighting men, remove the play from any touch of realism.

Guthrie's production was more romantic in feeling than the

new one, and consequently it dealt more effectively with the ghosts who haunt Richard the night before his defeat at Bosworth. Mr. Hirsch appears not to believe in ghosts, and even cuts some of them out of the text; such phantoms as are left roam the stage with the matter-of-fact air of tourists. This is a pity, for to neglect the supernatural element in Shakespeare is to rob him of an important and characteristic dimension.

But where Mr. Hirsch's production scores heavily over the earlier one is that he is able to cast the play strongly, and make an ensemble, rather than a star vehicle, of it. Leo Ciceri's watchful Duke of Buckingham, William Hutt's dignified (but not very poetic) Duke of Clarence, Zoe Caldwell's Lady Anne, Barbara Byrne's shrivelled Duchess of York, and Frances Hyland's Queen Margaret – a fine study in the enjoyment of malignance – all support Mr. Bates admirably, and show psychological subtleties in the play that usually lie hidden. As a company, this year's group is to the cast of fifteen years ago what a fine symphony orchestra is to a town brass band.

The play stands or falls by the principal character. Mr. Bates gives us a Richard who is attractive, cheerful, energetic, and keen-witted; he relishes his villainies as a schoolboy relishes practical jokes. He is a thorough-going crook, but he has tender feelings – for himself. The curses of his embittered female relatives really hurt him, for he is not armoured in malignancy. Consequently we are prepared for the end, when Richard invites Richmond to kill him; this passionate man might do precisely that, when he knew that the game was up. This was a convincing and interesting interpretation, though personally I prefer a Richard who fights to the death.

The speculation about what sort of classical actor Alan Bates would make may now be set at rest. He has the voice, the variety, and the physical strength for classic roles; he is magnetic and attractive; what he needs now is experience in handling audiences – the art of shutting up coughers. As a footnote, it may be added that as Richard he looks astonishingly like the great Richard of the early nineteenth century, George Frederick Cooke, another fattish, genial, magnetic actor. And Mr. Bates' ultra-modern side-whiskers are just like Cooke's. The more things change, the more they are the same.

The critics have, on the whole, agreed to dislike this production. I dissent. I manage to see a good deal of Shakespeare in the course of a year, and there is not much going that is better than this.

Stephen Leacock, in some invaluable advice to humorists, said, "Never be as funny as you can." The Stratford company, in their reworking of the production of *The Government Inspector* they took on tour last winter, have been as funny as they could, and the result is that the second half of their play is exhausting and a little alarming. They sweat and strain to squeeze more laughs out of the antics we have seen before, and we become quite concerned for their health. Will some overdriven mime positively have a stroke on the stage, we wonder, and when the strobe lights flicker and twitch, to indicate a change of scene, we wonder if perhaps we are having strokes ourselves. The version that was seen in the winter was better, because it was fully under control.

This is a pity, because Michael Langham's production is full of invention and splendid clowning; what is wanting is the courage to leave about a third of it out, so that the play by Nicolai Gogol can peer through. It is a queer play, not well-formed; the author is so fond of his moral point – that power breeds corruption – that he goes on hammering it home long after we have understood it. But before he gets into this trouble, Gogol is spare and sharp in his comment, and does not need the ultimate in funny makeup and athletics to support it. The Russians play it as wild farce, and everybody else has followed their lead, but Gogol said he meant it to be something much deeper and more alarming than farce. Even if we assume that the author did not know his business – always a dangerous assumption and one that has wrought great mischief in Shakespearean production – he ought to be given a fair chance.

This is what he did not get at Stratford. Beginning with Peter Raby's "adaptation" (which includes putting in a lot of dirty words that the Czar's censorship would certainly not have passed) and going on to some fashionable but distasteful dirty acting (it cannot otherwise be described for it would cause raised eyebrows at a rivetter's smoker), Gogol is buried under a mass of extraneous material. It is not for such horseplay as this that the Stratford Festival was founded.

It must be said that the first-night audience enjoyed it greatly. But audiences enjoy anything that is well done, including public executions. Audiences respond to excellence, and here was excellence in abundance. It just happened not to be excellence that arose from the Russian classic we had come to see.

Some of the actors stuck to the Gogol line, and happily one of them was William Hutt, whose performance of the impostor Khlestakov was in a fine tradition of elegant farce. So also was Leo Ciceri's performance of the corrupt local judge. That fine actor Tony Van Bridge did not fare so well; as the Mayor, he carries the weight of the play, and he appeared to have been goaded by the director beyond the bounds of his abilities, notable though these are.

It is good to see Stratford extending itself beyond Shakespeare; it has done so notably in the cases of Rostand and Chekhov. It is embarrassing to see this fine company driven to the edge of hysteria, as it was in *The Government Inspector* on its first night.

Compared with the demoralization and uproar of Gogol's Russian town, as Stratford chose to present it, Shakespeare's Windsor was almost sweetly pastoral. *The Merry Wives of Windsor* is essentially a farce in the vein English people like best – the vein which began with Chaucer, and has been so richly exploited by writers of every degree of talent ever since. But this farce has so much English town life mingled with it, and is so essentially good-natured, that its effect in presentation is likely to be gentle. It was not so when Stratford last offered it in 1956, when Mr. Langham tried to make a "dark comedy" of it, in which a fat crook exploited the vanity and stupidity of some small-town snobs. But this year we returned to the play that is to be found in the text, and it made a very jolly evening.

The ensemble at Stratford is so good that we are apt to undervalue the stars. Tony Van Bridge is a splendid Falstaff, capable of giving us all of the old man's dishonesty and mendacity without obscuring his essential greatness. Falstaff is great because he is greatly life-enhancing; the actor understands this and can make it palpable to us. Around this fine performance are grouped several notable creations: Zoe Caldwell's wittily self-righteous Mrs. Page, and Frances Hyland's delightful, warm Mrs. Ford; the contrasted outlanders, Dr. Caius and Sir Hugh Evans, the former like a self-important, high-tempered but charming hornet, and the latter like some small, costive, gnawing rodent – a learned hedgehog; Eric Christmas as Justice Shallow, giving us unexpected glimpses of sweetness in that old nuisance; Max Helpmann as a quieter, more human, and funnier Pistol than is common; Anna Wing, who as Mrs. Quickly, contrives to look more like Nellie Wallace than any Elizabethan should, bringing a spice of wit to a part that is sometimes merely noisy; Kenneth Pogue as an easy-going, but not inconsiderable Master Page. And, in the role of Master Ford, that comic study for Othello, we have Alan Bates, who never loses the humanity of this tortured man, and is both pitiable and funny. Surrounded by such riches, Mr. Van Bridge has to work hard to maintain his supremacy, and the fact that he does so is evidence of what a good actor he is.

In a play so fanciful and charming, it is curious to hear such a medley of accents, ranging from the High Cockney of Mr. Bates and Mr. Christmas to the Fine Old Rusted Saskatchewan of Messrs. Kozlik, Fox, and Monette. Surely some sort of agreement could be reached on manner of speech, so that Windsor did not sound like a meeting of the More or Less English-Speaking Union? Caius and Evans are meant to sound outlandish. Need so many others do so? Why don't they take Mr. Van Bridge as a standard?

So far, then, the Stratford season is a success and a good investment for your holiday money. The great test of *Antony and Cleopatra* is still to come and I shall report on it later. For the moment it only remains to be said that "O Canada" has replaced "God Save the Queen" as the opening number for each play. This is halfway to a really good custom – no patriotic airs except on occasions that obviously demand them. Mr. Lou Applebaum has made a beginning by cutting all the laborious rumpty-tum out of the middle of "O Canada," to its vast betterment.

Peterborough Examiner, 17 June 1967

A Stage in Our Past: 1969

The lot of the theatre historian is a hard one anywhere, for stage people are of all artists the most bemused, careless, and creatively mendacious in their records and recollections; the writer who attempts to bring even the most elementary kind of order to the story of the theatre in Canada deserves our special sympathy, for he must make what he can of the imperfect chronicles of touring companies, and the hardly traceable histories of ill-fated native ventures; he must piece out and weigh scant and often contradictory evidence. Canadians have never really taken the theatre seriously. Our attitude towards all the arts has until recently been poisoned by a mean puritanism – the puritanism of Stiggins and Podsnap rather than that of Milton – and we still tend to value them for the social prestige they confer rather than for any enrichment of spirit they might encourage. Honour, then, to Dr. Murray Edwards, who has tried to give form to the muddled and scrappy chronicle of 125 years of Canadian theatre in *A Stage in Our Past: English-language Theatre in Eastern Canada from the 1790s to 1914*.

The story seems to have begun in Halifax, and to have gone on to Montreal, where visiting regiments were diverted by companies so meagre that boys played subordinate female roles and (as Lambert wrote) the leads were entrusted to "an old superannuated demi-rep whose drunken Belvideras, Desdemonas and Isabellas have often enraptured a Canadian audience." The theatres were filthy adjuncts of taverns; the players too often, like their spectators, in Canada because England was too hot to hold them. Occasional stars like Kean, Kemble, and Macready passed through, groaning and cursing. Dickens amused himself with some touch-and-go farce performances, through which he carried his amateur supporters by the sheer exuberance of his spirit. Then, as the nineteenth century wore on, every town of more than 10,000 people, and many with a tenth of that number, acquired opera houses, often firetraps of the most alarming kind, built over ranks of shops; in these opera houses touring companies from England and the United States deployed the conventional drama of the time.

Nineteenth-century Canada was true to melodrama, and all that class of play which may be called "wholesome"; some of Dr. Edwards' saddest pages record our indifference to the new drama of Ibsen and Shaw. Robert B. Mantell's assaults on Shakespeare passed as classic theatre, and there were occasional visits from Irving, Forbes-Robertson, and Sothern and Marlowe for the more sophisticated. The incident lies outside Dr. Edwards' period, but as late as the 1920s Martin-Harvey was able to induce a theatre manager in our West to allow a performance of Reinhardt's great production of *Oedipus* only by explaining that it was really a Greek version of *Mutt and Jeff*; the plot as first described was considered too raw for a family audience.

It is unfortunate that Dr. Edwards' book is marred by a great many typographical errors, wrong dates, and misspellings of the names of players, and even the titles of plays, which will certainly mislead students who turn to him for guidance. One might have expected the University of Toronto Press and the author between them to do better than this.

From "Letters in Canada," *University of Toronto Quarterly*, 38 (1969)

Touring Fare in Canada 1920-35: 1979

What I offer you is not the result of patient research but an evocation of past experience in the theatre – the Canadian theatre during the last of that period when this country relied on touring
companies for its dramatic experience. When I first encountered
the theatre it was entirely an imported pleasure, and I never heard
anyone say a word of regret that it was so. Canada imported
pineapples and it imported plays for the same reason; such things
were appreciated here but they were not of Canadian growth.

Sometimes when I talk with students I find that they cannot
conceive of a Canada in which there was so little theatrical ambition and, as it appears to them, so little theatrical self-respect. It is
not easy to persuade them that we felt no misgiving on this subject whatever. We thought we had quite an active theatre. I draw
what I say not only from what I experienced myself, but from the
experience of my parents, who were keen theatre-goers and spoke
often and at length of the theatre they remembered from their
youth; the store of recollection on which I am drawing thus goes
back over ninety years. The self-conscious Canadianism of today
was then unknown. Canada did not cease to be a colony, psychologically, until long after I was born, and in matters relating to
the arts its colonialism was absolute. A national culture arises
from the depths of a people, and Canadians knew where those
depths were, and certainly it was not here. There were too many
Canadians who were physically loyal to the new land, but who
remained exiles in matters of the spirit. You might as well have
asked for an indigenous form of government, or an indigenous
religion, as ask for Canadian art. Theatre, music, and literature
did not originate here. They came from home, wherever home
might be.

As for the Canadians of long descent, among whom I am proud
to number my mother's family, they were in the main aesthetic
innocents. The Bible and *Pilgrim's Progress* served them for

literature; music, if it figured at all in their reckonings, meant church music of no very distinguished kind. As for theatre, a common attitude is summed up in a story my mother used to tell with glee. She, and some girls of her acquaintance, were making up a party to go to a nearby city to see a play. One of the girls said to her mother: "Ma, can I go to Hamilton to see *Ben Hur*?" "Who's he, Annie?" asked the mother, and when she found that he was a play-actor, letting on to have had direct experience of Jesus Christ, the matter was closed with a bang. The thirst for what the theatre could give was not strong among the majority of people outside a few large towns.

One need not retreat to the eighties to meet that attitude. My father, when a young man in Toronto about 1900, remembered very clearly a fiery sermon preached by a popular local clergyman who raged against the iniquity of a woman of known blemished reputation daring to show herself on the Toronto stage. The woman was Lily Langtry, and the clergyman was the late Canon H.J. Cody, who subsequently became President of the University of Toronto, and did not greatly abate his mistrust of the theatre. I may say that when I was a boy of fifteen a friend of mine was forbidden to bring me to his house, because his father had discovered that I was a reader of that notorious scoundrel Bernard Shaw. That was in the thirties of this century and Shaw had long before received the Nobel Prize. Canada's present hydroptic thirst for the delights of the theatre is a comparatively recent passion. Until 1933 touring companies served very well to satisfy the demands of those who frequented the playhouse.

When we speak of the touring theatre we are apt to concentrate on the cities and to look eagerly for evidence that Canada was not a cultural backwater. Nor do we look in vain. We now know, for instance, that a theatre-goer living in Toronto between 1830 and 1850 could have seen several – a majority – of the plays of Lord Byron, presented on the local stage. How well they were done we cannot accurately gauge, but the evidence suggests that they were not done badly. But that was an era of resident companies in big towns. What happened to touring groups we can discover from that delightful book *A Theatrical Trip for A Wager* by Captain Horton Rhys; they were greeted with suspicion, and their audiences were likely to be small and hard-bitten. We can reconstruct in imagination the entertainment offered by Rhys and his associates – Miss Catherine Lucette and Captain Bayly, the Primo Buffo of the celebrated A.B.C. Club – because he has given us their program in detail; it makes us feel sympathy for their audiences.

As a child, I lived in small towns, and I remember the touring companies that visited them. I once saw the famous Marks Troupe, though I was so small that my recollection is only of May Belle Marks, wrapped in a Union Jack and wearing a Roman helmet, singing "Rule Britannia," between the acts of a melodrama that has utterly escaped me. It was during the first Great War, and patriotism was lively theatrical fare. But later, in a different small town in the Ottawa Valley, I saw most of what came to our theatre, called, inevitably, the Opera House. It showed moving pictures, but these were easily set aside when we were visited by a play.

It was, I suppose, the irreducible minimum of what the touring theatre had to offer, though I recall two visits from Blackstone, the magician and hypnotist, who was by no means an inferior performer. But greatly below that level were the minstrel shows that visited us, which I was not allowed to attend because, I was told, they were "coarse," and luckier boys who had attended, assured me that this was so. But they were not as coarse as a kind of entertainment called generically Mutt-and-Jeff Shows. These were rough-and-ready musical comedies in which the leading roles were figures from the comic strips – Mutt and Jeff, or Maggie and Jiggs – who wore masks like the faces of the familiar figures they personated. There was a theme, expressed in the title, like *Mutt and Jeff in Paris*, and the show brought a small chorus of girls who were said to be of blemished virtue, though how anybody found out I was not encouraged to enquire. A rough audience attended; it was a lumber town and our audiences were unsophisticated playgoers who had to be hit over the head with a joke – even a dirty joke – before they saw it. Again, from hearsay, I learned that the show could get really dirty if the audience seemed to like it that way. If you are interested, a popular comic ploy was this: a girl walks across the stage in a very short skirt, making unmistakable gestures of sexual allurement; Jeff, or Mr. Jiggs, watches her go by, saying "Oh boy-o-boy-oboy!" then spits down into the depths of his baggy pants, to cool his lust. My parents were doubtless wise not to let me go to these things, but I am glad I heard about them from some of my friends, because I am able to report to you authentically what amused an audience of lumber-haulers in rural Canada in the early twenties.

If these Aristophanic shows moved them to laughter – and I have never seen any reason to believe that the plays of Aristophanes were much above the level of *Mutt and Jeff at Delphi* – what purged them with pity and terror? I can report from personal experience that even at that late date it was the evergreen *Uncle Tom's Cabin*. I saw two Tom-shows by the time I was ten, and my recollection of them is clear. Indeed, the local school was closed so that the children could attend a matinee of this improving drama. Even to my child's eye Little Eva seemed somewhat older than the text suggested – by a matter of twenty-five years at the least. But Simon Legree was satisfactorily villainous, and the scene in which he flogs the noble slave was terrifying, even though the lash was plainly striking on a padded jacket. Eliza's escape over the ice-floes of the Ohio river, bearing her child in her arms, was thrilling, though the scenic illusion was crude. We all applauded lustily when George Harris, the slave who is about to escape north cried: "And when I stand on the soil of Canada, beneath the British flag, I shall never call any man 'Massa' again!" We wept at the death of Eva, who expired in considerable musical style, for a choir of slaves knelt in her bedroom singing "Nearer, My God, To Thee" in close – very close – harmony. And when, in the final tableau, Uncle Tom rose from where he lay dead in the cotton field, cast his manacles from him and advanced up a rather short staircase to be greeted by Little Eva, robed as an angel, we were purged indeed, washed whiter than snow. This was melodrama and as such it evoked archetypes with unescapable power. I think myself lucky to have seen it when I was still innocent, before the coming of that critical spirit that robs us of so much pleasure.

There were other plays that attempted to strike the plangent melodramatic string. One was called *The Prodigal Son*; it was a Bible drama, to which even preachers went. The company included a camel, and we all agreed that it was a considerable advance in religious experience to have beheld a Bible animal of this sort. There were problem plays, too. Not Ibsen, of course, but the kind of problems our public could understand. I recall one, named *The Unwanted Child*; there were special matinees for women, who might feel some delicacy about seeing the play in the presence of men. I was not allowed to go, but I got a report on it from my mother's cook, who did. She did not want to tell me, for she was a woman of high principle who would have done nothing to smirch the pure mind of a child. But I persisted. "Please, Victoria," I begged, "what was it about?" She thought for perhaps a full minute, and then she found the answer. "Bobby," she said in a low, intense voice, "it was about a girl who Went The Limit." And with that dark revelation I had to be content, for I was at an age where the splendours and miseries of The Limit were still far in the future.

I must mention another kind of travelling drama, with which I was familiar in my childhood, but which I have never seen mentioned in any record. Only part of it travelled. The director, who was also the business manager and the musical director, would arrive in town with a carload of scenery and costumes, and would let it be known that he would shortly produce a splendid musical comedy. One of these, I remember, was called *In Sunny France*. He assembled a cast of local singing amateurs, and produced his show, under the patronage of the Oddfellows, or Knights of Columbus, or some such influential body. He cajoled everybody, directed everybody, provided romantic interest for everybody and within two days of his arrival in town, knew everybody.

These musical comedies were not tightly crafted, if I may borrow an expression popular in the modern theatre. They could be enlarged to include anything anybody in town could do, which included whistling and playing the musical saw. There was always a Prologue In Fairyland in which virtually every female child under thirteen appeared, dancing, sometimes rather morosely, to the music dispensed by the talented director at the piano. There was always a number called The Foxtrot of the Hours, or the Two Step of the Flowers, or something of that kind, in which every female schoolteacher under fifty had a brief solo, as an Hour or a Flower. The costumes were gorgeous but decent.

The highlight of the evening was when the talented director himself appeared on stage and sang a song filled with references to local notabilities. These were not pungent lampoons. I recall one which ran:

> *I taxi'd round to Mrs. Airth's*
> *To have a little frolic;*
> *I ate some cake the dear girl made*
> *And nearly died of colic.*

You appreciate the appeal of this. To take a taxi in our town, except for a wedding or a funeral, was mad big-city extravagance; the notion of a frolic with Mrs. Airth, who was the leading soprano in the Presbyterian choir, was suggestive if not downright salacious. But if anyone had been feeling sorry for Mr. Airth, a local furniture dealer, they knew that he was vindicated by the joke in the final lines. In their special way these were subtle dramas.

Where did these things originate? Where did the talented director come from? I cannot tell you. But I remember these affairs, and sometimes I think I am the only person who does. They were a form of touring theatre that stretched out a hand to amateurs. They were Broadway come to the Ottawa Valley.

I have told you of these performances to make the point that there was a considerable quantity of touring theatre that was of sociological rather than artistic interest, and some of it was not far removed from the shows given by the King and the Duke in *Huckleberry Finn*. Now I want to speak of the touring theatre as I experienced it later in my boyhood in the city of Kingston, which was a first-class touring town and had a yearly theatrical season, in that there was something to be seen in its theatre for two or three nights and a matinee, every week during the autumn and winter.

At least one popular musical comedy appeared each year, and sometimes more than one. They were of an innocence now unguessed at, for we have demanded of musical comedy a significance that has left it more seriously musical and hardly to be described at all as comedy. But *No, No, Nanette* and *Rose Marie* were meant only to please, and they were made in a durable mould where there were principal lovers – united to begin, parted by the caprice of fate, and united for the final curtain – secondary lovers, and comic lovers; given these and a set of comic parents, a villain or villainess, and a chorus, and you could not go wrong. Another necessity was a principal dancer, invariably a woman who could, in *Rose Marie* for instance, perform the Totem Dance with a rubbery sinuosity that was agreeably erotic and gymnastic in about equal proportions. Fantasy involving these gifted women was a prominent factor in the adolescent life of the period.

My recollections of this time inevitably mingle the theatre as I saw it in Kingston, and the theatre of Toronto, because I often came here with my parents to see plays, and for some years I attended a boarding-school here and every Saturday afternoon was passed in one of Toronto's theatres instead of in the fresh air. My present stunted growth is undoubtedly attributable to this unhealthy addiction. I shall not differentiate needlessly, because it was all theatre of the same general sort – that is to say, a theatrical mixed grill, a remarkable sampling of everything the theatre can offer. Music-hall artists of the first rank, like Harry Lauder and George Robey, appeared and I can assure you that they were every bit as funny as legend reports. There was some very old-fashioned fare, like Bransby Williams in *Treasure Island*, which was played straight and was rather hammy, and even *George Barnwell*, which was gently guyed in a production by Nigel Playfair, in which that brilliant actor Ernest Thesiger played the ill-fated Barnwell. I saw William C. Gillette in his own play *Sherlock Holmes*, and after several plays and movies about the great detective, Gillette, dry of voice and hawklike of profile, remains, for me, the best. Of course, the earliest illustrations of the stories were based on him. He was seventy-five when I saw him and remarkably swift on his feet.

There were productions described as "all-star" and they were starry indeed, but as we all know, the stars are immeasurably old. Such was *The School for Scandal*, with Ethel Barrymore, and the principal scandal was that she was demonstrably drunk. Such was *The Rivals*, in which James T. Powers played Bob Acres, and though not youthful, he had what used to be called the Old Comedy Manner in perfection. Such was an all-star production of *The Merry Wives of Windsor* with three stars legendary even then – Otis Skinner, Mrs. Fiske, and Henrietta Crosman. Their combined ages at that time numbered 190 years, but they certainly did not look it and their speech was a revelation of clarity and witty emphasis. Skinner played Falstaff as very much a gentleman who connived at and enjoyed his own troubles, and thus never really lost dignity. I remember still his delivery of the lines: ". . . Water swells a man; and what a thing should I have been, when I had been swelled! I should have been a mountain of mummy."

On the stage, of course, years are not so important as on the screen or (even more) on television. We now expect young characters to be young, and recently we had our way when we saw, on television, a Juliet who was authentically fourteen. As a girl of fourteen she was credible; but as Juliet she was incredible, because she hadn't learned her job. These senior players knew their job to perfection. I recall Seymour Hicks, who was supreme in that now rare thing, sophisticated comedy. He played in *The Man in Dress Clothes* and in *Mr. What's-His-Name*; in one of these he was a rake, irresistible to women and devoted to women. There was a scene in which he was so down on his luck that he ate the birdseed out of the canary's cage; what made it memorable was his sincere apology to the deprived bird. He was fifty-seven at the time, and rather plump, but he was more authentically a *bon viveur* than any thin actor of twenty-seven I have ever seen. It was because he knew how to be irresistible; he had a technique for it; he did not rely on personal endowments. And that is acting in one of its great modes. But one physical charm he possessed in high degree; he had a delightful, witty voice. Great voices are rarities on the stage at any time.

Walter Hampden was more easily resisted. When I saw him as the soldier-saint Caponsacchi in a play made from Browning's *The Ring and the Book*, he was certainly soldier and saint, but not a heart-warming lover. But then, perhaps, neither was Caponsacchi. As Hamlet he was deeply satisfactory. I choose those words with care, because he was fifty-four and though very handsome he was demonstrably middle-aged. But it was his understanding of the part, his mastery of nuance, the sense of nobility and tragic fate that he brought on the stage that made a production—he was accompanied by an admirable cast—that sent his audiences away fulfilled and sent me, as a schoolboy, treading on air, because a new heaven and a new earth had been opened to me. I have seen younger Hamlets subsequently, and some who were better: but none who were better simply because they were younger.

But age was not always splendid. An actor of the bad old school named Robert B. Mantell came to Toronto with a repertoire of Shakespeare, and also Bulwer's *Richelieu*, and lest you should think we were all humble acceptance and rustic wonderment, allow me to read what Laurence Mason of the Toronto *Globe* had to say:

The great, all-explaining fault of the production is that it is blindly clinging to nineteenth-century methods in a twentieth-century world, in complete ignorance of the revolution wrought by the new stage-craft. As a result, six whole scenes are silently omitted from *The Merchant of Venice*, including the colourful choosing of the caskets by Morocco and Aragon. Fragments of two other scenes (Act 2, scene 8 and Act 3, scene 1) are run together and bodily transported to the beginning of Act 4. Many lines are ruthlessly cut from other scenes, including some of the finest and most famous in the play. But then, to make up for this, Shylock is brought on twice where Shakespeare did not call for him, with words which Shakespeare did not write; Portia interpolates original lines; and several songs and dances are inserted. . . . There are ten or twelve pauses, some of them rather long instead of the continuous action which is so easily obtained with the use of a forestage. The scenery is very bad, as must be expected in an old-fashioned road company: for instance, jungle wings adjoin the Grand Canal in Venice, Portia's home is pretty clearly Macbeth's palace, the Court Room is even more incongruous; all this cumbrous apparatus of flats and cut-outs is obsolete anyhow. Jessica has no balcony, the caskets no curtains, etc. . . . Mr. Mantell is over seventy years of age, walks with great difficulty owing to a very bad limp, and lapses too often into gabble or rant. Miss Hamper is unfortunate in possessing an almost entirely expressionless voice. Worse still, the rest of the company was woefully inadequate. It is really not fair to Shakespeare or to the public to entrust these great parts to youthful amateurs not up to Hart House standards.

The critical position of Toronto reviewers at that time was that age was not a detriment to a first-rate player until it harmed the play; in the productions I have already mentioned this was certainly not the case.

It was unfortunate for Robert Mantell that his dismal *Merchant of Venice* visited Toronto when we were about to see a remarkable and beautiful production of that play with George Arliss and Peggy Wood at the head of the company. I doubt if, in the eyes of the Recording Angel, Arliss' egotism was less than that of Mantell, but Arliss wore it with a better grace. He had a trick of appearing to be caught unawares onstage at his curtain call; we were almost apologetic about demanding that this silvery artist listen to our cries of delight when he was so plainly eager to go to his dressing room. But he overcame his eagerness, set aside his own longing for privacy in order not to seem ungracious towards us, and took call after call—always apparently against his own wishes. He was the most subtle Shylock of this century; one marvelled that anybody could get the better of him. But he wanted villainy; the finest, most believable, and most paranoid Shylock of my experience was Randle Ayrton, a great actor, whose inability to get along with anybody else robbed him of top honours; but as Shylock, Lear, and Ford in *The Merry Wives* there was nobody to touch him for passion and tragic anguish. His later career was pretty much confined to the Memorial Theatre at Stratford-on-Avon.

From that Stratford there came some remarkable tours of Canada, playing Shakespearean repertoire in the admirable, clean, fast, and by no means unsubtle productions of Bridges-Adams. A company from Stratford under the leadership of Frank Benson had come to Canada in 1913, but the company in the early thirties brought a larger repertoire. The first visit included *Much Ado About Nothing, Richard II, Romeo and Juliet, The Merry Wives of Windsor, Julius Caesar, Twelfth Night, A Midsummer Night's Dream, Hamlet* and *Macbeth*. The principal actors were George Hayes, Wilfrid Walter (who was especially memorable as Claudius in *Hamlet*), and Roy Byford, a naturally fat actor who was a great Falstaff; that he was fat seemed unimportant, but that he was a wit and by far the most intelligent man in the play was palpable. These tours were a revelation to young people like myself, who had seen Shakespeare only with stars; here was ensemble acting of a high order, and Shakespeare very rapidly played, with the poetry always the first consideration – a treatment which brought out the structure and drama of the plays brilliantly.

At this time, by the way, we saw a production of *Macbeth* with scenery by Gordon Craig. The scenery swamped the play, and one tires of scenery very quickly. It is of interest that it was Robert B. Mantell who first played *Hamlet* in modern dress in Toronto. I fear that economy, rather than experiment, was at the back of this, and poor Mantell in evening dress looked like an old waiter.

Another favourite visitor in repertory was the D'Oyly Carte company, playing all of Gilbert and Sullivan except the unpopular last two operettas. This was before economy destroyed the musical and production qualities of that organization. I remember in particular the superb designs for *The Mikado* by Charles Ricketts. Musical standards, established by the conductor, Isidore Godfrey, were high, and the quality of the playing in a company headed by Henry Lytton, Bertha Lewis, Darrell Fancourt, and Leo Sheffield was still under the tradition of Gilbert himself and imparted by people who had worked with Gilbert. They possessed a distinction not to be suspected from what one sees in that company now. This was fossil theatre, for it was still Victorian in the marrow of its bones; but it was the best sort of Victorian staging, and that was very good indeed, and in the movement of the chorus as a single entity – which seems so intolerable now – there was great wit, for the chorus seemed to be a single character, multiplied by thirty.

We were ready to enjoy fossil theatre, but that was not all we enjoyed. Maurice Colborne and Barry Jones played in a repertoire drawn from the plays of Shaw; their company included a young actress, making the first of what was to be a fine reputation. She was Margaret Rawlings, brilliant as a Shavian heroine because she had in perfection the witty, dry style, the air of observing her character from without, as well as acting it from within, to which Shaw responds so well. This company did not confine itself to the most popular Shaw; its *John Bull's Other Island* was one of its greatest successes. Barry Jackson also sent a company that played what was then a modern repertoire, its newest play being *The Barretts of Wimpole Street*, with memorably beautiful designs; the part of Robert Browning was played by a young actor just coming into prominence as a leading man – Donald Wolfit. Mrs. Fiske appeared in Ibsen's *Ghosts*; Judith Anderson in Pirandello's *As You Desire Me*. We had popular London comedies, too, such as James B. Fagan's *And So To Bed*, in which Edmund Gwenn was amusing and endearing as Samuel Pepys. Nor should I forget to mention *The Chauve Souris*, which was splendid throughout, but never more splendid than when Nikita Baliev was introducing the numbers; he was named on the program as Theatre Autocrat, and that was manifestly what he was, and one was left with the impression that every theatre needed such an official.

It would be tedious to go further in this direction. I hope I have made my point that the theatre we enjoyed, in our days of cultural colonialism, was very good indeed, and it doubtless gained something in mystery and delight because it came from far away, and the quarrels that ravaged it and the wrangles about finance and pride of place were not the ugly gossip of our morning papers. Our situation was, no doubt, one of childlike artistic dependence, but it was an immensely enjoyable childhood.

I have spoken of fossil theatre, but I have not as yet said anything about the frequent tours of Sir John Martin-Harvey, who visited Canada, all told, eight times. His was fossil theatre in that it reproduced, and preserved, in many instances, productions and performances that had been originated by Sir Henry Irving, and what this actor undertook on his own volition was done in the Irving mode. But you must understand that when I talk of fossil theatre, I do not speak derisively; this mode of acting and direction belonged to a time past, and to see it, as I once did, very close to a production of Elmer Rice's *Street Scene*, which was accounted the ultimate in adventurous modernity, was to experience some of the astonishments of travel in time. To see it, as I did also, close to O'Neill's *Mourning Becomes Electra*, produced no such shock, for O'Neill's work had its roots in nineteenth-century melodrama, and one might imagine Martin-Harvey being very fine in, for instance, *A Touch of the Poet*.

Melodrama is a constant element in theatre; it is not tragedy, because it calls heavily on pathos for some of its effects, and it often makes use of grotesque juxtapositions of villainy and jocosity which tragedy is supposed to avoid, though Shakespeare never troubled to do so. The greatest tragedy – that of Greece – treats of a world in which the gods are expected to be capricious; the greatest melodrama takes place in a world where God is not expected to be capricious, but for a time, and unaccountably, seems to be asleep, and neglecting, or perhaps simply testing, His own. The cruel justice of the Greeks is very different from the justice of melodrama, which is poetic justice. Tragedy fears the gods; melodrama looks upon God as the final righter of all wrongs, the ultimate judge. Of course, if you test melodrama by its trashy examples, you will despise it, but if you glance sideways towards some remarkable examples of poetic art – towards Goethe's *Faust*, or Byron's *Manfred*, you will see shining about them a purplish light which can only be called the light of melodrama.

Martin-Harvey appeared in what used to be called Costume Drama. It was a sort of theatre which came into being in the nineteenth century at the same time as the Costume Novel, and there was always a whiff of Sir Walter Scott about it. Romance, as evidenced in high chivalry, elaborate codes of manners and morality, and extremes of love and hatred, was always more easily accepted when it was placed at a distance in time. Furthermore, Costume Drama gave actors and actresses an opportunity to display accomplishments that found little place in plays of contemporary life; the elegant management of the dress of a bygone era, of swords, capes, walking-sticks, plumed hats, combined with graceful bearing, refinement in the use of the snuffbox, the handkerchief, the fan, and all the variations of bowing, dancing, and exchanging salutations, required training and it was expected that in an accomplished player they would become so much second nature that any suggestion of training disappeared. Was the result false in impact? Did it suggest a pageant or a puppet theatre? No indeed, because these Costume Dramas, though at a distance in matters of scene and dress, were faithful to the accepted beliefs of the nineteenth century, and the passions and the humour were of the sort acceptable to people who read Dickens, Thackeray, Trollope, and Charles Reade.

You will say, surely this seemed strange in Canada during the late twenties and earliest thirties of this century? Yes, it seemed a little strange, but it was also pleasing, and if you will look at the moving pictures of the same era you will see that the morality of that time was not so far removed —in the mimetic arts, at any rate —from the nineteenth century as you might suppose. It was the era of the Hayes Office in Hollywood, when scenes of sexual involvement were hedged about with elaborate rules which make very peculiar reading. And Martin-Harvey, who was anything but a fool, did not press purely nineteenth-century conceptions to ridiculous lengths. . . .*

That is enough, I think. I could talk on about the touring theatre of my childhood and youth, but it would be self-indulgent, and self-indulgence is the vice of older playgoers, who love to harry their juniors with tales of wonders they have seen which will never come again. I do not feel like that, myself. I have seen acting during the past ten years as fine as anything I ever saw in my first twenty-five years, but it is of a different savour. It has gained much in psychological depth; it has lost nothing in refinement of technique; but it has lost the flair, the theatrical radiance of the sort of performance I have been talking about.

Is it lost forever? I greatly doubt it. Romance, like John Barleycorn, has a way of springing up again. It would be a delight to see some rebirth of the old style shorn of the old falsities.

From "Mixed Grill: Touring Fare in Canada 1920-35," an address given 2 August 1979 at the conference on "Theatrical Touring and Founding in North America" held at the University of Toronto.

---

*Here Davies noted ways that Martin-Harvey accommodated melodramas in his repertoire to the needs of the contemporary stage. He then went on to consider the strengths of melodrama and the virtues of the Martin-Harveys' romantic style of acting. Readers of *World of Wonders* will find this material of particular interest, for Davies' characters, the Tresizes, were modelled on the Martin-Harveys. The complete address (roughly half is omitted here) along with other papers given at the conference on "Theatrical Touring and Founding in North America" will shortly be published in book form, edited by L.W. Conolly.

II

LETTERS

Whiteoak Heritage: 1940

Miss Mazo de la Roche has written her seventh book about the Whiteoak family of Jalna; this is our own particular Canadian family saga. *Whiteoak Heritage* fills in a few gaps which the previous books have left in our knowledge of this odd tribe. Chronologically, this book is second in the series. It tells of Renny's return from the Great War to find that he must take charge of Jalna, which his uncles have seriously mismanaged. He has trouble also with his younger brothers, and his small stepbrother, the detestable Wakefield, is here shown at the beginning of his career as a nuisance. As always, old Adeline Whiteoak and her grandson Renny, are the most vivid characters in the book.

Much as this writer likes and admires the Whiteoak novels, he can never feel that they are distinctively Canadian. This family is an English family living in Canada, which is quite a different thing from a Canadian family. So far no novelist has ever succeeded in capturing the atmosphere of modern Canada; it is too elusive and too various. It is also a fact that we are a young and a self-conscious country, and too accurate an account of our daily life might prove unacceptable. Again, what is just as a description of life in Ontario is certainly not true of the Prairie Provinces or of the Maritimes, and the life of Quebec is even stranger, as Ringuet's *Thirty Acres* amply shows. There can be no novel which is true of all of Canada; we need regional novelists. And yet our population is not sufficiently large to make the sale of a book profitable even if all the nine provinces read it. There seems to be nothing for it but to go on as we are doing at present until an increase in population brings about the changes necessary to make literature about Canada, written for the Canadian market, economically possible.

From "Cap and Bells," *Peterborough Examiner,*
30 November 1940

As For Me and My House: 1941

Things are looking up in the world of Canadian literature. In less than a year we have produced three first-rate books. Two were novels and one was a book of poetry. That is by no means a bad record for a country which sometimes despairs of its literary growth. Of course there have been other Canadian books – a great number of them – during this period, but I am speaking now of books we may expect to be read outside Canada and which will reflect credit upon this country.

Readers will know at once the names of two of the books. First is *Thirty Acres* by the French-Canadian author Ringuet; second is Professor E.J. Pratt's excellent poem, *Brébeuf and His Brethren*. I doubt if many of you will yet have heard the name of the third. It is a novel called *As For Me and My House*, and its author is Sinclair Ross.

Mr. Ross was born in the province of Saskatchewan and has lived all his life in the Canadian West. He is a young man, and at present he works in a bank in Winnipeg. Writing is a spare-time occupation with him and his work on this, his first published novel, was long and laborious. The early life of most authors is one of double duty. It is rarely that a man has either the money or the talent to set up as a professional man of letters at the beginning of his career. More frequently, as in the case of Sinclair Ross, there is a job to be done during the day, and the writing to be done at night, and, however great the pleasure of creation may be, there is no denying that writing is also very hard work. If anyone doubts that, I advise him to try to write a book as good as *As For Me and My House* and he will see what I mean.

In the first place, the story is written in the first person by a woman, a technical difficulty which might daunt any author. But Mr. Ross accomplishes this feat in a manner which, to a male reader at least, seems entirely successful. The story concerns an unhappy marriage, and books about marriage are always full of pitfalls, particularly for authors who are themselves unmarried. But Mr. Ross seems to understand his characters perfectly, and the relationship between the husband and wife in his story, though complex and perverse, is entirely credible. Finally, the chief theme of the book is a love affair that went wrong, and here again Mr. Ross has been able to treat a sexual theme with restraint, so that although his picture is complete it never becomes dirty. As you may see, this author has set himself a difficult task, but he has accomplished it with remarkable skill and completeness.

The story is about a clergyman and his wife in the middle West. The man should have been a painter, but in order to make a living he has entered the ministry; because he has no real vocation for that work he becomes a hypocrite, but never one of those happy hypocrites who is unconscious of his own hypocrisy. He detests his work and the necessity which it places upon him to beg his salary and to lickspittle to his "flock." His wife, who tells the story, is a musician, or was until her marriage, but her love for her husband, and the feeling that he does not love her, robs her of her power of self-expression. Between them they drag out a life of frustration and misery until she finds that another woman is going to bear her husband's child. . . .

This story is told with great delicacy and sensitivity. Mr. Ross is keenly aware of the subtleties of the human mind but he knows when to let the reader draw his own inferences, and does not load his book with clinical detail. The book, though not precisely gay in tone, is deeply stimulating and is, as I have already said, a remarkable addition to our small stock of Canadian books of first-rate importance. There are passages in this book which give weight to my own personal feeling that Canadian literature, when it finally gets on its feet, will have a close resemblance to that of Russia. Similarity of climate begets a similarity of outlook, and while the Russians are Slavs and we are Nordic and Celtic in racial origin, Canadian literature at its best has a strongly Russian flavour.

It is pleasant to know that Mr. Ross is not suffering the usual fate of the author who is not without honour save in his own country. The West has received his book with a gratifying amount of acclaim, and it is rumoured that the University of

Manitoba may put *As For Me and My House* on the list of required reading for its course in the modern novel. The author is working at present on a new book, which is to be about farm life in the West.

It is no small honour to rank a young Canadian author with Ringuet and E.J. Pratt on the strength of his first book, but Sinclair Ross deserves it. Good as his first book is, it gives promise of others still better to come, and a representative man of Canadian letters to be made. When the time comes Canada will gain a professional author of first-rate importance and the Royal Bank of Canada will lose a clerk.

"Cap and Bells," *Peterborough Examiner*, 26 April 1941

Letters in Canada: 1940 / Canadian Literature Today: 1941

An interesting pamphlet has appeared called *Letters in Canada: 1940* which is reprinted from *The University of Toronto Quarterly*. It is a complete survey of the subject and it must have taken a great deal of laborious searching to make such a full compilation. All of us who are interested in Canadian letters must be grateful to the editors for the thorough job they have done, for it will be invaluable as a work of reference in future years. Although no promise is made in the book to that effect, it is clear that the editors of the Toronto University *Quarterly* have taken this task as their own, and that we may expect a similar volume next year and for many years to come.

Now, having handed a bouquet to the compilers of this excellent work, I must say that it is in some respects disappointing, as is Canadian letters itself. Looking through the book one is amazed by the number of factual articles which appear to be written and published in Canada and by the paucity of original works of imagination. Most of the writing which is done in Canada is done by people connected with universities, who write on academic subjects which are of little general interest, and it is the listing of these which helps to swell this survey of Canadian letters to its present size. I do not wish to belittle the work of our Canadian educationists, but it must be admitted that their works are not works of imagination, and it is only by the production of these that a country develops a literature which is of any importance. In the past year Canada has produced only three works which most of us will ever read; they are Professor Pratt's poem *Brébeuf and His Brethren*, the French-Canadian novel *Thirty Acres* by Dr. Philippe Panneton, who writes under the pseudonym of Ringuet, and the novel of Western Canada *As For Me and My House* by the Manitoba author Sinclair Ross.

At the risk of seeming ungrateful to our universities I must record my own conviction that imagination does not flourish in an academic atmosphere. Convention and rules are enemies of great inspiration. There is also a dangerous tendency among academic people towards that form of dishonest criticism which is vulgarly called "log-rolling." For instance, in *Letters in Canada: 1940* there is a highly complimentary criticism of *The Flying Bull, and Other Tales* by Watson Kirkconnell. The criticism is by E.K. Brown, who has a deservedly high reputation as a judge of verse. Now *The Flying Bull* was as commonplace a piece of work as can well be imagined; it proved, as conclusively as anything could, that Watson Kirkconnell is not a poet. This is nothing against him; no man as talented as Professor Watson Kirkconnell need regret that he has been denied the gift of song. But why does Professor Brown give serious consideration to such a work? It seems possible that Professor Brown either did not want to offend his colleague or that he felt that he must uphold the honour of the academic world by praising a work which he cannot have thought good. I do not wish to make too much of this isolated instance, for the book abounds with examples of this attempt to elevate commonplace work to a position it is not entitled to occupy. The cause of Canadian letters is not best served by that attitude. We must be honest with ourselves and abandon this family compact system of criticism or Canadian literature will always remain provincial, academic, unselective, and trifling.

Refreshing in its critical realism is W.S. Milne's survey of drama in Canada. He says: "The material this year is depressingly small in bulk. It would be pleasant to be able to say that its quality was high. That pleasure, however, is denied the reviewer, for most of the plays are pretty poor stuff." That is depressing but it is honest. Mr. Milne does not attempt to build the inferior material which he has to review up into something which it is not. The only play to which he gives detailed consideration is Alexander Knox's *Old Master*, and on this his comment is interesting. "With all its faults, this is probably the most professionally finished full-length comedy yet written by a Canadian. That there is nothing Canadian in its theme or characters . . . is less the fault of Mr. Knox than of a country which cannot keep its talented young artists at home."

Let us turn from *Letters in Canada: 1940* to another and, in my opinion, more honest volume, which is *Canadian Literature*

Today, a reprint of a series of talks on this subject which were given over the CBC in 1938. The first of these is called "The Contemporary Situation" and is by Professor E.K. Brown; in this Mr. Brown speaks his mind more honestly than he does in the later volume, and rightly, I think, attributes the poverty of good literary work in this country to the fact that a writer cannot hope to live on what he can make out of the Canadian market. To the academic evil Mr. Brown, understandably, makes no reference, but I think that this, quite as much as lack of money, hinders the production of imaginative work in this country. Canada as she really is, and Canada as she is seen through the eyes of our professors, are two very different places, and as long as our poetry and our criticism are in the hands of our cultured and well-meaning but essentially unpassionate and unimaginative educationists we cannot expect much from it.

"Cap and Bells," *Peterborough Examiner*, 17 June 1941

Barometer Rising: 1941

It is not every year that Canada produces two novels as good as Sinclair Ross' *As For Me and My House* and Hugh MacLennan's *Barometer Rising*. But whereas Mr. Ross' plot might have been laid in almost any Western town on this continent, Mr. MacLennan's is inescapably attached to Halifax, and its denouement is the disastrous explosion which ravaged that city in 1917. Few Canadian cities have been so well treated in fiction as is Halifax in this admirable novel.

The plot is simple but strong. Colonel Wain, a Halifax shipchandler and merchant, has made a disastrous mess of his career as a military leader. He succeeds in pinning most of the blame for his own incompetence upon his nephew Neil Macrae, who is one of his subordinate officers; the unpleasantness of a court-martial in which uncle and nephew appear is avoided because Macrae appears to have been blown up by a bomb. Nevertheless the Colonel is sent back to Canada to do unimportant work in Halifax. The action of the novel covers the eight days which include the return of Macrae, who was *not* killed, and the death of the Colonel in the Halifax explosion. Macrae is thus avenged, and is able to return to Penelope, the Colonel's daughter and the mother of his child.

The story is unfolded in a manner which is compact and exiguous without being bald. Mr. MacLennan has little to learn about constructing a novel or telling a story. He is not entirely happy, however, in drawing sympathetic characters. Neither Macrae nor Penelope is quite alive. The Colonel, on the other hand, is admirably drawn, and the author has been brilliantly successful in communicating the spirit of the city of Halifax to his readers.

In the opinion of this reviewer the most serious fault of Mr. MacLennan's book is that it is written in a good, but singularly rigid prose, which is pleasing for twenty pages but is monotonous when followed through 200 pages. This is a disability which the author will assuredly overcome, for in his description of the explosion of the *Mont Blanc* he shows a power and command of style which is nothing less than magnificent. It is this which raises the book from worthy mediocrity to the rank of a first novel of genuine importance. Mr. MacLennan's previous writing has been academic, and while he possesses the clarity and purity of style which is expected of a scholar, he has not yet overcome the scholar's dryness; but in his handling of the events of that fatal December Thursday in 1917 he shows a scholar's feeling for epic description and for several pages his prose is transformed.

This novel is an important addition to our Canadian literature and, unless something unforeseen happens, Mr. MacLennan will give us more books and better ones. Will they be on Canadian themes? That is entirely up to us. We are apt, in this country, to neglect our artists until they go to countries where they are appreciated, and it is high time that we overcame this unlovely national trait. By reading *Barometer Rising* now you will be doing something which will not only give you great satisfaction but will also be helping to cherish the tender sapling which is Canadian literature.

"Disaster and a Canadian Family," *Saturday Night*,
11 October 1941

Contemporary Verse: 1942

Threatened men live long, and invalids often bury those who have nursed them. Seemingly, Canadian verse belongs in the category of those things which are always upon the point of vanishing forever from this earth but which, somehow or other, continue to exist. Every now and again a group of enthusiasts appears, whose members give the pallid valetudinarian a shot in the arm, and it is saved for another few years. But its prolonged and interminable death agonies are a grim spectacle.

The fact is – and we may as well make up our minds to it now – that Canadian poetry simply is not going to die, however great the evidence to the contrary may be. The instinct to write verse is deeply rooted in the human heart, and nothing will ever drive it out. Ever since man acquired the gift of speech, he has delighted in intricate and lovely patterns of words, and has kept a special place in his society for men who can create them. Canada is no exception to this general rule.

But Canada has special handicaps as a land for poets. For one thing, she has no literary background of her own. Her literary history is, at a long stretch, 100 years old; her history has been shaped by politics and economics, rather than by the deeds of heroes, and she acquired her present form during a century which was certainly one of the most materialistic in all history. Her people are not indigenous to her soil; she has no peasantry who love the land and cherish its legends. She has, in fact, little of the usual stock-in-trade of poetry save for a wonderfully diversified and beautiful landscape. The man or woman who sets out to write poetry in Canada will find little help in the country or its people.

A great poet will write poetry anywhere, but great poets are remarkably scarce. Most people who write poetry are far from being great poets, but they have unusual sensitivity, a feeling for words, and – this is perhaps the most important thing of all – something which they wish to say. These are the minor poets, who produce so much that is beautiful; and there is always the chance that a minor poet may produce one or two great poems, if he has luck. We should like to see a great poet or so in Canada, but barring that piece of exceptional good fortune, we must be content with our minor poets, most of whom are very minor indeed. Asked to name our poets of distinction now living, most Canadians who are interested in the matter would speak of Charles G.D. Roberts, of Duncan Campbell Scott, of E.J. Pratt, of George Herbert Clarke, of a few more, and he would be forced to admit that of these only Pratt is read at all widely in this country or any other.

These reflections are provoked by an examination of the first two issues of a magazine called *Contemporary Verse, A Canadian Quarterly* which have come to hand. It originates on the Pacific Coast, and its head office is in Victoria. Its editor is Alan Crawley, who has done a great deal of hard and unselfish work to foster poetry and literature generally in this country. The men who are mentioned above as distinguished among Canadian poets are none of them young: Sir Charles Roberts is eighty-two, and Duncan Campbell Scott is two years his junior. Professor Pratt and Professor Clarke are both in middle life. Where are Canada's young poets going to appear? Presumably Mr. Crawley hopes that they will eventually turn up in the pages of his quarterly, and we sincerely hope so too. Candour, however, compels us to say that they have not made their appearance in the first two issues.

The verse which appears in these two small issues is, to use a damning critical adjective, intellectual. That is to say, it appears to have been written because the writers felt that they ought to write poetry, rather than because they felt any great compulsion to do so. Much of the work is excellent as far as it goes, and it is possible to read it with real pleasure, but it will never attract readers who are not, for some reason, professionally interested in poetry; such readers would be other poets and critics, and these make a poor audience. The themes chosen are not such as would attract general readers and the manner in which these themes are handled is positively calculated to frighten general readers away. This poetry is remote from life, and it will never get a hearing from people who have to snatch their poetry-reading hours from the rough-and-tumble, haphazard business of living.

Frankly, the poetry produced by the young writers in Canada today suffers from being flabby and precious. They do not appear to have much to say that anyone else would care to hear, and they elect to say it in an abstruse, over-refined way which puts more strain on the faculties of the reader than the verse itself warrants. Canadian poets, if they are not content to write merely for each other, must have more and better ideas, and they must express them more vigorously. Canadian poetry will not die; there is no fear of that. But at present the Canadian Muse is suffering from pernicious anaemia, and her persistent invalidism is a great bore.

"New Venture In Canadian Verse," *Peterborough Examiner*, 19 March 1942

Anthology of Canadian Poetry: 1942

Messrs. Collins, who are now publishing the excellent Penguin and Pelican books in this country, have brought out a first-rate *Anthology of Canadian Poetry* compiled for them by Ralph Gustafson and costing only twenty-five cents; there is, therefore, no possible excuse for not buying it. Any lover of poetry who has not a quarter will doubtless be able to find a friend who will lend him that sum.

To say that the anthology is a first-rate anthology of Canadian poetry is not quite the same thing as saying that it is an anthology of first-rate poetry by Canadians. It is of no use to pretend that this country has produced any volume of significant poetry. But it has produced some poetry which is excellent in its own way; great poets cannot be produced on demand, and Canada has done quite well with its second-raters. Like Australia and South Africa, countries with whom our artistic growth may fairly be compared, we have our minor poets, and their work has charm, polish, and freshness. But they are not the men and women to stun us with new ideas or blind us with sudden flashes of Promethean fire. In Mr. Gustafson's anthology only the work of E.J. Pratt and Robert Finch stands out; the first because it possesses in a generous measure that quality which is best called guts, and the second because it reveals a really keen and deeply intelligent mind. Guts and brains are as necessary to poets as to other people, and only these two seem to have either in any degree sufficient to make them remarkable.

Of the fifty-six poets whose work is included in the anthology thirteen are women. Every reader will find his own favourite in this group, and mine is Isabel Ecclestone Mackay whose lovely and deeply felt "First Love" is reprinted; on the whole the work of the women is undistinguished, as the poetry of men is apt to be. In all the centuries of English literature a bare hand-count of women have written poetry which anyone cares to remember.

Grace and ingenuity they have, but rarely strength or a deep understanding of things. Of the men, Mr. Gustafson has included many now dead, for poetry in the Dominion is a good three generations old. But it is notable that there are only two poems in the book which are not serious in intention. These are "The Wreck of the Julie Plante" by Dr. Drummond and "The Ahkoond of Swat" by George Thomas Lanigan, the founder of the Montreal *Star*; the others take life heavily. This is characteristic of our nation. We are nothing if not serious, in season and out.

Because the writer does not greet this anthology with noisy shouts of praise, let no reader imagine that he is an enemy of Canadian poetry. On the contrary, it is his desire to see this country produce genuinely great poetry which makes him critical of this. Canada, as a country and nation, had a difficult birth in the nineteenth century, and was forced to begin life in an era of almost unchecked materialism, without the background of a pastoral age to serve as a brake upon the dizzy speed of "progress." As a result our country has advanced most satisfactorily in the realm of commerce without any corresponding development in the realm of thought or the arts. Individuals have done their best, but the country as a whole has lagged, and spiritually we are still in the nineteenth century. None of our poets is strong enough to defy the age in which they live, and so they follow the trend of the times, instead of leading it. Is it any wonder then that our poetry is, in the main, timid and somewhat juiceless?

Mr. Gustafson, in his Preface, says: "In my task of compiler I have had to forgo, obviously, much good poetry; have had honestly to reject some material that had become falsely established. The yardstick in this task was plain and unvarnished. I have measured and judged my material not by historical significance nor by 'Canadianism' but in terms of vitality; is it alive or dead?" This sounds promising, and certainly Mr. Gustafson has omitted much time-honoured trash from his book. But he cannot draw blood out of a stone, and he cannot get more life from Canadian poets as a whole than exists in them. There are honourable exceptions. Pratt and Finch have been cited as having vigour and unusual intellectual quality; Duncan Campbell Scott writes as a man whose voice would be heard anywhere; Louis MacKay has character more than strength; and A.M. Klein's poetry with a

Jewish cast is richer than what we usually get in Canada. But the sound of big guns is notably absent.

It will be heard in time. But only when Canada has awakened from her nineteenth-century dream; only when we have troubled to find out what is going on in the world of thought that lies beyond our own shores. Perhaps we may hope for that time to come after this war? But it will only come when the country as a whole wants it. Our poets are not strong enough to arouse a reluctant country.

"New Anthology Of Poetry By Canadians," *Peterborough Examiner*, 6 June 1942

The Man Who Wrote "O Canada": 1942

Tomorrow is the seventy-fifth anniversary of the founding of our Dominion, and enough has already been said on that subject in the newspapers; but it may not be amiss to think for a while about a man who did much for Canada, for he wrote our national song. He was Calixa Lavallée, and this year is the centenary of his birth.

The British dominions have not been altogether happy in their national songs, for a Britisher abroad or in the colonies is a Britisher still and is content to go on singing "Rule Britannia" and "Hearts of Oak" till all is blue. But the French in Canada have different ideas and they were the first people here to seek a distinctively Canadian patriotic song. In 1880 the Lieutenant-Governor of Quebec asked Calixa Lavallée to write a musical setting of Judge Adolphe Routhier's poem, "O Canada, terre de nos aïeux," and the song which we know is the result. As a piece of music it has its merits and its faults. It is a simple development of one phrase, and consequently it is apt to become tiresome if it is heard too often; it has also a Victorian tendency towards sentimentality, and a somewhat square-toed musical pattern. But it has breadth and simplicity, and Routhier's poem is a fine one. Unfortunately, there is no first-rate English translation; Judge Weir's version is really an original poem rather than a translation, and the verse translation which exists is not a happy piece of work. It shows wisdom in the Dominion government that it has never adopted this song as a national anthem; it is unsuitable for many reasons, and it is better that "God Save the King" should serve the purpose of a national hymn throughout the empire. But "O Canada" is an admirable national song.

The Lavallée family had been in Canada for at least two centuries when Calixa was born in 1842. He was the son of Augustin, a blacksmith who was something of a musician himself. At least he advertised that he "repaired musical instruments and firearms." The lad learned to play the piano, violin, and cornet when he was still very young, and became interested in the organ when his father associated himself with Joseph Casavant, the founder of the great firm of organ builders.

In 1855, for some reason which is not clear, Calixa was adopted by a lover of music named Léon Derome who lived in Montreal. In that city the boy studied with a blind musician named Paul Letondal, who seems to have gathered up the threads of young Lavallée's disordered musical education and to have given him some notion of what artistry was. But the boy was possessed by that wild and roving disposition which is sometimes called "artistic temperament," and when he was fifteen he ran away with a theatrical troupe and ended up in New Orleans. Here a young Frenchman might find himself at home, and Lavallée soon formed a close association with a Spanish violinist, Olivera, and he toured in South America as accompanist to this artist.

When next we hear of Lavallée he is fighting in the American Civil War on the Northern side; he had acquired a dislike of slavery while in New Orleans. He fought at Bull Run and it is believed that he was wounded at Antietam. He was only twenty-one when he returned to Montreal and set up as a teacher of music, but he did not stay at this profession long. He was soon away again with a company of negro minstrels, and he wandered far and wide over the United States. He married a New England girl, and this experience seems to have steadied him for a time; at any rate he returned to Canada in 1870 and taught in Montreal and Quebec. But Lavallée was a roamer; soon he was off to New York where he became Musical Director of Pyke's Opera House, a noted home of minstrel shows. What attracted this gifted French-Canadian to this peculiarly American form of entertainment must remain a mystery; minstrel shows are rarely remarkable for the interest or complexity of their music. But after two years he was back in Montreal again and the ever-forgiving Derome received him with understanding and financial aid. Indeed, he dispatched Calixa, who was now thirty-two, to Paris, where he studied at the Conservatoire with Marmontel for two years. When he again returned to Montreal it was to become organist at St. James' Cathedral and to do his best to found a Conservatoire on the Parisian model. But Canada was unresponsive, and after a few years of gigantic effort Lavallée quitted this country in disgust and spent the remainder of his life in the States, where he became very well known as an accompanist of touring musicians. He died in Boston in 1891.

It cannot be claimed that Lavallée was a man of genius, but he was a musician far above the average, and if he had been given more encouragement he might have done much for his native land. But Canada was then, as it still is to a large extent, inclined to disregard native talent until it had fled over the border, and Lavallée was too mercurial in temperament to impress favourably the men who might have given the money to found his Conservatoire. Now he is known only by a handful of piano pieces and by "O Canada." He was before his time in his attempt to give Canadian music importance on this continent, but who is to say that our present enviable status in that respect does not stem from his efforts? Certainly tomorrow, when we are certain to hear "O Canada" played, we may spare a thought for the erratic, impatient, but fervidly Canadian Calixa Lavallée.

Peterborough Examiner, 30 June 1942

The Book of Small: 1942

It is about a year since the sickly child, Canadian Letters, was given the literary equivalent of a blood transfusion with the publication of Emily Carr's *Klee Wyck*; now she comes to the rescue of the invalid again with an even more stimulating dose called *The Book of Small*. Her publishers assure us that Miss Carr has material for many more books, and we may hope that these annual needlings will continue until the child is healthy and strong, deriving vigour from the lifeblood of the Victoria painter who has surprised us with her unique gifts as an author. It is no strained figure of speech to call these books the lifeblood of Emily Carr, for they are of her very essence. All the observation and understanding which have made her one of our finest painters are in them.

Emily Carr's writing is intensely personal. *Klee Wyck*, the title of her first book, is her own Indian name, and it means The Laughing One; and *The Book of Small* is so called because, of Richard Carr's eight children, she was the third of a group of girls. Two older sisters there were, and three boys who died young, and then three girls—Bigger, Middle, and Small; it is Small's life in a world where everyone seemed older and wiser and duller which supplies the matter of the book. But *The Book of Small* is not another of those molasses puddings which sentimental people concoct from dishonestly remembered fragments of their childhood; nor is it one of those Life With My Eccentric Victorian Father books which have cluttered the market recently, and which whisper unpleasantly of delayed revenge on a domestic tyrant. It is a genuine and truthful account of an intelligent small girl's response to an unusually interesting environment.

The dominating characteristics of the Carr household were Englishness and religion. Richard Carr did all that lay in his power to turn his part of Victoria Island into a replica of the dear land which he had left. He was a Devon man, and the lush yet orderly Devon countryside was his notion of what nature should be; the

159

grim Canadian forests were always alien to him. Miss Carr writes with restrained ridicule of those settlers who attempted to turn Victoria into a corner of England, but Victoria was her native land; she did not feel the pull of a divided loyalty. As for religion, it was given to the Carr children in large, regular, remorseless doses. As one reads of morning worship, evening prayers, church twice on Sundays, and Sunday School, and of those long Sabbaths when no food was cooked and no games played one's heart aches for the children who were subjected to this Hebraic regime, but a consideration of the results somewhat alters one's view; were not the children brought up in this glum, repressive creed better off than their grandchildren, who are frequently brought up with no ethical training of any kind? Miss Carr outgrew the grim faith of her childhood, but by that time its determination was an essential part of her character. It is surprising how much that is hard and unyielding children can survive; what invariably ruins them is weakness and lack of direction.

Bigger was a prim miss, fearful for the whiteness of her apron; she liked to play in the garden. Middle was a born mother; she liked to play with dolls. But Small was low in her tastes; "Small was wholly a Cow Yard child" as she admits herself. For some time the family cow was the only animal within the scope of her great love. For animals – "creatures" as she calls them with an unconscious echo of her English ancestors – were Small's chief delight in life. Yet it was many years before she was permitted to own a dog; a hard and painful passage in the book tells of how she hoped for a puppy for her birthday – she had been told that her gift began with a "p" – and of how she was given a picture which, ironically, showed a little girl fondling a puppy. But once she was allowed to have a canary, and when she wanted to confide her joy to the Bishop, he would not even look! Perhaps Small's doubt of his holiness began then, and her trend towards the Indians, who included animals in their religion and admitted them freely to the hereafter.

In *The Book of Small* Emily Carr has given another volume of first-rate importance to Canadian literature. Her writing is really Canadian, and not the dull copy of the cheaper sort of American work which Canadian writers are apt to turn out. She uses words sparingly and with delicacy; but the total impression is one of great strength. I am almost tempted to say that she writes in a Canadian vernacular, for although her writing is free of the conscious "style" of modern English authors it avoids the vulgarity of those American writers who sacrifice every grace to an impression of strenuosity. She can use a racy phrase with telling effect, but the staple of her vocabulary is Bible English with the thunder muted. Her writing, in short, is the natural expression of a distinguished and wholly original mind; one is almost tempted to guess that Miss Carr reads little, for there are no echoes in her work. This is Canadian writing as we have never seen it before, and there can be no doubt but that the publication of the works of Emily Carr mark a turning point in the literature of this country. I advise you strongly to read them now, so that your grandchildren will not blush for you when you confess that you lived in Emily Carr's time and failed to read her books.

"Childhood On Victoria Island," *Peterborough Examiner*,
10 November 1942

Emily Carr: 1945

During the eighties of the last century, a fifteen-year-old girl went to visit the Presbyterian missionaries at Ucluelet, a remote spot on the west coast of Canada. She learned to know the Indians, to sympathize with them, and to love many of them. They gave her the Chinook name of Klee Wyck, which means The Laughing One, for although she was no giggler, she was not so dour as the missionaries, nor so sober as the Indians themselves. On the second of March last, Klee Wyck died in Victoria; she was Emily Carr, one of Canada's greatest painters.

Although Miss Carr's eminence as a painter has been generally recognized during the past ten years, it may be that her fame as a writer will surpass it in time, when all her manuscripts have been sorted and made into books. She was a woman of comprehensive intellect, deep artistic insight, and rigorous honesty; there was no trace of cant in her mind, anywhere. She wrote as she painted, boldly and directly, without reference to accepted models; what she wrote was a true revelation of her mind, for she wrote without real intention of publishing. Her writings rank with the best that Canada has produced, and far surpass most of what we are pleased to accept as our native literature.

Artists of Emily Carr's stature are not put together with string and mucilage; they are shaped by circumstances sometimes too bitter to be borne without cries of anguish. Some of her writings contain such cries, but they are as short as they are poignant; she never pitied herself, and she never thought that her calling as a painter entitled her to special consideration from the world. She met the world squarely and pleasantly, as she met the Indians at Ucluelet; she was amazed and hurt that the world did not respond with equal candour.

A worldly-wise and understanding friend (if she had had such a thing) would have put her on her guard. She was an eccentric: she met the world with wide-open eyes, seeing everything as new and fresh; the people who saw everything through the smeared spectacles of convention could not forgive her for that. She was kind, and was eager to help those who seemed to need help; very often they accepted the help and then called her a fool for her pains. She insisted on living as she wanted to live, tramping to the butcher's to get scraps for her dogs, and dressing in the manner which pleased her; as she had neither money nor a great name to excuse these affronts to society, she was scoffed at as a crotchety old maid, probably not quite right in the head. Worst of all, she painted, not in the dainty convention of the Victoria Island Arts and Crafts Society, but as her great abilities told her to paint; this was unforgivable impertinence. Some very great people attract the particular attention of malignant and insignificant people, who are driven to insult and mock them whenever an opportunity comes; Emily Carr was such a butt, and she bore this irksome burden bravely for several decades.

Recognition as an artist came to her comparatively late in life. She was an original, working alone in a place where aesthetic appreciation, except on the lowest level, did not exist. But it came at last, and Emily Carr was able to sell her pictures, give up the drudgery of keeping an apartment house, and breed her Bobtail English sheepdogs for pleasure and not for profit. Friends of her own cast of mind made their appearance, and the misery and the loneliness lifted. It was one of these friends, Ira Dilworth of the CBC, who discovered Miss Carr as a writer, and communicated his discovery, with justifiable excitement, to W.H. Clarke, the Toronto publisher who, with his wife, made the journey to Victoria to visit the painter, who was not greatly impressed at first with the idea that she might be a writer as well. But in 1941 the first collection of her pieces appeared with her Indian name, *Klee Wyck*, as its title, and *The Book of Small* and *The House of All Sorts* have followed it. There is no other word but "pieces" to describe the random notes and impressions which make up these books. They are entirely coherent, but they are free of all the fallals with which writers usually fatten and connect the fragments of their works. She wrote as she painted, sparely, but with the brightest, the only possible, colours.

The death of Klee Wyck is not a matter for sanctimonious mourning in the manner of the Victoria Island Arts and Crafts

Society; no obituary of regretful commonplaces and obligatory groanings can add or detract from what she was. She wrote of death often with an understanding which shames the writer who would speak of her own passing; her work was done, and well done. But her fame is not done. It is only beginning, for Emily Carr was one of the great Canadians of the first forty years of the twentieth century, and we shall not see her in her true dimensions until some of the century's debris has been cleared away.

"The Death of Klee Wyck," *Peterborough Examiner*, 14 March 1945

Earth and High Heaven: 1945

During the twenties there used to be a good deal of talk about The Great Canadian Novel, which all young Canadian authors hoped to write, and which many reviewers hailed every month or so, only to discover afterwards that they had been deceived by a false dawn. The Great Canadian Novel has still to be written: that is to say, Canada has yet to produce a novel of first-rate literary merit which will be of interest to the whole English-speaking world. But in *Earth and High Heaven* Gwethalyn Graham has produced a novel which is likely to have a greater impact upon the world than any Canadian work written heretofore.

It is very pleasant for a Canadian to read a good novel about Canada, after ploughing dutifully through so many bad ones. Canada and its people have a distinctive character, but it is so slight and elusive that only an author of skill and sensitivity can capture it and convey it in print. We lack sensitive authors almost completely; Canada, in Canadian novels, is too often represented as a backwoods country, rugged and stark, peopled with rugged, stark men and women who are about as interesting as so many horses. To the majority of Canadians, this is not a rugged country in any sense; it is a soft country, and the people in it are those interesting hybrids, British North Americans. The flavour of Canada is exceptionally well conveyed in *Earth and High Heaven*, and if several thousand American tourists do not come to the city of Montreal to see if it measures up to Miss Graham's description, I shall be very greatly surprised.

The theme of the novel, as everybody knows by this time, is race prejudice. Erica Drake is the daughter of a prominent Montreal business man; she meets a Jewish lawyer, Marc Reiser, and they fall in love. But her parents refuse to meet Reiser because in their minds the fact that he is a Jew condemns him utterly. The situation, badly begun, feeds on its own venom until the Drake home is unhappy and Erica and Marc are unhappy too, and decide that marriage is out of the question for them. At last the problem is settled by a little application of common sense by Marc's brother, David.

The characters of the story are clearly and cleanly drawn. There is no laborious and cloudy "psychological" explanation of what they do, for their actions spring inevitably from what they are. We are spared the muddy introspections and soul scrubbings which mar so many novels of this kind. Charles Drake, Erica's father, is perhaps the most interesting creation of the lot; he is that fairly common type, the man of business who thinks that his success in business marks him as a man of unusual wisdom in every field of human experience; he is emotional and illogical, he does not think, he throbs. His prejudice against Jews is ignorant and silly, but he cherishes it and advances it with all the strength of his character. Erica's mother, her sister, and David Reiser are equally well drawn but they have not the strength of Charles; Charles, with the best intentions in the world, is an agent of evil, and evil is always powerful in works of art. Erica herself is a thoroughly believable character; she is quite human, and human heroines are very rare in fiction.

The principal adverse criticism which must be brought against the book is that the hero, Marc Reiser, is not human. He is not like a Jew; he is not like a Gentile; he is like nothing in the heavens above nor in the earth beneath, nor in the waters under the earth. This is how Erica's sister was impressed by him: ". . . She found it difficult to imagine anyone with a grain of sense not liking Marc. It was not only that he was attractive and intelligent, with charm and good manners and a marvelous smile, but he had another quality, still more important. He was completely straight. After talking to him for even a short time you knew that he would never lie nor take an advantage, and after a little longer, you knew also that he was incapable of consciously going out of his way to make an impression no matter who it was. . . ." Later on, in an intimate scene, it occurs to Erica that Marc looks like a Greek god. Marc, in short, is a little too good to be true.

But Marc is the only major blot on this excellent book. Miss Graham understands family life and writes about it well. As she is describing a well-bred, repressed, and unimaginative family, her family rows lack that violence, cantankerousness, and shrill acrimony which distinguish such conflicts at their worst. Her suggestion that Charles Drake's objection to his daughter's marriage is based in something deeper than anti-Semitic prejudice is conveyed with skill. She makes full use of the picturesqueness of the Montreal setting, though it is never obtrusive, and her dialogue is admirable; she knows how to be colloquial without becoming cheap. But the most important thing that her book does is to bring home to us the knowledge that in Canada there is a body of Nazi opinion just as malignant as any which has ever existed in Germany; that in Canada stupidity, smugness, and non-Christian cruelty disguise themselves as loyalty, common sense, and Christian charity; and that it is high time that we stopped shutting our eyes and ears to these facts.

"A Notable Canadian Novel," *Peterborough Examiner*,
11 April 1945

In Search of Myself: 1946

In his autobiography *In Search of Myself* Frederick Philip Grove passes on to us a dictum of his father's, to the effect that life is always either an adventure or a discipline. It is apparently Grove's idea that his own life has been an adventure: to me, if to no other reader, it appears as a discipline of the harshest sort. Time after time Grove might have echoed Gloucester's terrible cry – "As flies to wanton boys are we to the gods" – but not once does he do so. His life is a record of material defeat, misunderstanding, frustration, and cruel deprivation. Time after time his hopes have been raised, only to be dashed again when success seemed to be within his grasp. Now, in his old age and sadly broken in health, he is still a failure, as the greater part of the world judges such things; you will not find his name in *Who's Who In Canada* among the politicians and eminent manufacturers of toothpicks; and if you ask anyone to name, offhand, three or four of the most eminent writers in Canada, the chances are that you will not hear the name of Frederick Philip Grove.

Canada's taste in literature is still unformed and uncertain. We know what to admire if it comes to us from England or the United States with impressive recommendations from the critics of those countries. We pant eagerly after the taste of the rest of the world. But with our own writers we are at a loss; we dare not bestow the laurel crown, fearing that time may show that we were mistaken. We have no Book-of-the-Month, no Hollywood, to sift the wheat from the chaff for us and spare us the fatigue of making first-hand judgements. Our literary criticism is characterized in the main, by what Grove himself calls "utterly hopeless ineptitude": and, as he says on another page of his autobiography, "Intellectually, Canada is a chaos; the light has not been divided from the darkness." When, at last, light and darkness can be seen clearly for what they are, I think that Canada will wish that it had been a little more gentle in its treatment of Grove.

Grove is a literary artist of a type recognized in Europe, but hardly guessed-at in Canada. Without attempting to relate the men in any other way, or to make a comparison between their writings, he resembles Thomas Mann in his philosophical approach to his work, in his scholarly background, in his integrity, and in his essentially European estimate of the place of the artist in the community. His books have few charms for the ordinary reader; he makes demands on emotion and understanding which the average patron of a lending library cannot meet, and will not tolerate from a man who has not been labelled "great" by non-Canadian reviewers. He is chilly and austere; sometimes his books are "unpleasant," but not in the sniggering way that the public likes and the censor overlooks. He says himself: "The artist should always build his work as if it were meant to last through the centuries; and only the great commonplaces of life are worthy of being forever repeated and expounded anew." Is it surprising that this man's voice was drowned by the clamour of the literary hucksters in the market place? And will it be surprising if his voice is still heard 200 years from now when Canada has begun to take intelligent pride in her literature? But the posthumous fame which he will surely enjoy can do nothing for the living man.

Grove's book is painful reading, for the misfortunes come thick and fast and his occasional frosty twinkles of humour cannot soothe the hurt. But like many painful artistic experiences it leaves the reader with a feeling of triumph and new strength when he has closed it. Grove says that he has thought many times of writing a book about his devoted and courageous wife, to be called *The Life Heroic*; that might aptly serve as the title of his own book. Some day we shall be glad that this heroism had our young country as its setting.

From "Lives Heroic And Unheroic," *Peterborough Examiner*, 6 November 1946

Who Has Seen the Wind: 1947

Who Has Seen the Wind by W.O. Mitchell is the best novel about life in Canada that has come my way in a long time. It is the story of a boy's growth to manhood in a Saskatchewan prairie town, described in detail and with great love and understanding. Many a Canadian reader will find, as I have done, that the pace and tone and spirit of this book suit him better than the corresponding qualities in American books on the same theme. After all, books about a boy growing up in a small town are scarcely a novelty, and every book-reviewer has read several dozen of them; they commonly contain the old grandmother, the religious fanatic, the drunks and the bigots, the understanding parents, and the enlightened schoolteacher who appear in Mr. Mitchell's book. But he has so thoroughly captured the feeling of Canada and the Canadian people that we feel repeated shocks of recognition as we read; the kindness and stoicism of Canadian people, as well as the exasperating stupidity, fecklessness, and petty cruelty of which they are capable are rendered here in such a way that we know the characters as our kinsmen. Further, the book has an engaging humour, which is uncommon in Canadian writing, though by no means uncommon in Canadian life. This is that rare thing, a Canadian book which could not have been written equally well in the United States. It is a pity, by the way, that it is so poorly produced and bound. A book of this quality deserves a better physical embodiment. Why should a $2.50 book be so cheap and nasty?

From "Review Of Spring Novels," *Peterborough Examiner*, 12 March 1947

The Tin Flute: 1947

Written originally in French by Gabrielle Roy, *The Tin Flute* has achieved unusual success. It is not hard to understand why this is so. The book has a quality of understanding and charity towards mankind which is engaging, and a pleasant change from the "tough" school of novel-writing. I cannot honestly say that it is especially penetrating; its kindliness is the kindliness of the warm heart rather than that of the clever head. It tells, in a straightforward manner, about Florentine Lacasse, a girl who works in a ten-cent store in the St. Henri section of Montreal, and how she fell in love with Jean Levesque and, upon one occasion, yielded herself to him. But Jean was too ambitious to tie himself to any girl, and so she married Emmanuel Letourneau, who did not know that she was going to bear Levesque's child. (It is curious, by the way, that girls who fall once in novels always have children as a consequence; the world in reality is not so exacting.) The book also tells us about Florentine's unlucky father, Azarius, and her patient, drudging mother, Rose-Anna; her small brother Daniel, who dies of a deficiency disease, yearns for the tin flute which gives the book its name. . . . This competent and pleasant novel is not always well translated; it is much too easy to put such sentences as "Yes, Mother, it's all settled. The truck costs me nothing" back into French – much easier than it is to believe that a truck driver ever said them to his wife. Nor can we feel that "By Jove" and "By George" are good equivalents for "Mon Dieu." A more supple and sympathetic translation would have helped Miss Roy's book; we cannot tell how much of its flavour has been lost in a rather stiff rendering.

From "Five Spring Novels," *Peterborough Examiner*,
30 April 1947

The Diary of Samuel Marchbanks: 1947

*Can a mother's tender care
Fail toward the child she bare?*

So asks the hymn, and it might be asked with equal cogency if an author can be trusted to review his own book. Even though he may be a book-reviewer by trade—even though his opinions on books may be considered of some slight public interest—can he play fair when writing about a book of his own? I really do not know, but I shall try to find out, for in this article I shall deal with *The Diary of Samuel Marchbanks*.

And now, what about this fellow Marchbanks? Is he a Provincial Gentleman? No; he detests provinciality, and there is a widespread opinion that he is no gentleman. He is a shouter and a sneerer. Some other reviewers have used the word "urbane" in describing his *Diary*, but I don't think that he is urbane at all. He seems to be discontented with Canada—which we all know is The Greatest Country on Earth and he actually has the face to maintain that our beautiful country is intellectually arid, and full of complacent boobs. I would suggest that he be given a one-way ticket back to Moscow, or wherever he came from—but unfortunately he comes from Canada and we can't get rid of him. I strongly advise everybody who thinks that Canada is incapable of improvement to ignore this fellow Marchbanks.

Not, mind you, that the fellow is a Communist. He is something much worse; his political views seem to be utterly archaic. He doesn't believe in Inevitable Progress, he doesn't believe that a high standard of eating is the same thing as a high standard of living, and he often blasphemes against the sacredness of wealth. He makes fun of Service, and he keeps nagging away at his readers about music, books, and plays—things that only women have time for in a go-ahead country like this. Not that he is womanish in his attitude towards them; our Canadian women can be trusted not to get too excited about these fripperies – The Arts, as he calls them; our women maintain their Equilibrium – what some philosophers call their Essential Stodge – when confronted with artistic things. But not Marchbanks. The fellow is obviously a nut.

The worst of it is that he is not even serious in what he writes. Really good Canadian writers are so serious that you can hardly get through their stuff, but of course you don't have to; you know that whatever they say is perfectly safe. But Marchbanks is flippant, and even brokers from Bay Street in Toronto, and Scotchmen from the Maritimes, have been known to laugh at his nonsense. This is what makes the man dangerous, and a real threat to our Canadian Way of Life; once Canadians begin to laugh at themselves, who can see what may follow? And those decorations in the book, by some fellow named Clair Stewart – dangerous too, for the fellow is obviously an artist, and therefore suspect. . . . There, ladies and gentlemen, who could be fairer than that?

From "Delicate And Dangerous Diarists," *Peterborough Examiner*, 3 December 1947 (Until May 1948, Davies' regular book-review columns in the *Examiner* appeared under the pseudonym Samuel Marchbanks.)

The Wounded Prince: 1948

Douglas LePan's book of poems *The Wounded Prince* is now available in Canada, and should engage the attention of everyone in this country who is interested in poetry. LePan is very much a Canadian, and several of the poems in this collection have Canadian themes, but there is a richness and a breadth in his workmanship which is by no means characteristic of Canadian poetry, and which does not sound like the workmanship of the poets whose work reaches us from the United States. LePan's mind is of this continent and of this country, but it received its polish in Europe. In his work we find a linking of Canadian and European attitudes which is deeply interesting. It has been my privilege to know Douglas LePan for twelve years, and I formed this opinion some time ago. It is gratifying to have it corroborated by Cecil Day Lewis in an introduction to *The Wounded Prince* in which he says: "He is a Canadian. He is also in his poetic thoughts and themes a European. He is not the first poet in whom the New and the Old World have met; but I am not sure he may not be the first in whom this partnership will remain an equal one."

Douglas LePan has been an instructor in English at Toronto and Harvard; he saw varied service in the war, and until recently he has been first secretary to the Canadian High Commissioner in London. A fortnight ago the announcement was made that he had been awarded a Guggenheim fellowship which will provide him with a year's time in which to write a novel. This novel should be an extremely interesting production, for the feeling for words and the quality and analysis of emotion shown in *The Wounded Prince* will be sufficient to give it distinction, whatever other gifts it may reveal. It is plain that in Douglas LePan Canada has brought forth a writer of fine quality; the question now is, can it hold him? What rewards and honours has it for him? Does Canada want him, or will we relinquish him without struggle to the United States, or to Britain, as we have done with so many of our poets? These are not rhetorical questions, but practical ones, for there has never been a country of any consequence which did not take some thought for its poets. The first and best thing that his countrymen can do for Douglas LePan is to provide him with an audience.

From "Workers In Words," *Peterborough Examiner*, 28 April 1948

A Letter From Canada: 1950

It is difficult to say anything about Canadian writing as it is at present unless something is first said about Canada. The Canadian position in literary matters is rather like that of the United States a century ago, with this important exception – Canada has the richest and most vocal country in the world as its nearest neighbour. When American writers were trying to create a mode of thought and a literary idiom of their own, English money and English fame beckoned to them from across the ocean; American money and American fame do not beckon to Canadian writers.

In consequence, some Canadian writers declare that there is no point in struggling, and that we should all strive to become American writers as fast as we can. Others are cantankerously nationalist in their outlook. And at this moment a Royal Commission on the Arts and Sciences is trying to help us find some widely acceptable Canadian attitude and a state of being in which "Canadian author" means more than a writer who has not been able to find a New York publisher. Canadianism, though not easily apparent at a first glance, is real and deep, and will give rise to a literature of its own. Canadians are far more occupied with matters of politics than Americans are, and we are, politically, a very subtle people; our greatest statesmen have been our greatest artists. We have made our place in the world by brains, for we are too small a population to put our trust in brawn. But in matters relating to the arts we are shallow, distrustful of ourselves and forever following after American or English gods.

We are also, it is to be feared, lacking in humour. We have been to America as Scotland is to England, or as Scandinavia is to Europe – the dour, worthy, crafty men of the North who fear the joyous arts and demand of the magnificent creatures that they should be respectable and improving.

We are changing, however, and for the better. Canadian writers are beginning to get more money for their work, and as a result they are attaching less importance to medals and awards. Since the war a few novels have appeared which have tried to show Canadians to themselves as they are, and not as Americans wearing strategically placed maple leaves – such books as *Turvey* by the poet, Earl Birney, and *Chipmunk*, by Len Petersen.

What gives these books their particularly Canadian quality would be hard to define, but the first, in particular, could not have come from the United States. It is a humorous novel, and our humour, like our whisky, is not like the produce of Britain or the United States, but at its best it is very good. Was it said that we were lacking in humour? That is not quite true.

Our leading novelist continues to be Hugh MacLennan, and *The Precipice* is a searching and characteristically sober contrast of American with Canadian character. MacLennan has an American publisher. Nor would any consideration of current Canadian fiction be complete without a reference to Ringuet, which is the pen name of a Quebec physician who writes in French, and who is one of our most accomplished craftsmen. The French population is smaller than the English-speaking one, but more ready to spend its money on books. Ringuet's novels sell in numbers which make Canadian novelists who write in English wonder if they should brush up on their knowledge of our second language.

Except for E.J. Pratt, our poets continue to work in miniature, sometimes with great charm and accomplishment. Robert Finch of Toronto has lately advanced into the first rank, and A.M. Klein of Montreal is challenging Pratt's supremacy. A young and interesting poet is James Reaney, who has a pretty wit and can make words dance to an engaging rhythm of his own. Poetry here has fully emerged from that stage where every poet finds it obligatory to admire flowers and the more obvious manifestations of nature. And in the work of Klein, Finch, and Reaney we are getting poetry which is very much of our own – poetry which we could not import.

Perhaps our most unexpected development is in drama. A number of Canadian writers have turned their attention to the stage, which is just beginning to be a lively part of our national life. The appetite for Broadway and London successes has been dulled to the point where Canadian plays are now regarded with interest.

John Coulter has recently had an elaborate play on the rebellion of Louis Riel produced successfully, and Joseph Schull has written a fine war play, *The Bridge*. I myself labour in this vineyard which is, in every sense save the monetary one, hugely rewarding; Canadian drama is at its sunrise.

To sum up, Canadian writing, after a long and frosty spring, is moving slowly into its early summer. We are always happy to share what we have with the United States, though not at the cost of our individuality.

New York Times Book Review, 19 March 1950

Samuel Marchbanks Writes a Letter to Haubergeon Hydra: 1950

Dear Mr. Hydra:
I see that Parliament is much concerned about the quality of modern Canadianism. Apparently it is not Canadian enough – there are still big lumps of British influence and Colonial Inferiority Complex swimming around in it. May I make a suggestion to you as Deputy Assistant Sterilizer of Canadian Patriotism?

We need bigger and better Canadian heroes. We have the raw material, but we must work on it. You know how Canada hates anything raw. We have heroes, but we have not yet blown them up to full heroic stature.

Look at what has been done in the States with Washington, Lincoln, Barbara Frietchie, and others. Unpromising material to begin with. Just men and women. But by the use of gas and mirrors they have been given heroic stature. Think what that story about the Cherry Tree has done for Washington! We couldn't copy it, of course, for in Canada we still admire people who cut down trees, and could not see any particular nobility in admitting such an action. In Canada, a tree is still looked upon as a Big Weed, to be hoiked up or chopped down, or mutilated with impunity. But there are other stories which we could bend to our use, and I submit the following examples, for your consideration.

Sir John and the Spider
One day our Great National Hero, Sir John A. Macdonald, sat disconsolately in his lawyer's office in Kingston. Try as he would, he could not get the Canadian provinces to confederate. They simply wouldn't. As he sat, his eyes were attracted by a little spider which was trying to climb up a piece of string (or whatever that stuff is that spiders extrude so unpleasantly from their stomachs). He paid no attention, for spiders were then, as now, part of the standard furnishing of all lawyers' offices in Kingston.

Up the spider climbed, and down it fell. Sir John's left eyelid

179

twitched. Again the spider tried to climb the string, but again it fell with an arachnidal curse. And a third time it struggled up the string and immediately set to work to gobble up a juicy fly.

Sir John was now fully awake. "By George!" he cried (referring to George Brown of the Toronto *Globe* and thus uttering a terrible Conservative curse). "Shall yonder foolish insect put me to shame? I too shall strive, and strive again, until there is a Federal Government in Canada, gobbling up the richest flies the land affords." And hastily taking a drink of soda water (of which he was inordinately fond), he rushed out and confederated Canada in a twinkling.

MORAL: Never sweep your office.

Laurier and the Teakettle

One day Sir Wilfrid Laurier sat by the hearth in his parents' home musing and pondering in French (though being completely bilingual, he could just as easily have done it in English). Beside him on the hob, the kettle bubbled. "*Être ou non être?*" mused Sir Wilfrid. "*C'est la question.*" (This splendid line was later incorporated into the film of *Hamlet*, but it lost a great deal in translation.) "Blubbety-blub!" mused the kettle, in kettle-language. "*Qu'est-ce que c'est que vous avez dites?*" asked Sir Wilfrid. "Bloop!" said the kettle.

In that instant Sir Wilfrid conceived the whole theory of the steam-engine, and would have built a railway to the Yukon if the Senate had not vetoed the idea.

MORAL: The Senate should be reformed so as to consist entirely of the Cabinet.

Laura's Jewels

The constant companions of the great and good Laura Secord were her cows. Indeed, it was a cow which overheard the American officers planning their wicked attack upon Colonel Fitzgibbon's troops and warned Laura. The story that she herself listened at the keyhole is a vicious canard. Being immovably upright, she could not stoop to a keyhole.

One day she was entertaining a purse-proud friend who boasted immoderately of her riches and her articles of personal adornment. "And will you not show me your jewels, Mrs. Secord?" said she.

Smiling enigmatically, Laura called her cows to her. She put her arms around each brown neck and drew the wet noses close to her own. "These are my jewels," said she, with well-nigh unbearable simplicity.

MORAL: The cream of the cream can get along without diamonds, even of the first water.

There you have it Mr. Hydra. Fill our children up with that sort of thing, and in no time their patriotism will have surpassed even our most unreasonable expectations.

Yours for an aggressively Canadian Canada,

SAMUEL MARCHBANKS

From "The Marchbanks Correspondence," *Peterborough Examiner*, 10 June 1950

Samuel Marchbanks Writes a Letter to Chandos Fribble: 1950

Learned Fribble:

I have been reading a good deal of Canadian poetry lately, and it has disturbed me. But last Sunday I attempted to go for a country walk, and by the time I had reached home again, I knew what was wrong with Canadian poetry.

Canadian poets are not allowed to come into contact with Nature. The great English poets have, in most cases, refreshed themselves continually by spells of country life, or by excursions into the country. Canadian poets cannot do this. I walked about two miles in the country and although I did not count them I estimated that roughly 150 cars passed me in that time. I had no time for Nature; I was on the jump all the time. So I decided to walk across country. A farmer chased me, and told me not to tramp on his fall wheat, which I was not doing. However, I left his land and struck into the bush. This was a mistake, for a big dog came and pointed his nose at me and did his best to look like a bronze dog on a bookend. Soon two men with guns came crashing through the undergrowth, and seemed astonished when they saw me. "Say, what's that bird doing here?" cried one, and I knew at once that they had mistaken me for a partridge. But as they seemed about to blast my tailfeathers off I had the presence of mind to shout "I'm a game warden!" and they made off as fast as their legs would carry them. The dog was still pointing, and as stiff as a mackerel, so they snatched it up in one piece and bore it away with them.

That is what Nature means in Canada. Cars, grouchy landowners, people with guns. No wonder our poetry is thin.

Yours for a less cluttered countryside,

SAMUEL MARCHBANKS

From "The Marchbanks Correspondence," *Peterborough Examiner*, 11 November 1950

Canadian Quotations and Phrases: 1952

For several weeks past we have been browsing in *Canadian Quotations and Phrases*, a new and important book compiled by Robert M. Hamilton. So far as we know it is the first Canadian quotation book to appear, and it marks an important point in our national development, for without a measure of native wisdom, and a considerable native literature we could not produce a book of quotable passages. The compiler has wisely avoided any suggestion that these quotations are widely familiar; it is to be hoped, however, that they will become familiar, and that this book, slender at present, will run through as many editions as Bartlett, growing in bulk and quality with the years.

A book prepared on national lines such as this cannot hope to attain the richness of a quotation book which rifles the literature of the world. The fact, also, that so much of our history was made during the nineteenth century gives a predominantly Victorian cast to what is found in the pages of this collection. It was inevitable that politicians should be extensively quoted, and equally inevitable that some of their gold should be pinchbeck, if not downright brass. But the Canadian voice comes from these pages with refreshing strength. There are many passages from Sir William Osler which are pure gold. Macdonald and Laurier both appear in unfamiliar and becoming lights. Stephen Leacock, who said so much that was deeply true in a way that made us laugh, is extensively quoted, as he should be. And there are others, eminently quotable, including the neglected Lampman and a modern satirist with a brilliantly sharp pen, E.L. Mackay. T.C. Haliburton is extensively drawn upon, and those who find Sam Slick the Clockmaker funny will be glad of it; others will be grateful that Canadian humour did not dry up with Haliburton. This book is full of good things which deserve to be known as Canadian, and quoted by Canadians.

We are pleased that Canadian journalists have been able to add so much to this book. Bob Edwards of the Calgary *Eye-Opener* is quoted sixty-one times, and he is always witty and pungent. (Edwards, thou shouldst be living at this hour! The Canadian Press hath need of thee!) Nicholas Flood Davin, perhaps the ablest journalist ever to work in the Canadian West, is well represented; his verse appears to have taken colour and ease from that of his countryman Tom Moore – a colour and ease which Canadian verse has lost at present. Peter McArthur, the best of our Canadian writers about farm life, is quoted often, and so is Arthur Stringer. Charles Heavysege, whose work is not enlivening when read in bulk, provides some admirable and quotable scraps. We form the opinion, after a consideration of this book, that the political and literary life of this country has been better served by its press than is generally understood.

We wonder about the quotability of some parts of the book, but we would not wish them to be left out. The fact that E.B. Wood, M.P., was called "Big Thunder" by D'Arcy McGee is interesting, but we doubt if we shall ever wish to make use of it. On the other hand it is amusing to know that Egerton Ryerson was called "The Pope of Methodism," and we wish that this title might be continued in honour of whatever Canadian appears to deserve it. We note with lacklustre eyes that three Canadian politicians have been called "Honest John"; we instinctively mistrust anyone who bears such a nickname. But it delights us to learn that an indiscreet telegram won the late W.T.R. Preston the name of "Hug-the-machine Preston"; that name, too, should go to whatever modern politician deserves it. And although we once knew it, we had forgotten that Senator David Mills was called "The Sage of Bothwell"; has Bothwell ever had a sage since, we wonder? Sir John A. Macdonald might well be called "Old Tomorrow," and only Disraeli could have thought of calling Goldwin Smith "The wild man of the cloister."

A Canadian quotation book is a welcome and useful thing. We hope that it will get into all the school and university libraries, as well as to all the people in Canada who write. For there is a Canadian flavour about this book which is salty to the taste. Of course there is a great deal of pompous solemnity in it, and some solemnity which is vital and true without pomposity. But there is also an undercurrent of sly fun, of mockery, of intellectual anarchy, of the Old Adam, which is fine stuff, and a rebuttal of the oft-re-peated accusation that we are entirely a nation of dutiful asses, doing as our politicians and parsons tell us. The author and the publishers are to be congratulated on a good and lasting piece of work to which Canadians may turn when they want an apt phrase, or when they seek relief for their heaviness of heart.

"A Canadian Said It," *Peterborough Examiner*, 12 May 1952

Book Collecting and Canadians: 1953

It is always pleasant to receive a good new work on book collecting and the arrival of John Carter's *ABC For Book Collectors* gives me a chance to write about a pursuit which appears to be slighted and misunderstood in Canada. Our neglect of book collecting is, of course, only a part of our general neglect of books. A survey made a little over a year ago by the Gallup people showed that Canadians, with the exception of the inhabitants of the United States, read less than any other nation of the Western civilized world. Scandinavians, Netherlanders, the French, the British, Australians, and New Zealanders all read more than we do.

We are short of bookshops of all kinds, and antiquarian bookshops can hardly be said to exist within our borders. Some bookshops have a little group of what they call "fine editions"; these are modern reprints of classics, usually illustrated and bound in a manner which can only be called "fine" if one is rather easily contented. It would be more correct to describe them as "fashionable," and like all merely fashionable objects they are apt to lose their attraction in a decade or so.

As books, they have grave faults; they are often too heavy to hold in comfort; their bindings are frequently of easily soiled materials; their illustrations and decorations do not stand the test of time. They do not appeal to people who are deeply fond of books, and it is unlikely that they will ever be sought after by serious collectors, for they have neither rarity, special literary interest, nor beauty, and these are the qualities which collectors seek.

These books, however, reflect the taste of people who have some desire to collect books, but who do not know how to go about it. Their instinct is a commendable one, but it is not supported by knowledge. If they would take some pains to find out a little bit about books they could begin collections which would give them far greater satisfaction. Mr. Carter's book is an invaluable guide to such beginners, for it is a glossary of collectors' terms. And as such it is also of interest and value to old hands at collecting.

In my experience private libraries of real interest are uncommon in our country. I do not write now of collections made by very wealthy men and women who can buy almost anything they want: I mean libraries collected by people of moderate income which reflect their tastes and interests. Such libraries need not be large; they may not run to more than two or three hundred volumes; but they have about them an air of intimacy and completeness which no random collection of bestsellers and treatises on golf and dieting can hope to win.

Canadians do not read enough books, and they do not buy enough books, and in most Canadian homes the few bookshelves are loaded with miscellaneous trash – the rollerskate libraries of people with Buick incomes. Of course I shall be told that books are expensive, and I shall agree; a good book costs almost as much as a good dinner, and to buy a book once a week would certainly prove an intolerable burden to a person who thinks nothing of eating a dinner every day. But I do not speak of libraries of thousands of volumes – only of libraries which may be reckoned in scores of volumes.

I do not write, either, of libraries of beautifully bound antique books for, desirable as those are, they are costly to acquire. On this continent any binding better than cloth is accorded a ridiculous prestige. To find out what this amounts to in money, you have only to check the price of an eighteenth-century book in an English bookseller's catalogue against the price asked for the same book, in the same condition, by a New York bookseller. An increase of 300 per cent should not surprise you. Any old book, leather-bound, takes on some of the characteristics of the Holy Grail as it crosses the Atlantic.

This reverence, I may say, does not afflict the more reputable Canadian booksellers who deal in antique books. It is often possible to buy a good old book in Toronto cheaper than it could be bought in England because the demand is less, and the bookseller tires of keeping such merchandise. Canada is not an ideal place to buy antique books, but for those who know what they are doing it has certain advantages as compared with the United States.

A library, I repeat, is a collection of books which reflects the interests and temperament of its owner. It would be harsh indeed to insist that the books in the average Canadian home reflected the interests and temperament of the average Canadian. Therefore let us agree not to call such accumulations libraries. But anyone who wishes it can have a library, and if he sets out to acquire one he will inevitably have to buy some books which are not quite new, and may be quite old. He will want to get his books at a fair price, and in good condition. Therefore he must become, if only in a very limited sense, a collector, and as such he will have to know what he is doing. Therefore he had better buy a little book by Bernard J. Farmer called *The Gentle Art of Book Collecting*, and the new book by Mr. Carter which forms the excuse for this article.

Canadians are, of course, in the ideal situation to collect Canadiana. If you have any intention of doing so, you had better begin at once, for the field is not as open as it was even ten years ago, and prices are going up, though they are still not beyond the reach of an ordinary income. Many of the older Canadian books are rare, and as they were not often expensively produced, and were seldom prized, it is not easy to find them in good condition.

Let me warn you at once that you will be disappointed if you expect to buy some Canadiana now and sell it at a profit in a few years; if you hope to make money from your collection you will have to give endless time to that pursuit and you will work very hard for every dollar you get. But if you wish to have a collection of early Canadian books which will give you countless hours of pleasure and interest, and if you are willing to accept these as your sole gain, go at it by all means. Your children, or your grandchildren, may make a handsome profit on your books—provided they have not fallen prey to the damnable Canadian heresies that a book is something which lives in a Public Library, and that any clean book is superior to any old, worn one.

I purposely restrain myself from saying much about the pleasures of collecting and possessing books, great though these are. Too many people who are nervous and shy of books are frightened forever by those Professional Book Lovers who write affected nonsense about the delights of sitting in one's favourite armchair before an open fire, one's pipe (filled, doubtless with the Arcadia Mixture) in one's mouth and a friendly, warm, old, calf-bound volume in one's hand. Such literary posturers usually refer to themselves as "bookmen."

A pox on all such bookmen, I cry! Books, and a personal library, are amenities of civilized life, to be enjoyed as civilized people enjoy things; the bookman, who writes about his library as though it were a harem and he a caliph crammed to the muzzle with oysters and cantharides, is a mere sensualist, and he makes me sick. Of course books can become a mania, but you need not fear that it will be so in your case. As many Canadians are social drinkers, you may also become a social collector. I can see no sign that the book-drunk, shaken and consumed by his horrible bouts of bibliomania, is likely to become a common figure in our Dominion.

To return to John Carter's book: it is excellently arranged, sensible and complete without being tiresomely technical, and a good example of honest, tasteful, modern book-making in itself. I am not a greenhorn at collecting, and I have read it with pleasure and gratitude, and I shall keep it handy at all times. Can a man say more?

"Why Not Be a Collector?" *Saturday Night*, 20 June 1953

Light-Hearted Scholarship and Canada: 1953

A branch of literature little cultivated on this continent and almost unknown in Canada is what might be called Light-Hearted Scholarship. We have our learned men, of course, and some of them bear their learning with a fine dignity. They are scholars in the tradition of Duns Scotus. But where are our scholars in the tradition of Rabelais? Where are the men who cultivate learning, not for livelihood and in hope of a university chair, but for the glory of God and for the entertainment of themselves and, incidentally, for the amusement and instruction of mankind?

Offhand, I can think of only one such book by a Canadian writer. Doubtless there are others, but I do not remember them now. It is *The Four Jameses*, a study of four very minor Canadian poets, by William Arthur Deacon. *Sarah Binks*, admirable in its kind, is not such a book, for it deals not with fact, but with fancy which might very easily be fact. The scholarly approach, united to the merry heart, is a great rarity among us. We think of learning in terms of the snail-like progress towards the Ph.D., and the selection of a "field" or area of learning, in which the Ph.D. seeks to make a name. Having found his field he cultivates it with jealous care, elbowing and jostling all the other zealous husbandmen who are in it, until he is at last rewarded as "a big man in the James field" or even "*the* man in the Borrow field." It is all very worthy and no doubt it keeps the scholars out of the pubs, but it is of no general interest.

Light-Hearted Scholarship, on the other hand, is of general interest and it appeals to a person neglected in Canada, the Intelligent General Reader. The I.G.R., I maintain, is the foundation stone upon which any great national literature is built. Professors are happily able to live for generations by taking in each others' intellectual washing, but the books they write are not literature; they are works of scholarship, and they are growing duller and duller. There was a time when a work of scholarship might also be a work of literature; Gibbon's *Decline and Fall* is such a work and in our time Livingston Lowes' *The Road to Xanadu* is another. But books of this sort in which the I.G.R. can take pleasure are few, and Canada is not adding to their number.

Do I hear mutterings? Yes, of course such books demand much of the reader. Oho, is that so? Well, what makes you think that Canadian readers are not prepared or able to give so much? Let me tell you, whoever you are, that there are more I.G.R.s in Canada than you seem to think. Let's have some Light-Hearted Scholarship, and see what happens. . . .

From "For the Light of Heart," *Saturday Night*, 25 July 1953

Sincerity and Canadians: 1953

The book to which this article will be devoted does not at first seem to be a particularly important publication; it is a volume in the "Life, Literature and Thought Library" which appears under the general editorship of Dr. Vivian de Sola Pinto of the University of Nottingham, and its name is *The Pre-Raphaelites in Literature and Art*; its author is Dr. D.S.R. Welland. I picked it up from the top of a heap of review books merely to see if there were any pictures in it; I have always liked Pre-Raphaelite pictures. But then I glanced at the text, began to read, and went on until I finished the book. It seems to me to raise questions which are of great interest, and I shall attempt to discuss some of them briefly here.

It is interesting, to begin with, that this book is intended for use not only in universities, but in the upper classes of schools. Reading this, I was impressed once again by the standards set in English schools, and the sharp difference between them and the standards of our Canadian high schools. How many of our high-school students, I wonder, are expected to know anything about the Pre-Raphaelites, either as painters or writers? It is not vital that they should do so; life can be lived quite adequately without any such knowledge.

But it is part of general knowledge – of that loose mass of history, literature, art, music, architecture, science, and philosophy of which everyone calling himself an educated person should possess some smattering – and it is the scope of our general knowledge which gives flavour to life for most of us. To know nothing of Pre-Raphaelite art and literature is to be ignorant of a movement which once gave beauty and meaning to life for a great many people; to know something of such a movement may be helpful in finding beauty and meaning in our own lives, even if only because we shy away from the Pre-Raphaelites in horror.

It is desirable that Canadians generally and young Canadians in particular should know something about the Pre-Raphaelites because the mainspring of their movement, according to themselves, was utter sincerity. Now "sincerity" is one of the witchwords of our time, and nowhere does it exert a more powerful sway than in Canada. If it is said of a man in this country, be he artist or statesman, that he is not *sincere*, that man is as good as dead. What do we mean by sincerity? At best we mean integrity; at worst we mean a kind of humourless singleness of mind without overtones. Very rarely do we question our concept of sincerity; very rarely do we reflect that it is not especially commendable to be sincere unless we are sincere in some great cause, and that even sincerity in a great cause may bring us to grief.

That is exactly what happened to the Pre-Raphaelites. Sincerity in art and literature was the rock to which they clung, and the rock upon which they tore themselves to pieces. Paradoxically, when we look at their pictures and read their stories and poems today, we do not see sincerity, but a mass of affectation and mannerism, and unless we make a careful, conscious, and informed effort to understand these works we miss their point entirely. The blunt fact is that in art it is not sincerity and dogma, but genius and inspiration, which lie behind great creations.

The Pre-Raphaelite movement had its beginning in 1848, when seven earnest young men banded themselves together in a revolt against the materialism of their age. The movement took its inspiration from a German school of painting which attempted to return to the simplicity, rooted in faith, which was supposed to have inspired painters before the Renaissance. Of course we have little evidence to suggest that pre-Renaissance painters were particularly devout persons, but faith – the whole-souled abandonment to some form of belief – has always been strongly attractive to young artists, and particularly to young artists whose talent is not of the first rank.

We see this in our own day, and especially in the realm of literature. How many writers have taken a whirl at Communism, hoping that in its dogma, and in its woolly or hypocritical applications, they will find a rock to cling to and a never-failing source of inspiration! A number of writers, also, have become Catholic converts, for precisely similar reasons. They want dogma and they want a system; they seek an infallible answer to the great problems of life and they will pay a very high price in the coin of intellectual subjection for the comfort which such an infallible answer gives them. It very often seems that the great stream of humanism which began to flow at the Renaissance has run dry, or has become bitter to the taste; or it could also be that humanism demands a continued intellectual effort on the part of its followers which is too taxing for the lovers of dogma.

Dogma is like a railway track; set your handcar firmly upon the rails and pump away as hard as you like and you may confidently hope to fetch up in Moscow or in the City of God. The humanist, on the contrary, sets out upon the Atlantic in his dinghy and sweats all through the voyage of his life, with one eye on the stars and the other on his compass, one hand on the tiller and the other on the sheet; he would like to reach the Fortunate Isles, but he optimistically hopes to enjoy some parts of his voyage, as well.

This little book about the Pre-Raphaelites makes it plain that anything which they wrote or painted which was beautiful was done in spite of the dogma which they sought to impose upon art, and not because of it. They craved other-worldliness; they seemed to be in full flight not only from materialism, but from sex. Yet sex speaks plainly in their poetry and in their painting. They yearned to teach, and the pictures of Holman Hunt and Ford Madox Brown are so full of lessons that it takes quite a long essay, supplied by the painter, to give the key to them. Yet we admire these works, if we admire them at all, for the ingenuity of their drawing and colour, and for the naive yet stagey way in which they present their subjects. We are amused by the "lessons" taught in such pictures as "The Last Day in the Old Home," by Martineau, and "The Awakened Conscience" by Holman Hunt, but we like the pictures (at least, I like them) because it is possible, by studying them for a time, to get the feel of a particular kind of Victorianism – not merely its outward shows but its moral attitude.

So also it is with the poetry of D.G. Rossetti, his sister Christina, William Morris, and Swinburne: little of it is poetry of the first rank, but the worst of it has a flavour which we must heed if we hope to understand the thinking of the Victorians, and – perhaps more important than their thinking – their feeling. These people, in attempting to turn backward in time to what they believed to have been a better world, succeeded only in turning inward upon themselves, giving us their dreams and their wishes. Because they were people of deep feelings and strong individuality of thought, their dreams and wishes are rewarding and often fine. But what they achieved, and what they set out to achieve, were two very different things.

It was all done with the utmost sincerity. Let them stand as a lesson to young Canadians that sincerity is, at best, a shallow attribute of the mind, and has nothing to do with artistic creation. The integrity of the artist is not unquestioning adherence to an external line of belief or conduct; it is, rather, submissive attention to the voice of his own talent. The Pre-Raphaelites did their best to stick to a party line, but those of them who had true ability as artists were quite unable to do so, and it is their deviations which give their work vitality and interest now.

If this seems to say little about Dr. Welland's book, let me hasten to add that all that goes before arises from a reading of it, and that you will find it provocative of reflection. It is a well-planned book, containing an essay on the Pre-Raphaelites, some reproductions of their pictures, and a good selection of their prose and poetry.

"Brethren in Sincerity," *Saturday Night*, 21 November 1953

B.K. Sandwell: 1954

Since the death of John W. Dafoe, the late Bernard Keble Sandwell was unquestionably the most influential journalist in Canada. His influence was not of the obvious kind; he did not thunder or conduct long and calculated crusades; he did not consider himself a king-maker. But for more than twenty years he produced, every week, a considerable quantity of thoughtful, well-balanced, well-written opinion which came in time to carry great weight with countless people everywhere in the country. He was an unfailingly well-bred writer; he never shouted in print. But when the roars of lesser men were stilled, his quiet voice was still being heard, persuasive, amiable, and unyielding.

He thought highly of urbanity, and he was flattered when that word was applied to himself. But his urbanity was not that of Mr. Facing-Both-Ways. In conversation and in printed controversy he was so courteous that people sometimes thought that he was agreeing with them when in reality he was explaining that agreement was impossible; when this happened he was very much amused. But he never compromised on any question which he thought important; relaxed, quiet, and witty, he was prepared to argue for hours with angry or fanatical opponents, never yielding an inch but leaving them, at last, with the certainty that they had had their say. A surprising number of people who disagreed with him on virtually every important question regarded him with admiration.

For almost twenty years he was editor of *Saturday Night*. He was unusually well-qualified for such a post, for he was well-versed in economics, was a lifelong student of politics, and was an admirable critic of literature and the theatre. His predecessor, the late Hector Charlesworth, had given most of his attention to the arts and politics; Sandwell wrote, and wrote well, in a dozen different fields. It was some time before it was discovered that the penetrating articles on women's affairs, signed by Lucy Van Gogh, were from his pen.

He was never robust, and much of the astounding quantity of work which he produced was done while he was unwell. He had achieved a high degree of physical relaxation, but mentally he was never at rest. When so ill that he could not rise from his bed, he went on dictating articles and criticisms into a recording machine; when he was plainly in considerable pain he spoke in the same tone of light amusement, made jokes, and never lost his temper.

He was endlessly encouraging to young writers, and to poets in particular. "They have so few friends—and really, such difficult people!" he would say, after a session with an eager versifier. In temperament he was optimistic, but his optimism was held in check by a worldly wisdom which flirted with cynicism, but never embraced it. It was a pleasure to work for him, for he always assumed that his colleagues were as intelligent as himself—a high compliment. Those who knew him best will miss him most, but thousands of Canadians will mourn his loss. He was one of the great civilizing and liberalizing influences in our country for more than twenty years.

"The Late B.K. Sandwell," *Peterborough Examiner*, 10 December 1954

R.C. Wallace: 1955

We were sorry to record the death of Dr. R.C. Wallace, principal of Queen's University from 1936 to 1951, for he was the kind of man that Canada can ill spare, and at seventy-three it seemed that he still had much to do. Retirement was, for him, an empty figure of speech; he gave up his work at Queen's merely to give his great abilities to a dozen other projects which were near to his heart.

In him, intellect and character were one. His mind is better described as powerful than as keen, for he did not deal in flashing insights, but in sober and far-reaching judgements. He had, in the finest sense, the Scottish reverence for learning, and although he was a fine university administrator he was also a fine university liberal; with him, principles always took precedence over rules.

He came to Queen's at a time when that university had had a remarkable overhaul by Principal Hamilton Fyfe. Dr. Fyfe found Queen's in the intellectual doldrums, and he gave it a thorough stirring-up. He laid about him with a brilliant wit, and he made both staff and undergraduates realize that a university is expected to be a place of intellectual activity, and that seriousness does not necessarily involve dullness. Queen's needed Dr. Fyfe to get it out of the dumps. But after Dr. Fyfe had gone it needed someone to see that it did not sink gratefully back into the pit. It found precisely the right man in Dr. Wallace.

He thoroughly understood the Canadian undergraduate mind, which could not have been said of Dr. Fyfe. The underlying seriousness of that mind, so often obscured by inarticulateness and problems of social adjustment, was clear to him; he knew exactly where to help, where to be patient, where to be stern. He was a kind mentor to thousands of Canadian young men and women, and he provided them with an invaluable gift, of which we know that he himself was unconscious – a worthy pattern of a learned man. His name will be honoured among the makers of Queen's, and in consideration of the many men that Queen's sends into the public service it may truly be said that he was a maker of Canada.

"A Maker of Queen's," *Peterborough Examiner*, 1 February 1955

Literature in Canada: 1955

That very interesting appraisal of literature in Canada which appeared as the Middle Article in the *Times Literary Supplement* on November 5, 1954, has engaged my attention, at intervals, for the past four months. It does not appear to have attracted much attention in this country; a few newspapers wrote mildly resentful pieces about it, and that was all. It was anonymous, as all *Literary Supplement* articles are, and there is much to be said for anonymity; no writer's idiosyncrasies and personal vicissitudes are then called into court to give weakening testimony against his considered opinions. I thought that it was an important appraisal of the problems confronting the writer in what Patrick Anderson has called "America's attic," and I agreed with virtually all that it said; but I do not agree with the pessimism which darkened it.

Is the present condition of the writer in Canada "more difficult than anywhere else in the English-speaking world," as the *Times* writer (whom I shall henceforth call X) declares? Why does he think so? Because we lack a cultural capital, it seems, and thus our writers have a provincial, rather than a metropolitan, consciousness. Does he really equate these terms thus – "metropolitan; large in outlook and sympathies and contemporaneous in manner"; as opposed to "provincial; narrow in outlook and sympathies and dowdy and old-fashioned in manner"? If he does, a great part of the history of literature argues against him.

Certainly it is pleasant for writers to know one another, and to exchange ideas, and metropolitan groups have often produced notable work. But these same metropolitan groups produce also a rabble of imitators who copy mannerisms but cannot capture inspiration; such groups can bring artistic death to those writers who are so gregarious that they talk their books away among friends, and write little. Literature owes much to the solitary provincial, doggedly working in an environment which is indifferent to his writing, though not therefore hostile towards it. He gets little impetus to work from his surroundings, but on the other hand, the impetus which arises from within himself is not likely to be deflected or tarnished by contact with other writers.

Unquestionably X is right when he says that there is little genuine literary interest among the greater part of society in Canada; this is true of all countries, and it may be that we are no worse off, considering our small population, than others. In its intellectual outlook Canada remains a constant twenty-five years behind the rest of the English-speaking world. Our country was not settled by people with any cultural interests, and we have developed only far enough to be bourgeois play-safers at the present day. This is certainly hard on the writer who wants to be fashionable – to be "in the movement." Poets must suffer particularly in this respect, for the public here is as hostile towards what is new in verse as it is to what is new in painting.

But what is new in verse is a question of manner only. The sources of a poet's inspiration and the alchemy that produces his song is the same today in Canada as it was when Homer smote his blooming lyre. And poetic inspiration of a high order has a way of making itself apparent, whatever the manner of the poet may be. If Tennyson were living today in Medicine Hat, he would not write in the melodious and hypnotic fashion that we know, but that which made him a great poet would speak undeniably in a fashion suited to his time and place, and we should know him as a great poet. What ails many Canadian poets today is not society's hostility towards their manner of utterance, but the stunted and rickety stature of their innermost spirit.

The third element which X considers inimical to the writer in Canada is "the almost complete lack of discriminating criticism." On this point I wish to quote him at somewhat greater length:

> The example set by E.K. Brown, Mr. A.J. Smith, and a few other percipient critics has had no effect on the majority of the reviewers of the provincial Press who must be held responsible for the health of literature, lacking as it does the invigoration of a national Press or a single national journal of any intellectual calibre. The reviewers fall into two groups: the first are the bored apprentices to journalism; the second are well-intentioned people attempting to foster Canadian literature at the expense of every literary standard.

There is a measure of truth in this, if you like to put the cart before the horse. Personally I deny that reviewers in the provincial press or anywhere else are responsible for the health of literature; this is to give reviewers an importance out of all proportion to their powers or deserts. The health of literature lies in the hands of writers, and my great charge against X's article is that it is a spiritless whine that people other than authors are not doing enough for literature in Canada. This is an agreeable form of self-pity, and like much highbrow self-pity it has some justification and a certain degree of intellectual respectability; but it is self-pity none the less, and that is a force which has never advanced any cause.

That aside, it is true that criticism in Canada does not amount to much, if we except the work of a few academic critics and *Letters in Canada*. And it used to be true that critics now and then thumped the drum for a Canadian book in a way which was not, in the end, good for the book or the country. But as soon as we have admitted the general charges, we must begin to make exceptions. I could name perhaps a dozen Canadian critics, some on newspapers, some on radio, and some in universities, who do work which is consistently on a level quite as high as either the *Times Literary Supplement* or the Book Section of the *New York Times*. Of course, that level is not always quite so high as some people suppose, and anybody who reads those two publications consistently knows how shallow, how trite, how jejune, and how hopelessly provincial and mutton-headed they can be, at their worst. But their general standard is reasonably good, and if anyone in Canada wanted to start such a paper here, he could staff it with Canadians, and have no cause for shame. But as his probable circulation would be 3,000, nobody is likely to do it.

For X to bring in the provincial press is not altogether fair, for the best criticism in England, at least, is found in six or seven London papers, published weekly in most cases. I know what criticism in the English provincial press is, because I have read a good deal of it over a number of years, and it ranges from the London standard to one as hopelessly stupid and illiterate as anything to be found in Canada.

Defence, however, does not dispose of the charge. Our provincial papers in most cases have not recognized any responsibility to provide their readers with opinions on literature, or any of the arts. But if they were to do so, would we be better off? There are about ninety daily papers in Canada, and I do not know how many magazines and weeklies. Where are they to find critics? Good critics cost money, but money cannot create them. Perhaps we should be wise to know when we are well off, and recognize that no criticism may be better than a flood of bad criticism.

As for the charge that Canadian books are immoderately praised, it was once true, but it is true no longer. The good critics of whom I have spoken do not lend themselves to chauvinist enthusiasm. But it is a fact that they understand some things in Canadian books better than foreign critics, and thus their praise or blame may take a direction of its own.

The position of the Canadian writer is not a happy one. But what writer has ever had things his own way, and in what country? Writing, when it has real quality, is questioning, critical, and penetrating; or perhaps exultant, and celebratory; or it may be a groping in the dark immensities of the spirit. When have these things ever been widely popular? Let us not waste time in regretting our lack of what the earth has never afforded.

The Canadian writer is free to write what he likes; because public opinion is indifferent to him he can be indifferent to it; because there is no coherent school or clique of critics, they cannot knife him if he flouts or disappoints them. In these respects the Canadian writer is better off than he supposes. Perhaps this is negative comfort, though I do not offer it as such. But I say that there is really nothing to prevent a Canadian writer from doing the best work that is in him. And that is the most important thing of all. Of course, if a writer has little or nothing inside him, the voluptuous patronage of the most indulgent prince of the most book-eager state could not add a cubit to his stature.

"The Writer in the Attic," *Saturday Night*, 30 April 1955

Cousin Elva / Mortgage Manor / Shall We Join the Ladies?: 1955

An incident which took place many years ago, when I was a schoolboy, coloured my whole life. I was translating a passage of Virgil, and I thought I was doing rather well, when the master interjected, "Now that our licensed buffoon has given us his comic interpretation, suppose you take over, Jones, and tell us what Virgil really said." I presume that he meant to wound me, but instead I was perversely delighted to be called a licensed buffoon and I have been renewing my buffoon's licence every January 1 since that time. What is more, I have a brotherly, or guild, feeling towards other licensed buffoons, and today I want to write about new books by three of them: Eric Nicol, Lex Schrag, and Stuart Trueman.

It is no accident that all three are newspapermen. Canada's humour seems to flourish in its newspaper offices. True, it is unlikely soil, for if this planet boasts a more sober, responsible, slow-pulsed press than that of Canada, I have not heard about it. But if you are on the hunt for a Canadian humorist, you stand your best chance of finding one in the cloistral hush of a Canadian newsroom.

Canadian humorist, did I say? Perhaps it would be wiser to say "a humorist who is also a Canadian." There is a recognizable English humour, and a recognizable American humour, though much of the best funny writing done in both countries lies outside these immediately identifiable national bounds. Canadian humour does not come down strongly on either side and we have no national stereotypes of fun. The English funnyman, on an off day, can always dash off something about cheese or Brussels sprouts, for these are fixed stars in the English firmament of humour; mention them, and a few die-hards are sure to laugh. And in the United States the rich comicality of living in Brooklyn, or amorous intrigue with a blonde, are enough to amuse those who like the familiar and homely things in humour.

But Canada has no such sure-fire stuff. Canada, on the contrary, abounds in people who have no discernible sense of humour at all, but have in its place a highly developed sense of grievance: be funny about anything you can think of – it matters not how remote or innocuous it may seem to be – and you will get a few letters from these pugnacious and embittered spirits, demanding apologies. I speak as a man whose buffoon's licence has thus been endorsed hundreds of times. But in this fashion the Canadian humorist fulfils the chief duty of a journalist which is, as H.L. Mencken said, to comfort the afflicted and afflict the comfortable.

This core of national opposition to humour seems to strengthen our best wits. Many of our humorists, if we probe a little below the surface, are angry men, whose spirits are sore and stinging from the ineptitudes and inanities of the world about them. They choose to hurl, not the thunderbolts of Jove, but the spitballs of Momus. Behind the hilarities of Frank Tumpane, and the donnish waggeries of David Brock, this same indignant spirit is to be found. Sometimes, as with Lex Schrag, they make themselves their chief joke, and from behind this stalking horse, so to speak, they shoot sharp arrows into all who come near them. Canadian humorists, like all humorists worth their salt everywhere in the world, tend to be intellectual and discontented fellows.

But it is time to get on to the three gentlemen who are renewing their buffoon's licence this autumn. Mr. Trueman is the newest to the public; Mr. Schrag goes deepest into the dark caverns of human feeling; Mr. Nicol is the one with the widest range and the deftest touch. Let us look at Mr. Trueman's book first.

It is not quite a novel, and yet it is not entirely a book of disconnected sketches. It is about the misadventures of a man named Frank Lewellen Trimble, who undertakes to run a tourist home on the shores of the Bay of Fundy. Trimble is one of those unhappy creatures marked for failure, and his initial mistake is in imagining that he can run a hotel at all. His second mistake is his acceptance, with the hotel, of a permanent guest named Miss Elva Thwaite, who is a maiden lady of determined and eccentric character. In addition, the hotel has other disturbing guests, including a lecherous and deranged old party named Mr. Bogson, and a Dr. Fergus who has an exaggerated reverence for whatever is old.

The adventures of the wretched Trimble are chronicled in diary form, and at its best this book recalls that somewhat neglected classic of humour *The Diary of a Nobody* by the brothers Grossmith. But *Cousin Elva* seems to have been extended a little farther than the central idea can support it. Mr. Trueman, however, has an advantage in that he has been able to illustrate his own book, and the result is pleasing and should prove popular. Its best message is that another Canadian humorous writer of characteristic quality has made his appearance in book form, and will extend his audience.

The adventures of the Churl of Mortgage Manor are familiar to readers of the Toronto *Globe and Mail*. Personally I found them much more entertaining in collected form than as newspaper articles, which is by no means the usual response to collected essays. When we meet him in a book, the Churl emerges as a more varied and engaging character than he does in short pieces. The humours of developing a place in the country become subsidiary to the revelation of the Churl's own spirit, which is far from churlish. There is a philosophic weight to his indignation which I had missed before, and an implied criticism of Ontario suburban society which amused and enlightened me.

It is fatal to be serious about humour – or so I am assured. But after reading *Mortgage Manor* I hunted up a very different book, which I had not read since it was published in 1941; it is *Masochism in Modern Man* by the psychoanalyst Theodor Reik. In it there are passages on humour, and on the technique of the humorist who makes himself the principal butt, which apply perfectly to Mr. Schrag. Here is a humorist of real stature who has not yet, I am convinced, come fully into his own. He gets his fun, not from the shallows, but from the deeps of his nature. *Mortgage Manor* is a very funny book, but I am convinced that it is a mere overture to the books that Mr. Schrag has still to write. Meanwhile, you should not miss this one.

To recommend Eric Nicol is like recommending Santa Claus, or Fresh Air, or some other widely accepted public benefit. He has, I imagine, the largest and most faithful audience of any licensed buffoon in the Dominion.

In the last essay in *Shall We Join the Ladies?* he suggests that many people must think him a failure because he has not troubled

to acquire even that minimum accolade of Canadian acceptance – Success in Toronto. To be a real Canadian success, he says,
one must leave the country, but Success in Toronto is the first
step from provincial obscurity. Perhaps so. But Mr. Nicol is a
breaker of rules, and who shall deny that he has made all of Canada laugh (that part of Canada, that is to say, which can laugh) by
tossing the lightest and most prettily turned jokes at us from the
farther side of the Rockies? In his latest book he keeps up his very
high standard of craftsmanship, inventiveness, and wit. I read his
book at Thanksgiving, and promptly gave thanks for him. Can
one licensed buffoon, writing about another, say fairer than that?

"Let's See Your Licence," *Saturday Night*, 12 November 1955

The Sacrifice: 1956

The autumn fiction presses in upon me. Good. Let it press. I like fiction and nothing would please me better than to live like the late George Saintsbury, anchored to an armchair, reading three novels a day, every day, for years. But as matters stand, I cannot read all that I receive, and I have not space in which to review all that I read. Therefore, I shall waste no time on palaver, but will dive at once into the pile of new novels that I have read.

There will undoubtedly be a great deal of talk about Adele Wiseman's first novel *The Sacrifice*, for it is a remarkably meaty, and authoritative piece of work for the first production of a woman of twenty-eight. The story is of a Jewish immigrant family from the Ukraine, which seeks refuge from poverty and pogroms in a Western Canadian city – probably Winnipeg. Abraham the butcher begets Isaac the tailor, and we are left with a feeling that the obscurity and hardship of this family are about to be relieved in the life of Isaac's son Moses, who has talent as a musician. This is an emotionally mature retelling of the perennially good story of the immigrant. It is a story of which we Canadians, understandably enough, never tire, and Miss Wiseman has given it to us in a version which has great merit.

If it had less merit, I should not herewith proceed to be per-nickety about it. This book is so good that it should have been better. It could have been cut by forty pages, with great improve-ment, if the writer had not counted so heavily upon the folk-tale device of repetition as a means of making a point. She uses the English language garrulously and carelessly (she should not, for in-stance, refer to a beard as "freshly manicured") and blunts her effects thereby. And she has the understandable but dangerous desire of the Jewish novelist to take us too far into the ceremonies of the Jewish faith, which have become familiar. Every confirmed novel reader is well up in Bar Mitzvahs, weddings, funerals, name-givings, and similar proceedings as practised by the Jews, and unless they cast some special and necessary light on the story, they are not worth introducing for their colour.

And if I may say so, as a well-wishing Gentile, I am tired of the pattern of these novels, which suggests that Old Country Jews, bearded and humble, are necessarily the moral superiors of their sons, in whom some doubts about orthodox Jewry begin to appear; and that these doubting sons are in their turn better than the third-generation Jews, who make money, become liberal and even agnostic in belief, and enter the professions. I know several third-generation Jews who appear to be fully as good men as their simple grandfathers; the notion that the ghettos produced finer men than the universities, because they restricted freedom of thought, is romantic hokum.

But this is quite enough fault-finding. *The Sacrifice* is a deeply interesting novel by a writer who will not, let us hope, be lost to Canada, and I recommend it strongly.

From "Five From Autumn Fiction," *Saturday Night*,
13 October 1956

Poets Wander At Large In Canada: 1959

At a rough estimate there are 70,000 head of poets at large in Canada, roaming our plains, sheltered by our forests, and even venturing near to centres of population. Although the complaint is often heard that they are neglected, they seem to be on the increase; nevertheless, because of the general hostility of the population improvement in the breed is slow, and prime specimens are rare.

The word "poet" is used to cover them all, because it is short and convenient. But to speak truly, there are probably not more than ten real poets in Canada. Perhaps 500 of the others may be called Accomplished Versifiers, after which come the 69,490 poetasters, who occasionally assemble in mangy herds to sup milky tea or bad rye, and groan about their sorry lot.

Is there any hope for the poetasters? Can they aspire even to climb into the ranks of the Accomplished Versifiers? No, for that would mean acquiring a technique, and the most impressive single fact about these people is that they are utterly unteachable. To acquire the taste, the polish, the seriousness of self-criticism which distinguishes an Accomplished Versifier of the Apollonian type is utterly beyond them. They prefer to write straight from the heart. But, alas, their hearts have nothing to say.

If this seems bitter, I write as one who receives his full share of the work of poetasters, with requests that I read and comment. To all of them I reply: improve your technique. I have never known one of them to do it.

In future I shall tell them to study a book which has just appeared by one of the finest of living poets: it is *Steps*, by Robert Graves . . .

Toronto Daily Star, 7 February 1959

We Charitable Critics: 1959

Following some remarks I made about Canadian poets in this newspaper on February 7, a number of people have written to denounce me as an enemy of all that is good and pure in Canadian letters. I was prepared for this response, and I feel that I owe my correspondents an answer and an explanation. Some of those who wrote were poets, and some friends of particular poets; some were angry, but more were grieved, and the reason for their grief is summed up in one extract from one letter, thus – "How can you, a man of culture, discourage those who are trying, however humbly, to foster culture in this country?"

First of all, let me say that it always makes me shiver when somebody calls me a man of culture; I don't know what the phrase really means, but I fear what I think they mean. There is a widespread notion in Canada that culture is something which turns a man into less than a man; it is equated with intellectual cryptorchidism. Nothing in my modest experience of the world of art and letters supports this idea; people who are engaged in the arts are frequently aggressive and ferocious. All artists, even when not pugnacious, are tough-minded. So I prefer not to be called a man of culture, and if I am to be typed I suppose it must be as a writer who is occasionally a critic.

What is a critic? His tasks are many, and one of them is to insist upon the preservation of high standards in the art he criticizes. It was in defence of a decent standard of poetry that I wrote as I did about the majority of Canadian versifiers. Poets think of themselves as an oppressed group, but the fact is that too many of them are coddled and cosseted by their circle until they have an inflated idea of the merit of their work.

Proof arrives on my desk by mail several times a month. After my article on poets, several people unknown to me sent me examples of their work to ask if I thought there was any merit in it. Most of it was bad; none of it showed any spark.

Why bother with it then? Because I do not feel that Canadian critics are yet in a position to send out printed slips (as Edmund Wilson does in the United States, and small blame to him) saying that they will not read unsolicited manuscripts. There are too many Canadian writers who need help, and who do not know any other way of getting it. If I slighted a single Canadian writer of promise by refusing to look at his stuff when he sent it to me, I should feel that I had failed in something which is, in the present state of Canadian letters, my duty. I have no desire to figure in history alongside that Archbishop of Salzburg who kicked Mozart downstairs, or those unknown thugs who killed Edgar Allan Poe in an alley.

I beg my readers not to take what is written above as an invitation to send me anything and everything that they have written. I am not anxious to become the unpaid literary adviser of the unrecognized writers of Canada; not for the wealth of the Indies would I become a regular reader of manuscripts. But I know that every writer in this country who has by luck or industry or talent made his name known, receives his share of poetry and prose which he is asked to examine and advise upon, free.

A few of the letters were in irregular lines, meant for verse, and they throw much light on why I wrote as I did. Unfortunately there is room here for only one characteristic passage:

> To brand a poetaster with nothing in the heart,
>   And tell he who loves to paint, knows nothing of Art —
> Or ridicule a lad, who loves a lovely lass; —
>   The Critic has no charity, and his soul is lost, alas!

No, no, my friend, that simply is not true. The critic has great charity, for charity suffereth long, and is kind, and there is no critic in Canada who has not suffered, and been kind to masses of talentless, illiterate junk. But kindness does not always express itself in praise, and where praise would be a lie the critic dares not utter it, for fear that fire from heaven would sear his lips. In such cases the truest kindness lies in telling the would-be poet that he has no discernible talent, or else that his talent is hamstrung by his lack of poetic discipline and technique. Nobody blames the music critic for saying that the tuneless strumming of a tone-deaf child is not music; critics of poetry have at least an equal duty to truth and the standards they cherish. As well as being an art, poetry is a craft, and the craft part of it may be learned. It is not given to everybody to be an artist; but to be ignorant of one's craft, and yet to claim the respect owing to a craftsman is blameworthy, and certainly it will continue to be blamed by me, and by every critic who respects himself.

"Condemnation Can Be Kindness," *Toronto Daily Star*, 28 February 1959

The Watch That Ends the Night: 1959

If you are one of those people who likes to discuss the question of what is a Canadian novel, I direct your attention to Hugh Mac-Lennan's latest book, *The Watch That Ends the Night*. It is Canadian, in that it could not have been written by anyone but a Canadian. Its Canadian quality goes far beyond the facts that the setting of the book is Montreal, and that love and understanding for that city are part of the emotional fabric of the work; it is rather that the thinking and feeling which give the book its weight and worth are Canadian. I realize that such a comment asks for justification.

It is generally acknowledged that the work of the best writers of the American South has qualities which set it apart from the writings of other Americans; geography, economics, history, and some measure of local character give rise to these differences. I believe that this is also the case with Canadian writers, and especially those from the older part of the country.

We do not think or feel as people do in New England, or the American West; we have, many of us, British sympathies which we are sometimes reluctant to keep, yet afraid to cast away. Our climate sets its mark on us, making some of us moody and introspective in a fashion which is akin to the Scandinavians, or the Russians, and when we dig deep into ourselves we find matters which are very much our own. We are superficially a simple people, but our simplicity is deceptive; the roaring extrovert is only one kind of Canadian, and not any more representative than the nervous, self-concealing one.

For every Canadian who gets into a huff at the bitter tone of Norman Levine's *Canada Made Me*, there is another who can see the truth which in Levine has turned to gall. For every man who recalls his own childhood in terms of the boys in Ernest Thompson Seton's *Two Little Savages*, there is another who sees himself in the worrying, raw-nerved Harold Sondern, in Ralph

Allen's *Peace River Country*. If Canada gets another hundred years in which to present herself to the world through her books, this aspect of the Canadian character will become widely known, and will find affectionate understanding in the rest of the literate world. "Wild Hamlet with the features of Horatio," said Douglas LePan of the *coureur de bois*; never did anyone pack so much insight into the Canadian character in a single phrase.

In an excellent introduction to the New Canadian Library edition of *Barometer Rising*, Hugo McPherson says that Hugh MacLennan was a pioneer in exploring Canada's consciousness. He has continued so since the publication of that book in 1941, and he has received small thanks for it. Few critics appear to have been aware of what he was trying to do. Certainly his aim was not the production of neatly-turned novels which would sell well in the United States; that would have been entirely proper work for a craftsman, but MacLennan deserves a better name – he is an artist. A nice book with a Canadian icing slapped on it can be written, though not easily; a truly Canadian book is quite a different thing.

Hugh MacLennan has not written nice books, but the best books of which he was capable, and they have not always been easy or friendly reading. Always there has been that exploration of his own very Canadian consciousness, which has thrown up boulders of philosophical disquisition on what might have been the smooth lawns of his story-telling. He has refused to bury the rocks and roll the lawns, and has taken the consequences of his decision.

Now, in his fifth book, he has gained a new mastery over the two strongest elements in his work; the story-teller and the self-explorer are one. The effect is virtually to double his stature. The Canadian novel takes a great stride forward.

The story is of a woman greatly loved by two men. Catherine Carey was the first love of George Stewart, but whereas she was emotionally precocious, he was not, and so he lost her, and did not find her again until she was the wife of a rising surgeon, Jerome Martell. When Martell left Catherine, in pursuit of an ideal which took him to the Spanish War, George was her mainstay until Martell was reported dead, and then he was able to marry her. He continued to be her mainstay until her death.

The relations among these three are complex, and one indication of the quality of the book is that it is possible for three readers to interpret them in three different ways, and to provide evidence to support each point of view. My own feeling is that the two men give what is best in life to a woman whom I could not really like; Catherine is a fine example of the spiritual vampire, living on the vital force of others. To other readers she may well seem a true heroine – in Jungian terms, the soul of the hero.

Martell may appear to you as a truly great man, or merely as a man who mistakes his own abundant energy for thought; like all such people he is a two-edged sword, bringing fulfilment to some and ruin to others. George Stewart, who is the narrator and who presents himself (as narrators in books so often do) as a poor fish, is the strongest character, with the poorest sense of self-preservation. But it is his intelligence and insight and worth which engage us when we are impatient of the heroics of Martell, and the posturings of Catherine.

It takes a fine novelist, at the top of his form, to create people about whom we can feel, and argue, so strongly. I have talked to people who have read this book and who accept Catherine as the beautiful, rare person George Stewart believes her to be. One man tells me he thinks Martell is of heroic stature – too much so to be real. Yet another complains that the convention of the narrator is strained because Stewart reports things of which he could not have had any knowledge.

Still another is engrossed by the description of what Canada felt like during the Depression years – an aspect of the novel which is most skilfully brought forward and kept in focus, for the great part of the book. Two more are delighted with the descriptions of Montreal "the subtlest and most intricate city in North America," which is also among the best things MacLennan has done; I hope Montreal appreciates what has been said about it, but it is unlikely that this is so. (Is it true of Canadian cities, as an English friend of mine says of Canadian women, that they become hostile and suspicious when compliments are paid them?)

There will be downright souls, I fear, who will not think this book Canadian in feeling for the strange reason that it is so plainly the work of a man of extensive and subtle intellect. The emotions which it displays are not simple; the existence, side by side, of love and hate for the same woman in the mind of the man who cannot live without her is hard to get into words, and hard for the reader to swallow, if he has no personal experience of the feeling. Those who turn to novels for simple loyalties and happy loves will catch a Tartar in *The Watch That Ends the Night*.

But a literature has no hope of maturity until its writers embark on precisely this task of capturing the subtleties of human feeling and conduct, and revealing them as they are manifested in their countrymen. The people in this book could hardly be anything but Canadians; Catherine might perhaps exist elsewhere in the form MacLennan has given her, but I do not think so; Martell would be most unlikely in the United States; George Stewart is Canadian through and through. Their plight is a very old one, which has been explored in every mature literature.

MacLennan's triumph lies in working it out in our terms, in one of our own cities. The task has never before been attempted on this scale in the Canadian novel; it has rarely been done so well in any novel in our time. At what personal cost, no critic can know. MacLennan may say, as Whitman said: "Who touches this touches a man."

"MacLennan's Rising Sun," *Saturday Night*, 28 March 1959

A Red Carpet For The Sun: 1959

Irving Layton has included all the poems written during his first period which he wishes to preserve, in a volume called *A Red Carpet For The Sun* which will be on sale in a few days. This ought to be an event of importance to some thousands of Mr. Layton's countrymen; he is an undoubted poet and this signal that he has completed a phase of his work should be important to every Canadian who takes a moderate interest in the intellectual development of his country. But there are so many who, though not lacking in goodwill, are frightened of poetry. They have tried it, from time to time, and have been confused, then humbled, then made angry by it. I suggest that they make another try with Mr. Layton, and I should like to help them, if I can, to read him with a better degree of understanding.

First of all, what does he mean? He means exactly what he says. This is not poetry in which meaning is wrapped in veils of difficult language; he does not even bend his meaning to suit the needs of rhyme or strict rhythm. Readers who are not used to poetry may sometimes be reluctant to believe that he means what he says, for it is often blunt, and even coarse – and many people cherish the notion that "real" poetry is pretty and delicate. But pretty, delicate poetry – which may sometimes be very good poetry – belongs to a tradition against which Mr. Layton is in revolt. He wants to wake us up, to make us see life freshly, and not through Alfred Austin's spectacles.

He is so vexed with people who see life at second and third hand that he sometimes writes with savagery, and he employs physical and sexual imagery which prudish people do not like. Canadians are, he says, "a dull people" and his "songs, bawdy and raucous" are meant to jolt them out of their dullness. He is a Montreal poet, and when we remember Samuel Butler's "Psalm of Montreal," that great outcry against Philistinism, we may wonder if Montreal and not Toronto is the fountainhead of Canadian stupidity. Much of his comment on his fellow countrymen is invective, and those of us who share his wish that Canada should wake up from its snuffling, anti-Dionysian slumber find his vigorous outpouring of scorn refreshing. He seeks to confute the Philistines, not by persuasion but by direct attack and accusation.

If he were only scornful, dirty, and abusive, however, he would not be a poet. These things are only in his manner; what is his matter? It is a high-coloured, abounding delight in the physical world. Much of what he writes is about town life, the streets, the parks, the dance halls, and the girls. Yes, the girls, for Mr. Layton is not one of those poets who writes about the Muse, or Woman, or some other splendid female being more suggestive of a marble tombstone than of flesh. His poem "Earth Goddess" is addressed to Marilyn Monroe, and what he says is not meant for "the smelly puritan" or "the sulky christian," and will certainly not please them, either separately or in combination. In "Admonition and Reply" he tells of three of these puritans who ask him "Why do you write of the wenches?" saying:

> *They offend us,*
> *Your songs bawdy and raucous;*
> *Purify your soul, sing*
> *The glory of suffering.*

In answer he points to the wretched and unpleasing wives of these detractors. And how right he is! Only last week a friend of mine said, "You can best tell what a man is like by looking at the expression on his wife's face." An awesome reflection; fortunately it is only half true, for husbands' faces have as much to tell of wives.

Puritans will not like Mr. Layton's poetry, but there are millions of Canadians who are not thirty-third degree puritans. Nor are they all what he calls "The Barbari carrying their chromium gods on their sunburnt arms and shoulders." Many of them are people who would like poetry if they could break through the distaste for it which they acquired in school, when it was work, or if they could set aside the foolish notion that it is something too high, too fine, for the mere likes of them. They will search for a long time before they will find a volume which speaks to them more directly, or about simpler things, than *A Red Carpet For The*

Sun. But because it is simple, do not be deceived that it is trivial. These poems are the feelings and thoughts of a man who pierces through triviality to something that is enduring. His range is not wide, and he lacks music, but he has passion and poetic sincerity. Furthermore, he writes of the country and the people which we rarely see except through the spectacles of the politicians, the journalists, and the tight-lipped, thin-blooded uplifters whom Layton flogs so energetically.

"Layton Poems Not For Puritans," *Toronto Daily Star*, 12 September 1959

Mad Shadows: 1960

For several months rumours have come to us from French Canada about a new, very young, greatly gifted writer, Mademoiselle Marie-Claire Blais. Now her first novel *La Belle Bête* is available to us in a translation called *Mad Shadows*, and I, for one, hurried to read it with keen anticipation.

It was shrewd of the translator, Merloyd Lawrence, to give us a hint of the nature of the book by choosing an English title from a poem by Baudelaire, taken from *Flowers of Evil*. Marie-Claire Blais has sought to give us a flower of evil, and in a way she has succeeded. Certainly her book derives much from the hottest, steamiest sort of French romanticism. But Baudelaire was a master in the art of walking the tightrope between the splendours and miseries of romance, and the stupidities of Dickens' Fat Boy, who wanted to make our flesh creep. Baudelaire is a dangerous influence for a girl who writes a book like this at nineteen.

As we read the opening pages of the book we recognize, with dismay, the kind of writing familiar to anybody who has ever judged a high-school story contest. Gifted young writers have very often an impulsive and dishevelled style which comes from a flood of feeling trying to pass through the funnel of an inadequate technique. They are especially fond of what we may call the "unsupported adjective." For instance, in the early pages of this book a woman is described as having an "all-too supple wrist," but this quality is never mentioned again, is not needed where it occurs, and seems to have been introduced because it has a fine sound. So also the ugly girl who is at the heart of the story, Isabelle-Marie, is said to be "awkward in her black dress . . . and more awkward still in the flesh." Examine this, and what does it mean? It means that the author is manufacturing phrases, and that no kind friend has advised her to strike them out. This is schoolgirl's writing.

So also we read of the farmer who, "when he tilled the virgin loins of the earth, . . . was penetrating to the heart of God," of "the strange odour of earth," and of a girl whose sobs are like the moans of a stricken animal; we read of a seducer who had "the graceful, congealed laughter of marionettes," of a woman whose "contempt for her daughter spurted like pus from her fingernails," of lovers "who slept on top of each other" – a description which suggests a wholly theoretical notion of the sexual act.

This prose recalls the wildest excesses of French nineteenth-century romanticism; it also suggests Stella Gibbons' burlesque of the gloomy pastoral novel, *Cold Comfort Farm*. When we read about this family who, though well-off, subsist entirely on bread and drinks of water, and a rare drop of champagne, we seem to be with the Starkadders at Cold Comfort or, perhaps more charitably, with Mr. Salteena in the romance of an even younger author than Mlle. Blais.

It is altogether too easy to make fun of this hot, boozy, tumescent prose, and I have not said so much about it in order to be nasty to a highly gifted young writer, but to implore some wise friend to help her to moderate it. Unquestionably, Mlle. Blais has unusual talent, but from this work it is impossible to know how much or how sturdy. She writes like a schoolgirl, but few schoolgirls have her ability to carry a story so far as she has done. They have exhausted their monsters and their feverish, unexplained passions in two or three pages; she has written a short novel.

The story is of Louise who owns several farms, and has two children: Patrice, the boy, is exquisitely beautiful, but a moron; Isabelle-Marie, the girl, is ugly and jealous of her brother. Louise dotes upon her son, but marries a man of fashion who has a lame leg and walks with a golden cane; Isabelle-Marie tells Patrice that her mother no longer loves him, and ruins her brother's beauty by shoving his face in a pot of boiling water. The stepfather is killed. Louise dies of cancer of the face, having placed the now ugly Patrice in a madhouse.

The setting of the tale is the enclosed, high-coloured world of a child's fantasy; it has no relation to reality, and its impact is entirely emotional. If we give ourselves wholly to it, we are swept along on a powerful stream of adolescent passion, which the writer does not understand and makes no attempt to explain. This is primitive writing, very good of its kind, but certain to change its direction soon.

To mention Françoise Sagan on the cover as though she were a less powerful writer than Mlle. Blais is not kind to the latter. Mlle. Sagan, in her earliest novel, was already a gifted young woman; Mlle. Blais is still a gifted child, whatever her age may be. The uttermost critical judgement that can be risked on the evidence of *La Belle Bête* is that she has undoubted talent, which, under favourable stars, might develop into something remarkable. Let us hope that it will be so.

"Girl Has Unusual Talent But Should Moderate Prose," *Toronto Daily Star*, 8 October 1960

Pauline Johnson: 1961

Since the publication last September of *The Oxford Book of Canadian Verse*, edited by A.J.M. Smith, several readers have written to ask me why Pauline Johnson is not represented in it. Now that a long review of the book has appeared in the *Literary Supplement* of the *London Times*, in which much of the early Canadian verse is condemned as "unmitigated rubbish," more enquiries have come; is Pauline Johnson unfit even to be included among the trash? If so, why has the Canadian government celebrated her centennial this year with a commemorative stamp?

I am unable to answer either of these questions. Doubtless Professor Smith had excellent reasons for leaving Pauline Johnson out. Doubtless her work is as good as much of that which is included. Doubtless the Canadian government craftily wanted to please the Indian population and the literary people at once, and thought Pauline Johnson a more popular figure than, for instance, the truly considerable poet Archibald Lampman. But like all sentences which are opened with "Doubtless . . ." these things are somewhat in doubt.

Pauline Johnson's talent, such as it was, belonged to the bardic order. She barnstormed this continent, stirring audiences to enthusiasm by the spectacle of a handsome woman of agreeable personality, a member of the aboriginal race, reciting musical, sentimental verse of her own composition. Her reward, like that of any other public entertainer, was the immediate response of her hearers. In consequence, her verse bears the stamp of her trade; it is elocutionist fodder, and like the monologues of Ruth Draper, it is strangely flat without the personality it was designed to show off. I do not say this in derogation of her real gift, which was for entertaining. Thousands of people remember her public personality with pleasure; because she was essentially an elocutionist, we need not assume that she was entirely a mountebank. But her verses achieved their vogue because they were fashionable and easy, and they have ceased to be popular for precisely these reasons.

Pauline Johnson's father was an Indian, her mother an English-woman, and she grew up in conditions of comparative affluence near Brantford, Ontario. Her Indian name, with which she made great play in her professional career, was Tekahionwake, which means "Smoky Haze of Indian Summer." She began to make up verses before she could write, and all her later work shows the virtues and vices implicit in this early declaration of talent. The music of words, rather than depth of feeling or meaning, was what she had to offer, and she possessed a mastery of form, of rhyme, and of all that is mellifluous in the poet's gift, which makes her verses eminently speakable.

Her taste was uncertain. Noisy patriotism, as in "Canadian Born," came to her as readily as the music of "The Song My Paddle Sings," and rather more readily than the real feeling of "The Corn Husker." Nothing that I have been able to find out about her suggests that she was given to reflection; she enjoyed her bustling, successful career as a public entertainer, and who is to blame her? Nobody is obliged to forgo the sweets that lie most readily to hand.

If modern anthologists reject her, she keeps her attraction as a "period" figure. Perhaps her finest moment was when she recited for Queen Victoria. The picture is nineteenth-century, Imperial, and to me, both touching and funny. The half-Englishwoman, dressed in a costumier's version of Indian ceremonial garb, belting out her melodious numbers in her rich, actressy voice for that other tiny Englishwoman who symbolized the might of the British Empire at its greatest, had surely achieved as much as, for instance, Isabella Valancy Crawford, who still gets into Professor Smith's anthology as a reputable, if wispy, Canadian versifier. Poetry is undoubtedly a serious business, and nobody can say that we do not take it with graveyard seriousness nowadays. But the world also needs its entertainers, its bards, who remind us that poetry was not always a question of printed pages, hidden meanings, and dismal intellectual gropings; there was a time when poetry was for everybody, and had some fun in it.

Let us not grudge Tekahionwake her commemorative stamp, but we need not also assert that she ought to be in Professor A.J.M. Smith's carefully chosen anthology. Her fame came during her lifetime, which is what she – sensible woman – wanted.

"Why Pauline Didn't Make It," *Toronto Daily Star*, 8 April 1961

Mazo de la Roche: 1961

The Canadian travelling abroad during the past twenty years has been fairly sure of finding two Canadian authors represented in almost any big European bookshop, Stephen Leacock and Mazo de la Roche. Now both are dead, and both lie in the pleasant graveyard at Sibbald's Point.

Miss de la Roche was not a stylist or a philosopher; she was that rare creature in the literary world, a born story-teller. She made literally millions of readers eager to know what would happen next to the Whiteoak family, who would get the money, which marriages would ripen and which collapse, where unexpected talent would show itself, and where a fatal stupidity would blight a life; she created a world and peopled it, and invited the reader to lose himself inside her world for the duration of each novel. The creation of the *Jalna* books is the most protracted single feat of literary invention in the brief history of Canada's literature.

There were people who said that the Whiteoak family were not like Canadians – by which we must deduce that they meant the Whiteoaks were not like themselves. But there were many others who knew Canadians in whom there were all the Whiteoak strains – the colonial attachment to England mingled with a resentment of modern England, a democratic spirit at war with a desire for personal privilege, a pride in pioneer family blood with a consciousness that all the pioneer energy was being strained out of that blood. Oh, the Whiteoaks were Canadians, right enough! The Canadians who admired the American trend of the thirties towards Tough Guy novels and Social Consciousness novels could not see it, but Mazo de la Roche was writing about a Canada which was perfectly real, and which persists today.

Apart from her literary celebrity, Miss de la Roche lived very quietly. But it would not be suitable to end this brief comment on her life without some mention of her kindness and understanding towards young people, to whom she gave advice, affection, and money without stint. Nor was she a person who was interested only in backing winners; the young people who had not found their way, or who had lost it, or who were in some cases plainly no-good, were recipients of her kindness, as well as those who had ability and needed only a helping hand to make a place for themselves in the world.

Not only was Mazo de la Roche a novelist of unusual gifts; she was also a woman of uncommon breadth and vigour of spirit.

Peterborough Examiner, 13 July 1961

Canadian Literature: 1964

Canadian literature, like much else about the Northern Dominion, is deceptive. A non-Canadian trained in the attitudes of modern criticism – a post-doctoral student from California let us say – might think that in approaching Canadian literature he was entering a critic's paradise. A subarctic climate to produce the asperities of a Northern temperament; a dual culture with two living languages; a colonial background to revolt against; an expanding economy; a publishing industry closely associated with both Britain and the United States – here's richness indeed! But the critic would find, as he worked, that although all of these influences are present in Canadian literature, their effect has not always been positive. Only our travel posters are painted in primary colours; our history and our temperament use a darker palette.

Have we indeed a literature? Yes, and part of the dissatisfaction with ourselves that plagues us at present concerns it. It is not so impressive as many people, themselves uninvolved in the production of literature, would like it to be; but it is not trivial, and it is substantial in size. Compared with the literature of countries with which we have some kinship in spirit and history – Australia and New Zealand, for example – we have little cause for shame. But that does not satisfy us; we compare ourselves with England, with France, with the United States, and make ourselves miserable.

A young nation shares in the literatures of the lands from which its people came, and for Canada this means the British Isles and France. Geographical position and natural sympathy also give us a special interest in all writing in the United States. Indeed, Canada sees a greater variety of literature in English than any other country in the world, and the Canadian novelist, in a large bookshop, finds himself displayed in distinguished and sometimes eclipsing company; with Iris Murdoch and J.D. Salinger on either side of him, what are his chances of being chosen?

228

Yet he throws himself against this formidable competition and achieves a measure of success; indeed, his acceptance abroad is steadily increasing. He knows he has one great opponent of whose presence he can never be free: it is Canada's history and political composition. He has a powerful ally of whom he is less aware, because it exists within himself: the Canadian character, an element strong and more individual than many Canadians yet realize.

Let us consider history first. Canada's beginnings were as frosty as our winters. In this we are very different from our neighbours in the United States, who seized their destiny from the grasp of an empire, and had to make the best of it or expire in ignominy. That was bracing; it made for a tonic intellectual climate, and fostered the seeds of myth. But that same empire was our mother, and the navel cord was never cut; it withered as we grew.

In the national sense, Canada is a result of family planning. Certain colonies of British North America decided, peacefully and for admirable nineteenth-century reasons, to unite under a central government; they did so in a spirit of goodwill and compromise, with Queen Victoria as a benevolent but not deeply interested godmother. Result: the Dominion of Canada. Birthday: July 1, 1867.

This was a favoured, but not heroic, origin. We were not born of any passionate act; we were brought into the world peacefully. We wanted to unite, and Britain did not mind.

Today, as the centenary of our Confederation approaches we accuse ourselves of provincial dowdiness. The establishment of the Canada Council, in 1957, and some later provincial agencies to foster learning and the arts, are the results of a long, careful look in the mirror. We want to win distinction in the arts.

Can a country bring forth first-rate literature by desiring it? The problem of the Canadian writer is manifold. Whatever he writes will be criticized by the standards of England and the United States. He would not wish it otherwise. Nevertheless, the Canadian writer, if he chooses a Canadian theme or a Canadian setting for his work may not easily find an audience beyond our borders. Canada is not a country about which it is fashionable to read, and this question of fashion is more important in the literary world than is generally admitted.

Hugh MacLennan has had some success in giving Montreal a literary character, but I have heard Morley Callaghan's admirable novel, *The Loved and the Lost*, criticized in Canada for making that city the centre of a story which, it was thought, would be more appropriate to a city in the United States. Australian novelists, Patrick White in particular, have had some success in establishing Australia as a country with literary character, especially among English readers; but insofar as Canada is known in England through fiction, it is the romanticized Canada of Mazo de la Roche.

As with virtually everything about Canada, there must be a qualification to this. In the past five years Farley Mowat's books have become popular in the United States, and so has *The Incredible Journey*, by Sheila Burnford. But are they thought of as specifically Canadian?

Stephen Leacock, the most widely known of all our writers, is not always identified as a Canadian outside his own land. But he was very much a Canadian, and it is odd that many passages in his work which make this plain seem not to be understood by his readers elsewhere; his pungent but friendly criticism of both Britain and the United States could have come only from a Canadian.

Is it objected that Leacock was born in England? The whole question as to who is a Canadian writer is subject to similar complications, and we do not seem to know our own mind. We do not lay claim to Thomas B. Costain, who was born a Canadian but has done his work in the United States. On the other hand, we do claim Sir Gilbert Parker (whose once considerable popularity has utterly faded), although he did his work in England. But only recently have we remembered that Sara Jeannette Duncan, so much of whose life was passed in Calcutta, was a Canadian and wrote of Canada. Brian Moore sojourned among us for a while, but we never thought of him as a Canadian writer; Nicholas Monsarrat has made his home in Ottawa, but his celebrity was assured beforehand. Our greatest pastoral, *Maria Chapdelaine*, was the work of Louis Hémon, a continental Frenchman. We might lay claim to the great name of Goldwin Smith (who trounced us soundly in his writings), but we never do. Perhaps our finest hour of confusion was reached in 1954, when our highest literary award, the Governor General's Medal for fiction, was given to Igor Gouzenko, a Russian, for his book, *The Fall of a Titan*, a tale written in Russian on Canadian soil, about a Russian Communist official much like Stalin. The gesture was doubtless meant to assert Canada's largeness of soul in welcoming Mr. Gouzenko, who had sought political asylum among us; it was less effective in encouraging Canadian writers, writing in English or French about Canadian themes.

When we talk of Canadian poets we reach the firmer ground of Canadian character. Our poetry has developed in a manner which parallels our painting. In the eighteenth and early nineteenth century it was English poetry written abroad and guided by English sensibility, which was never at home in the new land. But as, during the latter part of the nineteenth century, the Canadian landscape, Canadian birds and creatures, the march of Canadian seasons, and the quality of Canadian light established themselves in the consciousness of the poets, their verse changed character, their language adapted itself to the new themes, and they wrote verse which could not have been written elsewhere. The yearning for "the lone shieling of the misty island," and the pathetic cry of the anonymous immigrant:

> *I canna ca' this forest home,*
> *And in it live and dee;*
> *Nor feel regret at my heart's core*
> *My native land, for thee.*

gave place to Archibald Lampman's

> *I think some blessed power*
> *Hath brought me wandering idly here:*
> *In the full furnace of this hour*
> *My thoughts grow keen and clear.*

Acceptance of the climate and landscape in Canadian poetry was followed in the twentieth century by acceptance of a Canadian cast of thought. This is not easy to identify, for there is nothing in this Canadian attitude towards man and nature which is unfamiliar; it would be strange indeed if Canadian poets found modes of thinking and feeling unknown elsewhere. But the sum of these elements is different. The sternness of the Canadian character at its best, the reserved but powerful feeling, and the strain of irony assert themselves in our poetry. These characteristics are common to the best of our writing in all forms, but poetry, by nature the product of refined, distilled, and compressed feeling, exhibits them most strongly.

This is no place to call a roll of Canadian poets of the first rank. Let E.J. Pratt stand for the stern strength and Douglas LePan for the heavily charged, controlled feeling; for the irony, there is F.R. Scott, whose verses called *The Canadian Authors Meet* end thus:

> *Shall we go round the mulberry bush,*
> *or shall*
> *We gather at the river, or shall we*
> *Appoint a poet laureate this Fall*
> *Or shall we have another cup of tea?*
>
> *O Canada, O Canada, Oh can*
> *A day go by without new authors*
> *springing*
> *To paint the native maple, or to plan*
> *More ways to set the selfsame welkin*
> *ringing?*

These are not the names of young men; a list of the outstanding Canadian poets born since 1924 would be a substantial one. In them the sternness is overshadowed by a complex sensibility – not a wincing sensibility, but a supple responsiveness to personal experience and the outside world. Yet the change is more apparent than real; in James Reaney and Jay Macpherson, for instance, the sternness and the irony are never completely concealed, although their expression ranges from mock naivety to elegance.

Even the poets who are aggressively in revolt possess a discernible kinship with those whose revolt is quieter (though possibly more enduring). Our strongest voice of poetic protest is that of Irving Layton, whose furious, large-spirited disgust with everything commonplace has obscured his stature as a moralist and critic of the times.

Vigorous protest about anything is an attitude adopted by few Canadian writers. Canada hates the direct attack on any problem, and, after an instant's flinching, ignores the attacker. An outsider, Wyndham Lewis, could not rouse us even with so fierce an onslaught as that in *Self-Condemned*, which portrayed the physical and intellectual misery of an Englishman in Canada. Norman Levine, whose *Canada Made Me* dwelt heavily on the provincial vulgarity which was all he found on returning to his native land, was as little heeded.

This resistance to direct and impassioned criticism recalls pre-Ibsen Norway. There is, of course, a literature of protest in Canada, but much of it is concerned with the wider world of literature and ideas; it is not purely national. Even the present vigorous assertion of Quebec's political independence has produced little influential writing, though in this realm of political and social protest our French writers greatly excel those who write in English. The Canadian writer who hopes to draw attention to faults in our life or government must treat his country as Peer Gynt learned to treat the Great Boyg, and set about his task by indirection.

Humour has been used to this end, but the humorist walks a tightrope. Stephen Leacock learned this lesson early in life, when his satiric book, *Sunshine Sketches of a Little Town*, earned him the fierce resentment of the little town itself. He was a notable ironist, and is doubtless laughing in Elysium because he is now the principal tourist attraction of the once-offended community, which annually presents a gilded medal bearing his likeness to the writer of what is judged the funniest Canadian book of the year; it is inscribed without shame, "The Sunshine Town." (The notion that the most useful author is a dead author is not, of course, exclusively Canadian.)

Canadian humour leads us to the element of irony in Canadian writing. An admirable anthology gathered by F.R. Scott and A.J.M. Smith, *The Blasted Pine*, shows that this has been constant and strong since our pioneer days. Indeed, pioneers have a natural tendency towards irony. Among ours were many people of education and intelligence who suffered from the intellectual famine of a raw new land. Two courses were open: those who tried to recreate England here were defeated, and their fate is not without pathos; the tougher-minded, who kept cool heads and tart tongues, succeeded. Perhaps they succeeded too well, for the Canadian intellect, like Canadian wine, is still a little too near to vinegar to encourage easy conviviality.

This astringent quality has marked our fiction. One of our

pioneers, Mrs. Susanna Moodie, made one of her characters say, in 1852: "Ghosts! There are no ghosts in Canada. The country is too new for ghosts. No Canadian is afearded of ghosts." Ninety-six years later Douglas LePan, in a poem significantly called "A Country Without a Mythology," could still write of the barren path "the passionate man must travel" here.

It was LePan also who wrote of that heroic, anonymous Canadian, the *coureur de bois*, as "Wild Hamlet with the features of Horatio." I believe this to be profoundly true of Canadians as a people. It is psychologically impossible for any people to live forever without some communion with those deeps of the spirit which nourish other countries – even countries as comparatively young as the United States – and which reveal themselves in national mythologies. But this is what Canada has attempted to do, and now the pretence that we have no ghosts, no unconscious, is wearing thin. The features of Horatio we may bear, but the Hamlet-like division of spirit asserts itself increasingly in the stresses of a bicultural, officially bilingual land, and in the tensions created by the powerful pulls of British and United States economic and governmental sympathies.

No ghosts in Canada? The country which too vigorously asserts its normality and rationalism is like a man who declares that he is without imagination; suddenly the ghosts he has denied may overcome him, and then his imaginative flights make poets stare. Unfortunately, he also needs the help of the psychiatrist, and there are no psychiatrists who minister to whole nations.

However, nations have a way of whispering the inner truth about themselves, sufficiently disguised to deceive those who would keep the truth hidden. In poetry Canada has been well served; its poets have uttered oracles which some of us have understood. But what of fiction?

Since 1957 a Toronto firm of publishers, McClelland and Stewart, has been bringing out a paperback selection called New Canadian Library; it is of interest because it gathers together a great deal of what is significant in Canadian writing since 1769.

This early date is not contrived by a trick. *The History of Emily Montague*, by Frances Brookes, is an excellent epistolary novel by an English lady, wife of an army chaplain, who knew Quebec at first hand and thought well of Canadians. It deserves its revival.

So does *The Stepsure Letters*, by Thomas McCulloch, a finer piece of Canadian irony than the much praised Sam Slick stories by Judge Haliburton. It was not until the twentieth century that Canadian publishers were ready to risk much on Canadian books, and so our nineteenth-century productions were usually pitched to catch the ear of publishers in London or New York, and it sometimes requires divination to discover anything Canadian about them. But if a Canadian novel is not a novel written in Canada by a resident of the country, what is it? There were a few, like Sara Jeannette Duncan, who wrote of the land they knew, and achieved reputation; others, like Grant Allen and Gilbert Parker, were Canadians by birth but Englishmen by choice.

In the present century we have produced a body of fiction about Canada which is as varied in texture as the country itself. The tale of pioneer endurance is only one thread in the tapestry. The overheated gothic tales of Marie-Claire Blais are Canadian also, and they have been greeted with keen interest in Paris. Gabrielle Roy is one of our few novelists writing in French who enjoys an equal popularity in English. Ethel Wilson produces fiction as elegantly fashioned as any that is written elsewhere; she is especially successful in what Willa Cather called "the thing not named, the overtone divined by the ear but not heard by it," and this sets her apart from most of her contemporaries, who are not primarily stylists. Indeed, a lack of strong feeling for language is one of the principal weaknesses of Canadian prose writers, but perhaps in this they are truly Canadian; examine the Canadian entries in Partridge's *Dictionary of Slang and Unconventional English*, and it appears that we are, as a people, uninventive and heavy in our dealings with words.

Again there are exceptions. Two painters, who did not think of themselves as writers, were notable stylists. The short pieces of Emily Carr and the letters of David Milne are among the best-written things in Canadian literature.

In the United States the names of Hugh MacLennan and Morley Callaghan are familiar; the latter has been singled out for warm praise by Edmund Wilson. Both handle with ease nuances of character and incident that are subtly and unmistakably Canadian.

Yet our fiction would be poorer without novels which deal with matters that seem, at first glance, to be unCanadian; for example, Henry Kreisel's *The Rich Man* and Abraham Klein's Talmudic *The Second Scroll* are among our finest works of fiction. The novels of Mordecai Richler, though less completely successful in achieving artistic unity, are full of promise for splendid things to come; Richler relieves his bitterness of feeling with splendid passages of humour, occasionally disruptive but welcome for their own sake.

To the names of Kreisel, Klein, and Richler, all of them Canadian novelists writing in the Jewish tradition, can be added the name of Leonard Cohen. His first novel, *The Favourite Game*, would hardly attract attention were it not that he has already made a name as a poet; he stands out as a follower of Irving Layton but is of a finer poetic fibre.

A complaint often voiced is that there is not enough Canadian literature. I have for the past two years helped to form a library which hopes to gather together a representative collection of our fiction alone. Statistics are futile in matters of literature; it can only be said that the collection is larger than anyone not engaged in such work could conceive, and that the impression it gives is of a nation which writes not too little, but too much.

If Canadian books are mingled with books from England and the United States and all the other lands that publish in English, they are likely to be lost, for their tone is not aggressive or eccentric. But gather them together as a Canadian library, and consider them as the production of a land and a people, and they assume a more impressive stature.

They tell of a country which is a political rather than a geographical or racial fact. They tell of a people self-effacing and self-doubting who are being pitchforked by history into new self-appraisal. They tell of a people who have pretended they had no ghosts, but who now find themselves troubled by all the importunate ghosts of a bicultural civilization.

This self-appraisal now begins to reveal, among much else, that the Canadian writers of the past have been more perceptive, more prophetic and disenchanted, than their readers have guessed. In the land which pretends to have no ghosts, they have seen ghosts; in the country without a mythology, they have heard the ground bass of myth; in a country born not of love and struggle but of politics, they have fought battles; and, with reserve and irony, they have offered their country love.

"Party of One: The Northern Muse," *Holiday*, April 1964
(This article ended originally with a list of "Fifty Canadian Books" chosen as significant statements about Canada and Canadians. It included books in three categories: general, poetry, and fiction.)

The Stone Angel / The Tomorrow-Tamer: 1964

Because two of Margaret Laurence's books of fiction appear under the imprint of her American publisher in mid-June of this year, there will be many people – quite sensible people in most ways – who will talk of her having been "discovered." Of course, every writer laughs at such talk. He knows when the true discovery happened.

Mrs. Laurence, for instance, discovered herself thirty years ago. Though she is still under forty, she began writing when she was eight, in her native Manitoba. Her discovery by the public came in 1954, in Somaliland, where she produced the first English translation of Somali tales and poetry. She then wrote *This Side Jordan*, about the emergence of Ghana. She lived in West Africa for several years with her husband, a civil engineer. During that time she wrote many admirable short stories, some of which appeared first in Canada.

Though she now lives in England, Canada will hope to claim her as one of its own – and with justice. Not only was it the land of her birth, it is also the setting of her new novel, *The Stone Angel*.

The theme of this fine book is pride; and, as we turn its pages, we acknowledge once again the wisdom of those early theologians who ranked it foremost of the sins. Pride endangers a soul because, more than any other of the Deadly Seven – even more than the arch-disguiser Envy – it can be made to look like something else. In this short novel it wears its favourite North American false-faces. It looks like sturdy independence, like courage, like "character." The novelist puts us in a position from which we can also see that it is pigheadedness, domineering possessiveness, sheer cussedness.

Not until the day of her death does Hagar Shipley hear her decent, dull, dutiful son, Marvin, confide to a nurse: "She's a holy terror." Even then, as she approaches a measure of self-recognition, we cannot tell quite how she takes it. Probably she thinks that a holy terror is a fine thing to be. Better, doubtless, than such a nonentity as Marvin, whose good qualities have never commanded her love.

Hagar is a woman of the Canadian prairies, born just after the first rigours of the pioneering days have passed. Even as a child she is a great keeper of moral accounts. We sense in her the spirit of the Shorter Catechism, that remarkable document which makes it clear that mercy is an attribute of God only, and which enjoins no spirit of pity or compassion upon God's creatures.

This sharp, strong-minded child grows up into a sharp, strong-minded young woman, who marries a handsome, shiftless man against her father's wishes. Being the kind of father who would beget and rear such a child, he casts her off and cuts her out of his will.

Does Hagar care? Not greatly. She herself sees life in these terms. She has made her bed and is ready to lie in it. As she lies in it with her husband, he gives her many experiences of fulfilled passion, but Hagar never lets him know that he has stirred her. Mrs. Laurence does not use it, but there is a Canadian expression for this attitude: "I wouldn't give it to him to say."

This is the pattern of Hagar's life. Beneath a courtesy which is in itself a weapon to keep the world at bay (she learned ladylike behaviour in a private girls' school in Toronto, the Canadian Athens), she is as harsh with her husband and her children as she is with herself. The effect of this, and a measure of Mrs. Laurence's insight as a novelist, is not to make Hagar a monster, but a prisoner. We meet her when she is ninety. Her granite spirit despises the body which is now betraying her; a final blaze of pride gives her strength to run away; but there can be no flight from age and death.

Our sympathy is with her, but we may also feel keenly for Marvin and his wife, Doris, in spite of their dowdy sentimentality, their muddled thinking about whether Mother would not be better off in a home, and their lack of flair. This is a familiar story, but the author's freshness of approach, her individuality of insight, her gift for significant detail, and the justice tempered by mercy with which she sees the common predicaments of life, make its retelling distinguished.

The most arresting thing about Mrs. Laurence's talent, however, is not the assembly of good parts listed above, but her control of them all by form and style. Not, let it be said at once, that she has a "style" in any self-conscious or obtrusive sense. The style is in the grain.

She has chosen to relate the story of Hagar in a series of flashbacks, and in the work of writers whose sense of form is defective this device can be wearisome and confusing. Mrs. Laurence slips in and out of the past with the greatest of ease, without arousing any doubts about chronology.

She tells her tale, furthermore, in a good, firm vocabulary, congruous with the mind of Hagar herself. The rhythms are those of Canada before the turn of this century, and there is a sprinkling of words that give us a feeling of time and place. But there is no question of character-acting in print. This is revelation, not impersonation. The effect of such skilled use of language is to lead the reader towards the self-recognition that Hagar misses.

The same feeling for language distinguishes *The Tomorrow-Tamer*. These are tales of modern Africa, where white men are quickly being displaced by native African administrators and Caucasians who have learned to call Africa home find themselves bereft. Here is the Africa where a young pharmacist may be caught up with a dwarf prophet and jester; contemporaneous, these two are yet divided by centuries. This is the Africa where a missionary's son finds his affection for the land of his birth offensively nostalgic to his black foster-brother. There has not been much in fiction since the early novels of Joyce Cary, which explains so perceptively the atmosphere of disquiet in that explosive land.

The needs of a writer are many: a story to tell, a sense of drama, insight beyond the common, a reasonably coherent notion of what life is about – all of these are wanted. But such gifts of imagination and spirit are not rare. It is the gifts of artistic control and of language that are rare and cannot be counterfeited. Mrs. Laurence has these, as of right, and they give her work its distinguished quality.

"Self-Imprisoned to Keep the World at Bay," *New York Times Book Review*, 14 June 1964

O Canada: An American's Notes on Canadian Culture: 1965

Edmund Wilson's authority as a literary critic rests on his reputation for exploring his subjects at length and with unusual insight. Even when he sets aside literature to write of something else – the condition of the Iroquois, for instance – his habit of thoroughness does not leave him. Therefore, however carefully he may describe his latest book as "notes" on a "culture," there will be many who will overlook his disclaimers and believe that he has written about Canadian literature in his usual painstaking fashion.

This time, however, "notes" are indeed what he offers us. His book is discursive, changing course in a manner that will bewilder readers not already well informed about Canadian affairs, and mislead those who accept it as a balanced view of Canadian writing or Canadian politics. Canadians will be complimented that Mr. Wilson has chosen to publish such a book, for attention on this level is sufficiently unaccustomed to be welcome, but they will be sorry to hear it quoted as authoritative – which is likely to happen.

Canada is a country of deceptively innocent appearances – "Wild Hamlet with the features of Horatio," as Douglas LePan has put it. Mr. Wilson has fallen into an error unworthy of a man of his subtlety: he has cast French Canada for the meaty role of Hamlet and English Canada for – well, sometimes for Horatio, but more often for Fortinbras, sometimes for the impatient Laertes, and very frequently for Laertes' father, the crafty, sententious Polonius. Admitting the justice of this (so far as it goes), it does not go nearly far enough; English Canada is very well fitted to play Hamlet, but its performance does not appeal to Mr. Wilson.

A great friend of the oppressed, he is powerfully attracted by the revolt of French-speaking Canada against economic domination by English-speaking Canada, and against intellectual domination by the Church of Rome. But when he pulls on his scarlet Liberty cap, Mr. Wilson's normally cool intellect becomes overheated and causes him to write thrilling melodrama but bad politics. Coarse and stupid people on both sides of the Canadian argument have said and written foolish and wounding things; but by no means all Canadians are coarse and stupid, and the best among them desire and work towards a nation in which two languages and two cultures can exist and nourish one another. There is a quantity of intelligent goodwill on both sides which is ignored in these "notes."

In the last 135 pages of the book, politics gradually gains supremacy over a discussion of some Canadian writing in French. The earlier pages contain Mr. Wilson's warm appreciation of Morley Callaghan, whom he describes as a writer whose work may be compared without absurdity to Chekhov and Turgenev. The only other writer in English to whom substantial attention is given is Hugh MacLennan, who is awarded a lower mark, though a clear pass. It is refreshing to find that Mr. Wilson thinks our fiction better than our poetry: a considerable body of opinion in Canada has run the other way, and the poets have had, on the whole, an easy time of it. Mr. Wilson points out the narrowness of their range; narrowness of scope is certainly not the fault of our fiction.

Without clamouring foolishly for "equal time" or "fair play for English-Canadian writers," I do not think the author offers much of a counterweight to his extensive consideration of what is being written and thought in French. Mr. Wilson seems to think that the writers in English are not interested in defining and exploring the Canadian identity. He is wrong. He is not interested in what they have to say, which is another matter. Why? There are hints throughout the book which may provide an answer.

Anybody who has read Mr. Wilson's literary criticism extensively is aware of the bee he has in his bonnet about the English: though he admires their literature he considers them a treacherous people, paradoxically combining the effeteness of Imperial Rome with the rapacity of the barbarians. He seems to assume that the English-speaking Canadians are of the same low breed.

Did they not, after all, decline to join the glorious uproar in 1776 (as did also the French, but that is another matter) and throw off their colonial shackles? They must, therefore, be crypto-Englishmen still – those who are not Scots, another race Mr.

Wilson regards with suspicious distaste. He is not so naive as to ignore our substantial non-British immigration, but he seems convinced that the English dominate us. His paraphrase of the opinion of the separatist Marcel Chaput about "English" (meaning Canadian) judges in our Supreme Court, who are assumed not to be impartial in their consideration of Quebec affairs is but one unhappy instance where anti-British spleen stifles good sense. Several of those judges, and until recently the Chief Justice, are Canadians of French descent; nobody thinks that this fact colours their opinions.

Upon the whole, then, though we must all be glad that Mr. Wilson has said his say, let us be careful to remember that he disclaims any attempt to be comprehensive in his comment or decisive in judgement. What he offers is, as he made plain in the title of another of his books, a piece of his mind. It is a fine mind and this is a pretty piece of it, but that is all.

"More Pieces of a Fine Mind," *New York Times Book Review*, 16 May 1965

A Season in the Life of Emmanuel: 1966

Emmanuel is the sixteenth child of a French-Canadian farm family, and this novel is the story of their life during his first year. The day he is born, Grand-mère Antoinette tells him that he can give his life into her keeping, and we feel sorry for the child immediately. His mother is a child-producing drudge, his father a lustful illiterate, but Grand-mère is that dreariest of fictional characters, a peasant philosopher.

Emmanuel has several brothers, of whom the most interesting is Jean LeMaigre, a tuberculous genius who feeds on the vitality of an unfortunate junior usually called Number Seven. Both Jean LeMaigre and his sister Héloise are ravaged by unappeasable sexual craving, but Number Seven, who seems to be about twelve, has taken to drink. Jean LeMaigre is sent to a noviciate, where his death is hastened by an incompetent and homosexual infirmarian; Héloise is cast out of a nunnery and accepts an appointment in a bawdy house.

Another brother, Pomme, loses three fingers in a shoe factory; Number Seven finds his vocation as a thief; Jean LeMaigre writes some admirable biographical letters and dies; Héloise establishes herself in her new life, where she displays her crucifix prominently over her bed, among the lewd photographs. These are the main events in Emmanuel's first year, and they are played out with high passion against a background of squalor, ignorance, and spiritual destitution.

Unquestionably, this is piling on the agony, but Marie-Claire Blais relates her grotesqueries with such vigorous and compelling fantasy that most of the time we are acquiescent. Not at all times, however. We grow restless, and wish that some of the horrors could be pruned away, and others controlled so that our shudders and waves of pity might be cumulative in effect, not merely spasmodic. We wish – and a dangerous wish it is, for it might seriously impair her talent – that Mlle. Blais had a dash of humour in her composition, so that she could tell a gothic phantom from a Halloween pumpkin. But in the end we are grateful for another display of her uncommon talent, even though we wish it would grow, and not be content to proliferate.

It is futile to wish for these things. Mlle. Blais is a genius – that is to say, a writer with an extraordinary capacity for imaginative creation, subject to laws of her own, and not amenable to discipline. Still in her twenties, she began publishing novels in her teens. Already she can sound a string that few writers possess, and she can tell a tale we want to hear to the end, even though we sometimes laugh in the wrong places. To expect her to have the gifts she possesses and a self-critical faculty as well is perhaps to ask too much. We must accept her as she is.

Her earlier books (*La Belle Bête*, *Tête Blanche*) took us by surprise, because of the special imaginative colour they displayed. She seemed to be writing a modern version of the gothic novel of the first years of the nineteenth century. But those first books were not attached to any place, or to any specific time, though anyone who knew Quebec could find a flavour of that province in them. *A Season in the Life of Emmanuel* is recognizably a Quebec novel, and there are dangers in this local attachment.

To be blunt, the book uncomfortably suggests that large group of novels that Stella Gibbons knocked on the head in 1932 with *Cold Comfort Farm*. Nobody in those books was a homosexual, so far as I can recall, and nobody actually got to the point of masturbating, or ravishing a hunchback, but the flavour was the same: Nature was morose, and Man was vile. The revival of this sort of novel in our post-Gibbons era is dangerous even to a talent so strong as that of Mlle. Blais, and we hope she will think better of it when next she publishes.

"Cold Comfort Farm," *New York Times Book Review*, 21 August 1966

Letters: The Unfashionable Canadians: 1967

Our national attitude towards literature is ambiguous. We ask gloomy questions about it: where is our great poet? when will we produce a novel that cultivated people everywhere will think it necessary to read? when will our writers reveal our national identity? But when a book which is unmistakably about Canadians appears – Hugh MacLennan's *The Watch That Ends the Night* or Douglas LePan's *The Deserter* to name two – it is greeted with some embarrassment. Our demand for a national literature is like an outcry for portrait painters in a country where nobody wants to be a sitter.

This is only to say that in respect to literature Canada is still a naive country. Literature is, of course, the art of which anybody who can read considers himself to be a judge. We are relatively sophisticated in matters of painting, architecture, and music, and we are hospitable to performing artists who reveal to us the treasures of other cultures. But we are not yet comfortable with creative artists who may draw inspiration from some familiar and perhaps unflattering local source, or from the unexamined depths of the spirit; writers, beyond all other artists, belong to this group. As a nation we detest the kind of introspection that a serious national literature provokes.

Why do we fear self-examination? Why are we prepared to accept almost any belittling terms for ourselves as a people – colourless, second rate, dowdy – rather than embark on that journey towards the truth which so many other nations have made by means of a national literature?

When this question arises there is much talk of our innate conservatism. It is thought to be this quality that led us to refuse an invitation towards autonomy in 1776, and again in 1812. We were loyal to Britain in the spirit of the daughter who chooses to stay at home with mother. Mother accepted the loyalty, but thought her daughter a spiritless creature. As for the United States, it treats us with the scrupulous politeness we reserve for those from whom we must conceal the fact of their own second-rateness. We have no right to complain of either of these attitudes; we have brought them upon ourselves.

We are beginning to dislike our situation, and we have indulged in orgies of self-blame that are superficially like criticism, but cure nothing. We have even begun to ask some of the questions that may bring us to a better understanding of what Canadian literature may be in the future. But if we are to go far with that work, we must recognize that the Canadian literature of the past was better and more significant than most of us have understood.

I write these words in a room above the Library of Massey College, which contains about 4,000 volumes of Canadian fiction and poetry. Almost everyone who visits it is surprised by the extent of the collection, which is nevertheless only a little more than half-way to completeness. Why do so many of us assume that our Canadian past was meagre in literary production? "Ah, but where are the *great* books?" say some visitors, shaking their heads regretfully, as though my failure to pick from the shelves a Canadian *Chartreuse de Parme* or *War and Peace* reduced the whole collection to insignificance. The answer must be that the great books are where they were in an English library in 1350 – they are in the future, but their roots are all about us. Some of these roots are stronger and more promising than any but a handful of well-read enthusiasts suppose. After all, the decision to offer a course in Canadian Literature in the Honours English School of the University of Toronto was taken only in December 1964, and in our day the general taste in reading follows the universities to a remarkable and somewhat undesirable extent.

How good are these Canadian books of the past? I can answer only by analogy. How recently have you read a book by any of the following: Bjornstjerne Bjornson, Selma Lagerlof, K.A. Gjellerup, Knut Hamsun, F.E. Sillanpaa, Henrik Pontoppidan? If some of these writers are unfamiliar to you, let me explain that I have chosen them because they have all been winners of the Nobel Prize for Literature, which surely establishes their credentials. But I can find books for you by Canadian writers which are in my opinion, fully up to the standard of these.

Why then has there been no Canadian winner of this literary

award? I think the answer must be that Canadians are not a fashionable people; the rest of the civilized world does not look to us for nourishment for the imagination, or cheer for the heart. You disagree that nations can be classed as fashionable and unfashionable? How then do you account for the enthusiasm for Irish and Scottish books which was so striking a circumstance of the literary scene during the last ten years of the nineteenth century, and which has persisted in the case of the Irish, while failing in the case of the Scots? How else account for the interest in Scandinavian writing during the twenties? How else account for the failure of even so enthusiastic a publisher as Alfred Knopf to interest this continent in South American novels, demonstrably of excellent quality, except by saying that South America is not a literary fashion? Canada is unfashionable. No writer who, like myself, has been invited to change the location of a play from Canada to the United States, in order to improve its chances of interesting a large public, can doubt it.

Will you accept my assurance that there are already in existence a creditable number of Canadian novels of merit, allowing that no work of superlative merit has yet appeared? Our poetry has been generously praised – perhaps over-praised – but our writers of fiction, history, and *belles lettres* have had less than their due. If in their works the roots of a future literature may be discerned, what will it be like?

There are strong indications that it will be less a single literature than a group of regional literatures, among which one may achieve supremacy. People who talk loosely of Russian literature rarely reflect how much of it comes from a comparatively small area to the northwest of that country. Canada's literary growth might equally well be most vigorous in the Atlantic Provinces, on the Prairies or on the West Coast, and the likelihood is that readers beyond our shores will accept this regional literature as a portrait of the country as a whole.

For a considerable period it will be a literature of introspection, and much of it will certainly give pain to those who dislike self-analysis. But analysis it will be, if we are ever to see ourselves plainly and discover what we are. We have a consciousness of difference now; we know that we are not quite like our neighbours to the south, just as we are not Englishmen, or recognizable members of any of the other nationalities who have contributed heavily to our settlement. We must dig deep to find out what we are, and there are few people and fewer peoples with enough mordant humour to find deep exploration anything but painful. But if the work is undertaken honestly, the result is more likely to be good than bad.

Certainly we cannot count on self-exploration to support and corroborate some of our present self-honouring fantasies. Neither will it be that wholesale slaughter of sacred cows so dear to the hearts of the rebellious young; unfortunately people who set out to kill a sacred cow have in most cases some tuberculous animal they wish to put in its place. Rebellion and discontent may be the beginnings of self-analysis but they are not the forces that carry the work to a successful conclusion.

Regional in inspiration, introspective in tone, cleansing in effect—there is nothing extraordinary about any of this. But it must be remembered that Canada appears rather late in the day for literary innovation—so late indeed that one of Canada's most original thinkers, Marshall McLuhan, declares that the day of the book is already over. The book will probably last for a few centuries longer, even if in decline; Canada will certainly build a national literature on the foundations already laid, and as I have stressed, much better laid than is usually understood. There will be only one thing that will distinguish it radically from the literatures of other countries whose language is English: it will be ours. It will speak for us, and to us. The great question is, do we care?

So far we have not cared much. True, anxious questions are asked about what may be done to improve the status of the writer. This seems always to be phrased as though giving writers money would seriously improve their work. True, medals and awards are offered, but they are too many for the number of books we produce annually, and carry no importance in the eyes of the public. They probably do no good, and may do harm; too many mediocre books carry these laurels. But the questions are asked and the medals given by the 25,000 people in Canada who seriously care about the arts. The Canadian public at large, which has begun to concern itself with the arts that can be superficially appreciated without too much personal exertion, has not yet turned its eyes towards Canadian books, which demand a special and sometimes uncomfortable kind of attention. The serious writer speaks from deep feeling and can only be understood if he meets some sympathetic feeling in his reader; the writer speaks, and the reader must listen before he brings his critical faculty to work. Literature of quality is born of a union of serious writer with serious reader; it is understood, of course, that "serious" does not mean "solemn"; we are amply supplied now with the solemnity which is no more than pompous, joyless triviality.

Canada has had writers, and has them now, and they have not been trivial in their achievement. What Canada needs is serious, demanding readers. Before a nation demands masterworks it must be certain that it really wants them. Strong demand brings rich supply.

Century, 1867-1967: The Canadian Saga, edited by John D. Harbron, a Supplement to the *Toronto Daily Star*, 14 February 1967

Leacock as a Literary Artist: 1971

Stephen Leacock was a man of complex character, extensive formal education, and substantial vanity: any suggestion, therefore, that his most characteristic writing was what W.S. Gilbert called "A sudden ebullition of unmitigated jollity" seems to me to be totally mistaken. Yet the tradition of the naive Leacock persists, for the sufficient reason that he invented it and fostered it himself. Nobody who reads his work carefully is taken in by the tradition, but then–who reads his work carefully? You do, and I do, and we are not deceived. However, there are hundreds of thousands of Leacock's readers who are not members of our mystic and devoted group. They are middle-aged people who are either tired or think themselves tired, and who will read anything labelled Humour because they imagine that it will not tax their exhausted intellects. And there are a certain number of young people who think that Leacock is, on the whole, pretty poor stuff. Some of these are high-school students, and when I talk to them I find that their attitude towards Leacock is respectful, rather than admiring; they accept him as a pinnacle–a kind of Hamilton Mountain–in the broad, level steppes of Canadian Literature. Canadian literature is, as the schoolboy wrote about the works of Matthew Arnold, "no place to go for a laugh." But Leacock is still some place to go for a laugh and that is the quality that maintains his popularity, without adding to his reputation. Leacock's reputation is in the trough that gapes for the reputations of literary men after they have died, and from which reputations do not usually emerge for twenty-five years or so.

That emergence has begun. You and I, ladies and gentlemen, are the living proof of it. What are we doing here, on a Saturday afternoon–a portion of the week sacred to entertainment and refreshment–listening to serious discussion of Leacock as a literary artist? Why are we not at a football game, or a pornographic movie? Because we are pace-setters and trend-sniffers, that's why.

So let us to our holy task at once. Let us pace-set: let us trend-sniff. Let us see if we can find out anything about Leacock as a writer that we did not know before, and perhaps raise his reputation to higher ground.

He wrote a great deal of the work of his most productive period for magazines, and some examination of these magazines is illuminating, for they are of a kind now utterly out of fashion. Some of us here remember them; indeed, I remember them myself, from a period of my boyhood when the purchase of two or three magazines was a necessary preparation for a train journey. They were to be found in the reading rooms of clubs, in the parlour cars of trains, and of course in the offices of doctors and dentists. There were several of them; one of the most durable was *Judge*, which was a successor to *Puck*, and another was *Life*. In addition to the magazines with a predominatingly humorous bias, virtually all magazines that published fiction and articles of comment had a section for funny pieces; if you recall *Saturday Evening Post, Harper's, Scribner's, Vanity Fair,* and *The Atlantic Monthly* as they were in the twenties and thirties, you know the sort of thing I mean. And to Leacock the English publications were also a market; not only *Punch*, but *Pearson's*, and *The Strand* were interested in the kind of thing he wrote. Here in Canada was *Goblin*, which was not to be despised. Leacock had a large, well-paying market for his short pieces, and he cultivated it in a businesslike fashion.

I remember all of these magazines, for they all came to my home when I was a boy. It was not that my family were unusually devoted to periodical literature, but it was a way of getting whatever was new from the most popular writers of the day. Conan Doyle, P.G. Wodehouse, W.W. Jacobs, Stacy Aumonier, Roland Pertwee, Hugh Walpole, Somerset Maugham, Irvin Cobb, George Ade, Ring Lardner, Octavus Roy Cohen, Robert Benchley, Donald Ogden Stewart, Harry Leon Wilson – it was a remarkable list and perhaps the most remarkable thing about it from today's standpoint is that every one of these men thought of himself as an entertainer, as a man whose principal aim was to divert his readers, and not to hector, or depress, or bully them about that widespread modern disease The Human Condition. The readers responded with gratitude and fidelity, and the magazines paid their contributors highly, in terms of the times. Some of the writers I have mentioned – and I could have trebled the list – were artists, but all of them were craftsmen. They knew how to make themselves readable. Leacock was certainly a craftsman, and like all the rest he got what was to be gained from the magazines, and once a year he bundled up the year's successful productions and re-published them in a book with a catchy title, usually directed at the Christmas trade.

What were the conditions imposed on him by this sort of highly professional work? One, which should not be underestimated, is that he had to produce a substantial bulk of material, so that the editors, and the public, would not forget about him. Another was that he must not experiment too boldly, or write at a length unsuited to the pattern of the specifically funny sections of popular magazines, which usually contained a funny piece or two, and some light verse. Yet another was that he must not be too sharply satirical, for the prevailing mode in humour was playful and somewhat bland. *Punch* gives us a key to the taste of the day, as it existed on both sides of the Atlantic. The editor of *Punch* from 1906 to 1932 was Owen Seaman, who became a friend of Leacock's; Seaman combined in himself the best elements of an Edwardian popular humorist, for he was learned, perceptive, a brilliant parodist and versifier, and he had a sure grip on public taste. Seaman was also immovably opposed to anything that was even slightly off-colour, and he detested humour that had a cruel edge. Very little of what Leacock wrote appeared in *Punch*, and it is probable that Seaman thought his style outside the *Punch* range. But Leacock regarded *Punch* as a model, and in *My Discovery of England* he regrets his lack of that ability to write skilful light verse which was Seaman's particular glory. And Leacock certainly followed the *Punch* line in avoiding anything that was risqué in his writing. Now and then some hint appears in his work that he was aware of a world in which sexual irregularity existed; in *Arcadian Adventures with the Idle Rich* we get strong whiffs of it; but it was not a theme he explored. I think we must say that, like Owen Seaman, he thought it below the dignity of a gentleman. There was also the plain fact that such stuff did not sell in the market he had made his own.

Where did people turn for off-colour humour in those days?

The question is interesting now, when *Punch* has become almost as gamy as *La Vie Parisienne* used to be, and when there are plenty of publications that specialize in off-colour jokes. But during Leacock's heyday many daring young sprigs of the twenties turned to *College Humour* for sexually sophisticated humour. I remember it well; my elder brother never missed it, and I used to sneak his copy out of the drawer of his dressing-table and read it in order to acquaint myself with the way the world wagged. There were innumerable jokes between fraternity-house drunks who were comically called Frosh and Slosh; there were daring exchanges between girls who were called Debs and Co-eds about garments called Teddies; there were many pictures by John Held Jr. of boys and girls with heads like billiard balls and noses like cribbage pegs, who wore either Oxford bags containing hipflasks, or rolled stockings and Teddies. I remember one drawing of a girl shrugging herself into a transparent nightdress, under which was printed the words:

> *Highty-tighty*
> *Aphrodite*
> *Acting thus*
> *On Saturday nighty!*

It very nearly fused my entire nervous system for a week.

I recall yet another, which showed a tiny mouse looking with a speculative eye at a girl's legs. The verse was:

> *Hickory, dickory dock;*
> *The mouse ran up the clock.*
> *Good gracious, how shocking*
> *'Twas the clock of a stocking!*
> *Hickory dickory dock.*

Later, in my undergraduate days, when I was reading the works of Sigmund Freud, I realized that this was a sophisticated and deep rhyme, for it provided a diverted discharge of energy from the Primal Fear felt by all women that a mouse will run up their legs and impregnate them; it is of course a displacement from the fear of rape which is part of the Great Primal Fear that engulfs us all, and which manifests itself in the male as *Mausgeschlechtlich-likeitsbesorgnis* or Jealousy of the Superior Potency of Mice.

It was not to such racy pages that Leacock contributed; he seems to have had a fully Victorian sense of public propriety, and it would never have done for him. He was a thorough craftsman in writing for the best-paying market of his day, and if his books seem to us now to be composed of rather short-winded pieces, that is the explanation. Furthermore, if we can take the time to look back through the files of such magazines as *Judge* and *Life*, we see how superior Leacock's contribution was to most of what appears there. There is in every age a considerable amount of light literature that is amusing only so long as it meets the demands of a current fashion. Once that fashion has passed, it is as dead as any kind of writing can be – deader even than out-of-date theology.

But the point I am making – that Leacock paid careful attention to the demands of his market and established himself as a craftsman – is quite enough to dispose of any idea that he wrote naively. He was even less naive than Mark Twain, that hard-bitten old purveyor of fancy goods to the nobility and gentry. Mark Twain has left us a few things that he could not publish in his time, either because they were too dirty or too blasphemous; obviously he wrote them simply because he wanted to – because he could not help it. So far as I know, there are no Leacock manuscripts that have to be kept under cover until the right moment comes to publish them. Leacock seems never to have written anything he could not sell. During the latter part of his life, when his desire for money outweighed considerations of pride or propriety, he wrote advertisements – pamphlets and even books to order. To produce them Leacock had to trade on his name and reputation and he seems to have been a hard trader. He did not need the money; he was quite well off when he died, and lived in the kind of luxury he liked; he did not *need* it, but apparently he wanted it. As a craftsman he knew how to get it.

But I have undertaken to talk to you about Leacock as a literary artist. Had he anything that could be called artistry, and how did he exercise it? I think he possessed a considerable degree of conscious artistry, and I think he was fully aware of it. It may even be that he exaggerated it.

His artistry may be approached in terms of what it was not. He was not an artist in form. His frequent attempts at parody prove it. *Nonsense Novels* is one of Leacock's most popular books, and one of his funniest. It is quite funny enough to distract our attention from the fact that he meant its contents to be a series of parodies. But he never had the gift of the first-rate parodist. When we look at the work of the great parodists, like Max Beerbohm and Wolcott Gibbs, we see that their power comes from a thorough—indeed, almost an uncanny—appreciation of the style of the writer who is being parodied. Beerbohm certainly admired Meredith, Henry James, Shaw, Chesterton, Belloc, and the other writers of great attainment whose work he parodies in *A Christmas Garland*; even those whom he dislikes and despises, like Kipling, Wells, and Maurice Hewlett, he thoroughly understands. This is true also of Gibbs, who usually parodied writers he did not admire, but whom he deeply understood, and his satire is deadly. The form, the vesture of a man's mind, were very clear to Beerbohm and Gibbs, and they wrote as their subjects might have written if the gods had suddenly struck them with madness. Leacock cannot do that, and I doubt if he would have wanted to do it. The work of a great parodist is a combination of love, hate, derision, and a Protean ability to put on another man's style which is a rare and not entirely agreeable gift. Leacock's mind was certainly not simple, but it was strong, direct, and masculine; he did not want to strike any other man down with that man's own sword, which is what the parodist does; he would rather flatten the subject of his wrath with a sword of his own—or even with a club, if a club was more convenient. And so, although *Nonsense Novels* is a delightful book, and contains some of Leacock's best inventions, we do not think of it as a volume of parody. The fabric of Leacock's mind was all his own and he could not and did not want to disguise it.

He was not an artist in the creation of character, though if he had desired it I am sure that he could have been so. Two books of his are the work of a man who could have been a novelist—*Sunshine Sketches of a Little Town* and *Arcadian Adventures with the Idle Rich*—and in them we can find much evidence of the kind of observation and selection that are among the gifts of a man who seeks to create character. But these gifts are secondary to a principal quality which for want of a better term I shall call Impersonation. Leacock wrote about his people from the outside; he never got into their skins. And though they amused him, he did not really like them. The people in *Sunshine Sketches* were people he had left behind: in *Arcadian Adventures* they are people it gives him little pleasure to know. Has it ever occurred to you that there is not one character in either of those books to whom we would liken a person we did not wish to deride? Leacock's idol, Dickens, created scores of characters who are both absurd and immensely likable. Leacock, never. If I say to a man, "You remind me of Mr. Pickwick," he knows that Mr. Pickwick had a very foolish side to him, but on the whole he is pleased. But if I were to say to any one of you, "You put me in mind of Dean Drone, or Josh Smith, or Jefferson Thorpe," you would bear me a grudge to your dying day. And it is not because the people in these books are the creations of a young man; young men jeer at all sorts of people and flail about fiercely because they are trying to find out what they themselves are like. When Leacock wrote these books he was in his early forties, and if he was ever going to see more in his characters than their faults, that time had certainly arrived. Over and over again in his writings Leacock assures us that the greatest humour is kindly: over and over again much of his best work contradicts him. But a man who wants to be a novelist must see people, if not in the round, at least in the quarter-round; Leacock always saw them flat – very funny, but flat, and from above.

I should like to dwell on this aspect of his character and writing a little longer, because it is a sensitive area, and greatly open to misunderstanding. Last summer, on Dominion Day, the CBC broadcast a program about Leacock which contained some opinions about him by people in Orillia who had known him. One was a taxi-driver who, when asked if he liked Leacock, replied, "No, I didn't like him because he didn't like us." My response to this was: "Well, what about it? Why is it assumed that Leacock had to like the people of Orillia, or indeed anybody? We know that his family affections were strong, and that he had some friends whom he valued greatly. He was – except when his hot temper was aroused – courteous in his public demeanour. Why this suggestion that he somehow fell short of his duty in not liking everybody?"

The answer, I think, is that the obligation to like everybody is one that mankind lays on its humorists, and for a very good reason: humorists are feared. They are likened to capricious surgeons who may suddenly lance a boil at a party, or chop off somebody's leg at a dance. They have a gift which is not only delightful but somewhat uncanny, and they may exercise it without warning. Therefore we want our funny men to give us constant reassurance that they like us; that when they are with us, they will draw in their claws. They may say things that will not immediately be understood or which, if understood, will cause some humiliation, or even pain. I think this explains the general opinion that it is very much more praiseworthy to write tragedy, rather than comedy: everybody can, in some measure, comprehend what is sad, but not everybody understands what is comic.

Now Leacock was not only comic, but deeply ironic, as well, and the ironist is a man who says one thing and means its opposite; irony is to sarcasm what the stiletto is to the lash. Another of his characteristics was that he had little patience or sympathy with failure. Like many successful men, he seems to have thought that those who had not succeeded lacked either industry, gifts, or character. I do not propose to discuss the rights or wrongs of this point of view. I am content to point out that successful men who wish to be liked – politicians, for instance – use an impressive amount of their energy in persuading mankind in general that they are themselves very ordinary fellows whose success is the result of blind fortune – a mere fluke. Leacock had no time for that sort of thing. As I have already said, his character was powerfully masculine and essentially honest. He did not waste time in pretending to like people about whom he cared nothing unless there was some pressing reason to do so – if, for instance, they were his readers or his hearers at one of his immensely effective public appearances.

I hope that I am not making Leacock sound a hateful man; he was nothing of the kind. But in a very broad area he was an honest man, and he was also a wounded man. His childhood, which he associated with Orillia, had not been a happy one. Orillia may have meant to him a narrow world from which he had escaped, and to which he returned in triumph. None of this was Orillia's fault. The feeling was a subjective one, residing in Leacock.

As for liking everyone, a lot of dreadful nonsense is talked about that. It is part of an extremely watered-down and sentimental concept of Christianity, for which Leacock had no use at all. He was a Stoic, rather than a Christian. It may be noted in passing that Our Lord, when He hung upon the Cross between two thieves, did not feel moved to say that He liked them both. Leacock's somewhat haughty attitude towards the generality of mankind limited his art as a writer, but when has there ever been a writer upon whose limitations the critic did not delight to dwell? Let us talk of his strengths, and in my opinion the greatest of these – apart from the disposition of mind that made him a humorist – was his gift for language.

Leacock did not use language elaborately; he did not pluck all the strings of the harp. I think it would be false to suggest that he exercised a conscious art in his writing, and I base that remark on the commonplace and often muddle-headed stuff he wrote in his book *How to Write*; if he had himself written as he counselled the readers of that book to write, he would not have been half the man he was. His art seems to have been instinctive, but there is nothing wrong with that. When he tried to write with conscious art, as in the tricky little piece called *Number Fifty-Six* which he included in *Literary Lapses*, he was not in his best form. His best writing seems to take its rhythms and cadences from ordinary speech, but that is not to say that ordinary speech transcribed comes out as Stephen Leacock.

Sometimes people make the mistake of thinking that this is so, and they dramatize Leacock's short pieces by the simple expedient of extracting all the dialogue, and expecting it to be dramatic. The results are dismal. When Leacock wanted to write a play, he very sensibly collaborated with an experienced playwright, Basil Macdonald Hastings, and did the job properly. The result is the amusing and successful one-act farce "Q," in which the great comedian Charles Hawtrey appeared in 1915. In it we have dramatic dialogue that moves forward in a brisk fashion from beginning to end. In the amateur dramatic versions of which I speak, there is no progress, and often the action is barely comprehensible. It is because Leacock, like Dickens, wrote dramatically, but most of the drama lies in the portions that are not dialogue. Dickens does not dramatize effectively unless he is completely rewritten, with all the loss entailed therein, and the same is true of Leacock.

This rhythm of common speech is deceptive. Mark Twain had it. Dickens had it, too, though it is only one of the manners in which he could write, and the rhythm of Dickens' era, and Dickens' country, does not seem particularly colloquial to us here and now. But Leacock is a master in this prose of brief sentences, ordinary vocabulary and apparent simplicity. But what a variety of nuances he wrings from it! And what brilliant use he makes of that subtle rhetorical device, the Disappointed Climax! If you doubt me, try re-writing a characteristic piece of Leacock's prose, to see if you can say what he says in fewer and better words. Within a limited range, he has utter mastery, and I think we may deduce that it comes from an inborn feeling for his medium, rather than from any conscious art.

How do we deduce this? By reference to what Leacock says in that book *How to Write*. Personally I have little trust in books with such titles. People who can write, in any case I can think of, have taught themselves, by one means or another. But there is a confident tone in Leacock's title that puts me on my guard: to know that one can write oneself is an admission that one may make to oneself in the secret watches of the night, though it is better to receive the assurance from the outside world: but to assert that one can teach somebody else to write is to tempt the gods to visit their most exquisite ironies upon one's offending head. *How to Write* – it seems to echo other confident, hollow titles: *How to be a Success at Parties* or *How to be a Ventriloquist*.

How false it is, this twaddle about writing! It is hard enough to learn an interpretative art – playing the piano or the French horn, for instance. But to learn a creative art is an impossibility; a teacher may provide some hints, some cautionary words, but the creative artist teaches himself. Leacock taught himself: what possessed him to think he could teach others?

What his book called *How to Write* really teaches is not how Leacock wrote, but how he read. His taste in writing, as he reveals it in this book and in his other writings, was undistinguished. Dickens appears to have been the only writer of genius for whom he had unstinting admiration, and even in his biographical and critical book about Dickens, Leacock cannot take the trouble to get the names of Dickens' characters quite right, and from some of his judgements one is inclined to wonder if he had really read all of Dickens' work. He jeers at Shakespeare; he jeers at Ibsen. He had no ear for poetry, though he wrote some humorous verses himself that are by no means bad. He persistently misquotes poetry in *How to Write* – an inexcusable carelessness which any competent student could have helped him to avoid if he had thought accuracy important. Leacock seems to have admired, and recommended, O. Henry more than any other author of his day – a taste that the passing of time has rendered incomprehensible. He appears to have had a spotty knowledge of literature and no taste. I have already said that he was no parodist; parodists have great taste, and cannot get along without it.

Now I do not really believe that this matters in the least. It is a romantic delusion to suppose that writers all have the minds of professors of literature, that they refresh themselves by constant ecstatic gloating over the classics, and that they bring an exquisite critical consideration to the work of their contemporaries, and especially to new writers of promise. The biographies of authors of the highest rank show that they very often read little themselves, didn't like the classics, and loathed their contemporaries, especially the young and threatening ones. Writers are artists, and often men of strong and passionate nature; they are creators, not critics and appreciators, and the two types of mind are widely different. The fact that Leacock's taste was patchy and sometimes absurd makes no difference at all to his achievements as a writer: it does, however, mean that he was giving himself away with both hands when he wrote a book and called it *How to Write*.

On several occasions, on the platform and in print, I have said that Stephen Leacock was a genius, and by that I mean simply that he could do with comparative ease and repeatedly what most people cannot do by the uttermost application of their abilities. What he could do was to write brilliantly funny short pieces, that still delight us. He could also write in another vein – the vein of the essayist, in which his opinions about education, politics, and society are set down with vigour, and illuminated by the same brilliant perception of the absurdity of human pretension, the same wit and cogency, that make his purely funny writing great. He was an artist in his command of a colloquial, spare style that, even at its most extravagant, owes a great deal to the classical foundation of his education. He may be extravagant, but he is never baroque; in the true sense of the word, his best writing is chaste. But he could be false to himself, and when he became didactic – as in *How to Write* – that is what happened. He was himself doing what he mocked so shrewdly when others did it – he was pretending. But a genius he certainly was, and like many a genius he did what he did without being in the least able to explain how he did it. I say this with caution, for I do not want to be misunderstood: his primary gift was for feeling, not for thinking, and this was what lay behind his best writing. Writers *may* think, but they *must* feel.

A thinker may write, but he had better not write poetry or fiction. Bertrand Russell wrote fine prose but it was a pity that, towards the end of his life, he offered the public some facetious, wizened little short stories. Bernard Shaw, though unquestionably he thought, wrote his best plays from a ground of feeling. I stress this point because we in universities have a tendency to deal with literature in terms of thought – probably because it is easier to fake thought, both as professor and student, than it is to fake feeling. The trashiness of pretended feeling is easily detected; pretended thought evades detection for varying lengths of time, but sometimes it can fool the public for a generation or two.

Other speakers today have dealt with Leacock as a thinker, and you have heard what they have said. I have tried to talk about him as a feeler, as a man of emotions and sympathies which were not invariably of the broadest or the noblest, but which were strong and wholly his own. It was this Leacock – the man of feeling, and I may say the man of passion – who wrote the works that give him his place as a literary artist. Heinrich Heine wrote: "Out of my great sorrows I write my little songs." It was from his stoically endured disenchantments that Leacock wrote what he himself called "Funny pieces, just to laugh at."

University of Toronto Graduate, 3, No. 4 (1970-71)
An address given 31 October 1970 at "The Other Leacock," a symposium held at Massey College honouring the centenary of Leacock's birth.

Canadian Nationalism in Arts and Science: 1975

To speak effectively on such a theme as Canadian nationalism in the arts and sciences one ought really to be filled with zeal – zeal either for Canadian nationalism or against it. One ought to be able to draw a clear line between nationalism and patriotism. Now I, alas, have no zeal for what is commonly called nationalism; nationalism in the broad sense belongs to an area of Romance that has little appeal for me; therefore its relevance to art and science must be discussed with all the coolness I can command. As for patriotism, I am by no means wanting in it, but sometimes it brings me into company that reminds me of Dr. Johnson's dictum that it was the last refuge of a scoundrel.

I must control merely personal feeling, for nationalism is very much in the air at present. I can sympathize with its desires and respect its ideals. As the practical and pragmatic advance of internationalism continues on its Juggernaut course, I feel for the people who deeply desire a national home, rather than simply a geographical area; I understand their longing for a body of accepted belief and a common past; I know why they want to call some men brothers in a particular rather than in a general acceptance of the human state.

It is not as if Canada were the only country where such a desire asserts itself; nor is it the country where that desire is most intense. We need look no farther away than Scotland and Wales where the cry is: "See me not as a citizen of the world, not as a member of the Common Market, but as a man who lives in the light of a special heritage." This is the longing to be, if not unique in oneself, a partaker of a unique nationhood.

Extremists seem almost to seek a rejection of the European culture of the past 2,000 years: that greatest of cultures known to history, for it is scientific in scope as well as humane. Luckily they cannot reject it, any more than they can unscramble an omelette, but they can belittle and betray that great culture, and sometimes in their blind zeal they do so. It is not of extremists we need speak here, but of those who want a unique Canada without having any very clear notion of where uniqueness is to be found, or what form it may take.

We understand and we sympathize in principle, if not in full commitment. At a time when the world's population is growing at an astonishing and perhaps an alarming rate, and when the easy movement of the world's peoples produces what might be called a Blenderized Population in countries which once had a racial homogeneity, we may sometimes feel that things are moving too fast for us. And if we are not so much caught up in present fashions in idealism that we have lost the use of our eyes and ears, we are aware of undercurrents of resentment. We see race riots and racial persecutions not only as ugly evidence of prejudice, but as signs of an *idealism*, however perverse and ignorant in its application; the resentment is evidence of a sense of loss and a growing fear. Governments, those mighty purveyors of popular idealism and cheap, short-term philosophies, throw open their gates to new and unfamiliar peoples. (Or, if they do not actually throw them open, they leave them slightly ajar, and avert their gaze.) The appeal of homeless and unhappy children is given immediate attention; indeed, it is exploited without any apparent thought for what will happen in twenty years when these children may well have become disaffected and unappealing adults. Now many of the people who are represented by such governments express their fear and restlessness in "ethnic" jokes, and "Paki" jokes, and all sorts of jokes that leave a bitter taste in the mouth. Nobody dares to speak out against anything that is labelled humanitarianism, for humanitarianism has taken the unassailable place once occupied by Motherhood and the Flag. But the cry for a vigorous nationalism grows, and it is a cry *against* the popular trend. It is a cry for identity in a world that is moving towards Blenderized Man.

Does the cry come too late? I cannot tell you. Indeed, in what I am saying today I do not pretend to tell you anything: the most I shall be able to do is to state a few problems and perhaps clarify their nature. But if I may comment on the question I have just put — Does the cry for nationalism in Canada come too late? — I must say at once that Canada has always seemed to me to be a country which moves slowly in the realms of thought and feeling. We are not innovators and we are tenacious of whatever is familiar. When a cry for change is heard *here*, the hour is the eleventh hour.

The comparatively recent dispute about our national flag offers evidence of what I mean. When the question arose as to what our national flag should be – when we had discarded the Union Jack and the Red Ensign as evidences of our past, rather than our present state – we had a chance to lead the world by declaring that we would have no flag at all. For, after all, what is a flag? It is a banner formerly used in battle for identifying friendly forces; its present significance is that of a totem-object, used at ceremonials of a nationalist kind. Its nature, in our world, is divisive.

If we had chosen to declare that we would henceforward fly the United Nations flag, as a sign of our goodwill towards all men, we should have startled the world and greatly strengthened the hand of the United Nations. We should also have shown ourselves to be a nation of unique quality of spirit. What we did, in fact, was to haggle like a club committee choosing new curtains, and arrive at what looks very much like the creation of a committee. We also gave rise to a situation in which provincial flags, all rooted in a significant past, have achieved a popularity undreamed of before. The time came when we might have taken a giant step, but after a great deal of ungraceful clog-dancing, we remained very much where we had been before.

Let us learn from that experience. If we are sincere in our desire for national identity, we are going to have to move, and move rapidly, with a determination and clarity of thought that has not characterized us in the past.

In what direction? Fortunately I am not called upon to speculate on the whole of that question, but to talk only of Canadian nationalism in the arts and sciences. And at once I disclaim any intention of speaking about science, for I am wholly unfitted to do so. I shall go no further than this: if my colleagues in this discussion advocate a nationalist stand in matters of science, I'm a Dutchman.

That is a thoroughly Canadian declaration, by the way, for on my mother's side, and somewhat distantly, I am a Dutchman. So, like a real Canadian, I have protected myself before making any serious commitment.

But in the arts? Nationalism in the arts is thoroughly familiar. In painting, in music, and literature, we know of great achievements that seemed to spring from a particular national spirit. Even those of us who are simply amateurs are quite capable of telling an Italian picture of the Renaissance from a Rembrandt or a Hals. When we go to the opera we are in no danger of mistaking Verdi for Wagner or Debussy. These are obvious distinctions, but expert connoisseurs make distinctions so fine that we may doubt them, until they are suddenly shown to be correct by the discovery of some new evidence.

In literature we do not always talk of national schools, but we are seldom in any doubt about the place of origin of a work we know well. The world of literary criticism is a world in which refinement of sensibility is of uttermost importance, and if national considerations played no part in it, criticism would be the poorer, and an invaluable instrument for placing and assessing works of literary art would be lost. No, in the arts the question of nationalism is relevant; it is not to be confused with patriotism, the aggressive assertion that "our boys are better than your boys"; but it is like the distinctions that oenophilists make between the wine of one country and that of another. Perhaps I should add the proviso that the critic must not be dealing with either hocussed wine or hocussed literature, and both impostures are not unknown.

The Canadian problem is simply stated as: *Who are we?* Have we anything to say that others have not already said as well or better? Let me be bold enough to give an answer: We are who we are; we are the civilized people of the northernmost portion of North America. And what we have to say is what mankind has always had to say in its literature. The themes are Love, War, and Death; our task is to write of these things in our own way, without fretting about originality or novelty, which are both delusions. Every writer of worth, whether poet or novelist or dramatist, writes of the passions and aspirations of man as he sees them; originality lies in himself, far more than in the mode of life and racial makeup of the people he writes about; novelty lies in the quality of his perception rather than in eccentricities of form. If literature had always to be new, it would have stopped long ago with the composition of a few works of which the Bible, the epics of Homer, and the Arabian Nights come quickly to mind. But literature is renewed every time a writer of individual observation and understanding bends himself to his work, because he speaks to his time; and perhaps if he is a writer of high worth the time he speaks to extends well beyond the period of his own life.

But nationalism? Is it our first aim? I could tell you of national literatures, and great ones, of which we in Canada are almost wholly innocent. Argentina has such a literature, and what I have read of it in translation impresses me greatly. If you look over the list of winners of the Nobel Prize for Literature since it was first offered, you will be a learned man indeed if you do not discover the names of writers of whom you have never heard, or, if you have heard of them, of whose works you know nothing. Yet they were not solitary writers, but men who were judged, in some ways, to be the best their country had produced. In that same list you will notice omissions that will astonish you – the names of men worthy of international recognition to whom it was not accorded in this form. Nationalism is not in the centre of a discussion of literature, and works of literature that are most admired as national achievements are not always the best a country has to offer.

This is a hot subject, so I had better illustrate it with a cool example. Let us talk of Scottish nationalism, and one of its foremost exemplars, Sir Walter Scott. It is fair, I think, to say that the Scottish sense of national significance and self-esteem would not be what it is today had Sir Walter confined himself to the practice of the law. He was inspired by tales of Scottish gallantry, outlawry, and ambition that he heard as a child, and he touched these often bloody and unedifying chronicles with a splendid sense of romance. Where he found naked greed he offered it to the world as derring-do, and where the fearful interchange of women was the key to large tracts of real estate, Sir Walter represented it to the world as gallantry. Not everyone was deceived. I well recall as a young man discovering in the Bodleian Library an early nineteenth-century parody of *The Lay of the Last Minstrel*, the opening lines of which were:

> *The way was long, the mud was thick,*
> *The minstrel's name was Dirty Dick;*
> *The last of all the bards was he*
> *To sing of rape and buggery;*

Somebody, contemporaneous with Sir Walter, had a firm grasp on the realities that lay behind the romance. But as the romance was golden coin, and the realism was leaden, it was the romance that prevailed, and prevails still. Sir Walter, to a remarkable degree, invented the popular idea of archetypal Scotland. If you disbelieve me, walk along Princes Street in Edinburgh any summer day, and watch the American and Canadian tourists eagerly buying lengths of tartans to which they assert a romantic claim, and outfitting themselves with little tartan-bound histories of the clans, in which a version of history is offered that might fittingly be called Scott-and-water. They are asserting their claim to a national heritage more vivid and comprehensible than their own. And who would wish it otherwise? What Sir Walter gave to Scotland was a burning sense of national identity which the cruel facts of history had done much to wear away. Millions have sought to ally themselves with that national identity.

Was Sir Walter's picture false? No more false, I think, than if he had written of half-naked peasants starving under a cruel regime, with every instance of their degradation gloatingly detailed in the manner of a modern pseudo-realistic novel. Part of his achievement was his uniting in a picture of Scotland two races who felt themselves far apart in heritage and aspiration – the clansmen of the Highlands, and the dour, thriving folk of the Lowlands. The genius of the literary artist is, as Thomas Mann so often pointed out, not interested in common concerns of fact and balance; it is a poetic, coaxing, alchemical kind of genius, somewhat more akin to the spirit of the confidence man and the criminal than we care to think. Sir Walter had his own work to do. Did he, in his inmost heart, give a toss of a button for the advancement of Scottish nationalism? Read his *Journals* and answer the question for yourself.

He was, of course, through the circumstances of his time,

nearer to bedrock Scotland than any writer today. When he wrote, his quill may very well have come from an Abbotsford goose that he had known in its lifetime, and he wrote with ink made in Edinburgh on paper that was also made in Edinburgh. He was published by Scotsmen. But did these things make much difference? To Scott, as a literary artist, I doubt if they mattered at all. He did not write as he did because he was a Scot, but because he was Scott.

That is more than a play on words. Consider the great figures of other literatures; was the quality of their nationalism something external? Were Dostoevsky and Turgenev any less Russian when they were writing in Germany or Paris? Was not Ibsen at his most intransigently Norwegian when he was living in Rome? Which was the more truly Russian – Tolstoy when he was playing the peasant at Yasnaya Polyana, or Dostoevsky when he was playing the fine gentleman in Baden? What I suggest to you is that if national literatures are something above the triviality of, for instance, the Kailyard School in Scotland – an exploitation of dialect speech and provincial manners – they do not have their origins in national problems, but in men, who dare greatly in being themselves, and in whose achievements of self-realization their countrymen find something which they claim as a national possession.

The nationalism of Canadian literature, therefore, is not to be achieved by external pressures or ultra-nationalist posturings. It is not to be discovered in keys to survival. In saying so I do not wish to set myself against those people who strive for a better deal for Canadian writers and Canadian publishers, when they keep within the confines of common sense. I applaud their efforts to persuade the Canadian government to make some Canadian books available, through our ministries abroad, to people who might like to find out about us.

They have made notable progress. I recall that in 1947 an experimental theatre in Oslo wanted to perform a play of mine, and appealed to the Canadian Embassy in Norway for assistance in getting the details of setting, dress, and so forth as right as they might be. They received, not assistance, but a sharp warning that the Canadian Embassy discouraged the performance of my play, as in the opinion of the ambassador it did not present a fair picture

269

of Canada. That could not happen today. A wider sophistication prevails, even in government circles, and it is owing to the hard work of Canadians who have striven for a recognition of Canadian literature as something more than the hobby of a few hundred Canadians of uncharacteristic opinions and dubious loyalty. What such people can do is more than welcome to all Canadian writers. What has been done through such agencies as the Canada Council has given Canadian writing firmer ground under its feet. But not all the goodwill in the world, and not all the funds of the Canada Council from now till the year 2000, can produce a single Canadian book of worth. Only a writer can do that. And the book he writes will be first of all a fine book: only in a secondary sense will it be a Canadian book.

Will it offer some clue to the Canadian identity? First of all it will establish the identity of the writer: only in a secondary sense will it establish an identity recognizable in other Canadians. But it *will* do that, have no doubt about it.

At this point I ask leave of those among you who are scientists to talk in a fashion that may seem to you irrational. But I assure you that my irrationality arises only from the fact that I cannot establish a clear line of reasoning from my causes to my effects. If I were writing a novel or a play, I should have no problem whatever at this point: I should simply assert what I want to establish with as much persuasiveness as I could muster, hopeful and pretty confident that I should carry you along with me, and convince you without a lot of tedious and wholly unnecessary reasoning. But I am aware that this is the Royal Society, and that I must offer some poor scraps of logical argument, or risk being thrown out as an impostor. Be at ease: I am sure that when my scientific colleagues speak to you they will give you all the logic and reason you can possibly want. They are experts at fitting causes to effects. Of course, I know their secret: it is precisely the same as my own. I know it because Professor Polanyi once confided it to me in a moment of friendly indiscretion. "You scientists," I said to him, "are awesome reasoners, but do you ever –?" and I paused. "Of course we do," he said. "We get a good idea and we simply know it's true; we feel it in our bones; when we are certain of it, we construct whatever logical scaffold is needed to support it." There, you see. That cat is out of the bag. That's what I do, too, except that I have not the scientist's persuasive skill in reasoning. I just say what I know to be true.

Canadian identity, I dare to assert, will follow the leads given to it by Canadian literature, and the other arts as they emerge in Canada. You see how it works elsewhere. Did anyone before Cervantes see the qualities of Don Quixote in the Spanish people? No, but plenty of people do so now, and they are not wrong. Don Quixote is there to be seen, not because some disingenuous Spaniard is acting a role to make himself interesting, but because Cervantes gave birth to a portion of his soul, fetched it up out of the unconscious and made it known to the world – including Spaniards who had not previously been aware of a whole train of kindred response in themselves.

Dickens invented a great many Englishmen, in the sense that he made it possible for us to see them, and we can all spot Mr. Micawber, and Rosa Dartle, and Scrooge, and Miss Havisham, and Dick Swiveller, and Dolly Varden, when we meet them now – and meet them we do, in modern dress and speaking in the most up-to-date lingo. And don't we meet people, as we say, "out of" E.M. Forster and Arnold Bennett, to speak only of writers who are dead? Would American sensibility be what it is now without Mark Twain, yes, and Henry James, and Sinclair Lewis and – the list could go on for a long time. I say nothing of the literature of France, or of Russia, or of many another nation; you can draw up the lists for yourself. It is not that authors invent these people; they release them, and when they have been released everybody can see them, as they can see the figures Michelangelo released from marble. But who saw them when the marble was still in the quarry? Who sees national character until poets and novelists have shown it to be there?

Will Canadian writers do this? Of course they will. Indeed, I assert that they began long ago, and that if we read widely in the very considerable body of Canadian writing in both our principal languages we shall find a Canada and a variety of Canadians that will surprise us. Last Saturday I had a conversation with Sir John Betjeman, the Poet Laureate: he had just finished reading *The Oxford Book of Canadian Verse* and what he found in it of Canadian individuality of mind and poetic inspiration delighted me. But, I thought, it takes an Englishman, and a very special English-

271

man, to see that. How many Canadians have seen it? Until very recently the fault has lain with Canadian readers, rather than with Canadian writers. The readers in my youth picked up a Canadian book with two conflicting emotions: they powerfully desired that it would be the Great Canadian Novel or the Great Canadian Poem – there was apparently only to be one of each – but they were tormented also with a conviction that they were in for another disappointment. They wanted *War and Peace* or *The Excursion* in Canadian terms, and of course they didn't get it, and assumed that what they had actually been given was of less value than was often the case. They mistrusted themselves, and as is so often the case with people who mistrust themselves, they could not see what was in front of their noses.

The situation today is changed. Courses in Canadian literature are common in our high schools and universities. They are, of course, extremely variable in quality. Like every other Canadian writer, I am accustomed to being summoned to the telephone by some plaintive high-school student who tells me that he has to present an analysis of my work that will satisfy his teacher within the next few days, and will I please tell him what to say? He has read one or two of my books, and he wants to know what other writer – English or American – I model myself upon, where I get my plots from, and if I copy my characters from people I know. If I speak of imagination, he grows impatient. He doesn't believe in imagination. He is especially troubled by my attitude towards life and fate, and would like to have it explained, so that he can write it down. He charges me with irony, mysticism, and other crimes against comprehensibility. He is especially severe about my regrettable sense of humour and asks me solemnly if I think it will work against the eternal endurance of my books.* Will I defend my proneness to these objectionable lapses? I do the best I can for him because he represents a hope. It is a hope that Canadians will learn to take some pride in their own literature. Because, although the questions I have just told you about are the usual ones (and I swear that I have not invented or coloured them), every now and then a student calls who is really excited about literature, who

*If I say I don't expect to last forever he scorns me: if I don't expect immortality I am obviously one of those base creatures who writes only for the big money it notoriously brings.

understands what a writer is saying to him, and who feels that the literature of his country is a live thing. He takes writing seriously. That is of the uttermost importance. He takes writing seriously, and not with a shallow solemnity, which has for too long been the Canadian response. I was greatly struck a fortnight ago to read an interview in the Toronto *Globe and Mail* with one of the greatest writers of our day, Isaac Bashevis Singer. Singer writes in Yiddish, but his stories are translated into English for the delight of those of us who know no Yiddish. They are splendid expositions of the timeless problems and joys of mankind, and because many of them are laid in the Poland of the nineteenth century, and are about poor but devout Jews whose culture is at once narrow and deep, they rely on rabbinical attitudes and Polish-Jewish folklore to give substance to the thoughts and actions of the people in them. What did the *Globe* say? "He relies heavily on the supernatural beings, the imps, the dybbuks, the demons of Jewish folklore in his stories so that one is never sure how seriously to take him." In other words, he does what so many great writers have done: he calls upon the unseen, insubstantial but very real world of the psyche to support and explain the actions of his characters.

Can one take him seriously, the very Canadian interviewer asks us. My reply is, yes, take him with the uttermost seriousness, because he is talking about the things that really count in the idiom in which they are most cogently expressed. He is talking about the soul of man, and before he can do that the writer must swim in strange waters. Whatever the intellectual fashion of the day may be – and we live in a country where the depths of the spirit are too often sealed wells, and where the human psyche, which is the womb and matrix of all great art, including poetry and great fable, is regarded with mistrust – the writer who speaks profoundly of himself, and in doing so speaks profoundly of his fellow men, must make the descent into the depths of the spirit where he finds not only himself but his people.

If he does so, should we, in the words of the *Globe*'s writer, "take him seriously"? If we don't, we do not deserve to have him among us. We are worse than a people who mistrust art: we are a people who mistrust life.

The turn that my argument has taken reminds me that this

year we celebrate two centenaries that are relevant to what I am saying; 1875 saw the birth of Carl Gustav Jung on July 26, and Thomas Mann on June 6. Perhaps I may make so bold as to offer Jung to my scientific colleagues, for although he probed some very strange realms, he insisted all through his life that he was a pragmatist and a scientist, and the pattern in which he presented the fruits of his research was, as it was with Sigmund Freud, scientific. Mann was, of course, one of the great writers of the past century whose explorations of the German spirit, and the European spirit, were always part of an inner journey of his own, never more feelingly described than in his great address given in 1936 in celebration of Freud's eightieth birthday. (It was like Mann to choose the occasion also to make a handsome tribute to Jung, which must have astonished the guest of honour no little.) I speak of these men because they are relevant to my subject and to the position of our country and its literature now.

Canada is not going to have a national literature in the mode of those European lands where a long history has bound the people together, and where a homogeneous racial inheritance has given them a language, customs, and even a national dress of their own. We are not an externally picturesque people: we are a people of today, upon whom the marks of the nineteenth century are still clearly to be seen. But Canada has at present, and may have in greater measure in the future, a literature fully national in being the work of writers who have made an inner exploration which has taken them to the depths of their innermost being, where they have discovered not only truths about themselves, but truths that are relevant, revelatory, and healing about the people among whom they live. If we hope to understand their work, and make it part of our national heritage, we must take them seriously – seriously as the interviewer in the *Globe* doubted that Isaac Singer could be taken; we must be prepared to find ourselves discussed in terms which may seem strange, but are not for that reason untrue. For we are the heirs of Jung and Mann, and must recognize that the great literary explorations of the future will be made by the inner journey, and not only on the great waters and the uncharted portions of our land. And these writers will speak not of a single, racially coherent nation, but of a nation that belongs to a constantly growing international community.

We must do what we have until now been reluctant to do in our artistic life. We must forgo our trust and delight in the surface of things. We must explore and sound our depths, and we must embrace our modernity, for only through that can we discover whatever there is about us which belongs to all time and all men.

Proceedings and Transactions of the Royal Society of Canada, Series 4, Volume 13 (Ottawa: Royal Society of Canada, 1975)

The Manticore: 1977

You ask me to tell the readers of *The Advocate* why, when I wrote my novel *The Manticore*, I chose to make its principal character (its hero, I suppose one must say) a lawyer.

This is a much more complicated question than I at first supposed. To begin with, I did not *make* David Staunton a lawyer; he was a lawyer when he first appeared in my imagination. Authors do not – or perhaps I should be more modest and say this particular author does not – outfit characters with professions or physical characteristics; when the author is pondering the story he means to tell, the characters appear with all these things complete. The author's job is then to make the acquaintance of the character, and write about what he does and what he feels, either from the point of view of the character himself, or from an outside, objective position. I chose to write about David from inside, because I came to know him well.

This is what makes it hard for me to answer your question, which implies that David has no autonomy. He is not my creature; by that I mean that I cannot write about him in any way I please, or make him do anything that occurs to me. Characters, when they appear to an author, have a fate and a mind of their own, and woe betide the author who goes against it, for the falsity of what he has done will weaken his novel, or his play, or whatever it may be. This does not mean that authors are haunted people, recorders of an inner film; it means that creative thinking happens below the level on which mere whim has relevance.

Why was David Staunton a lawyer? There are many answers. First, he was the son of a rich man and had to find a place in the world where such a person might fit in; not all professions are open to the rich and socially prominent. Next, he was by nature suspicious and cynical; such a temperament would rule out medicine, because a doctor may have reservations about his patients, but he certainly must not dislike them. Law and architecture are the professions for those who wish to keep people at a distance. Consciously or unconsciously, this is why many people choose to be lawyers. Undoubtedly David's impulse came from a desire to have work in which his powerful, attractive, persuasive, multimillionaire father could not interfere; this might have been so if David had become a corporation lawyer, but he chose to be an advocate, a courtroom gladiator, and he proved to be a very good one. For the advocate, his relationship with his client is intimate yet not affectionate; his most important work is done in solitary combat, however many assistants he may rely on before he goes into court. The reputation or fame he achieves attaches to him alone, because in his hours of courtroom glory he cannot rely on his background, his wealth, or on anyone else's influence. He is a star of a particular kind, and David wanted to be a star because he did not want to be obliged to his father.

Most of all, David loved the ambiguity of his profession. Although he made his decision to be a lawyer with some idealistic notions of championing the right, he soon learned that the concept of right as it appears in the courts – not as it appears in the written law – is inextricably mingled with the character and achievement of the lawyers involved. If a murderer is on trial, and his lawyer is a star, the murderer stands a better chance than if his lawyer is a careful, learned, scrupulous man who, however, has no gifts as a spellbinder and who desires that strict justice may be done more than he desires to win his case. David wanted to win, and he did win often enough to make him a lawyer with a particular sort of reputation – the reputation of a winner.

This is not to say that he was a crook. A winner need not be a crook, but he may sometimes put victory above what he would regard, if he were seated on the Bench, as strict justice. He puts victory above everything else. The great advocate is not engaged in the work which will make him the richest kind of lawyer; corporation work will bring him greater rewards. But the great advocate is in an ambiguous, sometimes dangerous, and potentially shady area of legal practice. He may rise to a fame the corporation lawyer cannot rival, and among the criminal classes he is revered as a wonder-worker whose brilliance of mind and powers of persuasion may represent the Last Chance to somebody who is in deep trouble.

I have never been in deep trouble of the kind that puts people in the dock. But if I were, and had to choose a lawyer, I would certainly not ask the man of my choice, "Are you honest?" Not a bit of it! My question would be, "Are you a winner?"

Why was David so eager to be a winner? The year with an analyst that reveals his life and character in *The Manticore* goes deeply into that question. He wanted to top his father, and in his legal character that is what he did. But he was not a happy man. Indeed, he sought the help of the analyst because he knew himself to be a drunk, and feared that he might lose his mind. Why was that?

It was because of the ambiguity that lay at the heart of his character. He wanted to rise triumphant above his father because he hated him for what he had done to his mother and himself. For those who have not read the book – and few of the lawyers I know are great readers of novels – I should explain that David's father, Boy Staunton, had neglected and destroyed his wife because he discovered that she could not keep up with his own intellectual and social advancement; and Boy Staunton had dominated his son even to the extent of interfering in and destroying his earliest love affair, when David was young, defenceless, and idealistic. Reason enough to hate him. But complex people do not regard their parents with a single emotional bias. As well as hating his father, David loved him, because from infancy his father had exemplified for him an ideal of manhood. Boy Staunton was clever, suave, attractive, and successful; in fact, a really great winner. To be torn between love and hate of the same person is ambiguity indeed, and quite enough to make a man rebellious, cynical, a drunkard, and perhaps – if things go too far – a madman.

If, in the pages of *The Advocate*, this should come to the notice of any subtle legal minds, I am sure they will smile that covered smile which is a special possession of lawyers, and decide that I am an extremist who sees life in absurdly vivid colours. Of course I am; I am a novelist and I do not see life in shades of legal grey, but I see it through what I must call the artist's temperament, though I dislike that phrase. I know that modern advocates do not bray at juries in the gaudy rhetoric of the nineteenth-century spellbinder. Indeed I know many lawyers – some of them successful – who can hardly put a grammatical sentence together and whose voices in the courtroom are scarcely audible. I know, too, that the old-fashioned notion of "a madman" is quite out of tune with modern psychiatric treatment; the raving lunatic is a rarity nowadays, and when he occurs he embarrasses his doctors. But I do know that great modern advocates have their own rhetorical devices that are just as subtle and delusive as those of the kind of barrister caricatured by Dickens as Sergeant Buzfuz. And I know that the suffering of the man who is under treatment for what we call a nervous breakdown is fully as agonizing as that of the madman rattling his chains in Bedlam. It is the externals that have changed, not the reality.

So there you are. David Staunton was a lawyer because the profession gave scope to the ambiguity that lay deep in his nature; as a lawyer he could appear as a champion of justice and at the same time flirt with criminality. He was a just man, yet he feasted with tigers. Such ambiguity is delightful, but it has its price, and for David the price might have been ruin.

Are any readers of *The Advocate* headed towards the law because of some ambiguity deep in their own souls? I have my own opinion, but of course it is a novelist's opinion and could not possibly be accepted as evidence in a court. But if I were studying law I would ask myself that question before I sat for my Bar examinations.

"Lawyer as Protagonist: A Star of a Particular Kind," *The Advocate* (the magazine of the Students' Law Society at the University of Toronto), 12, No. 1 (1977)

The Novels of Mavis Gallant: 1978

Mavis Gallant's novels are so much in the modern mode that if we approach them carelessly we are apt to see them merely as explorations of the shadow side of life, resolutely turning their backs on any hint of the heroic or the romantic. But as we read we become aware that they are finely shaped, and at the farthest extreme from those works which hope to suggest the incoherence of life by a want of artistic form; these three novels are classically spare, their feeling for the significant detail is unerring, the tone controlled, ironic, and wryly humorous. Her novels, like her short stories, are works of art, and produce in the reader the special, unmistakable satisfaction that belongs to literary art.

They are marked by lucidity, elegance, and individuality. These qualities are not to be achieved unless they are inherent in the writer's mind; art may refine and polish them, but it cannot bring them into being. Individuality is the product of the other two, for writers are never lucid and elegant in the same way, and the inimitable quality of a good writer's prose may only be analyzed up to a point. Mavis Gallant's stories of miserable women stand apart from most writing of the kind because there is no current of anti-masculine grievance in them – no sound of an axe being remorselessly ground without ever achieving an edge; they are pathetic and compassionate, but they are also reserved in tone and touched with a humour that is ironic rather than exuberant. The language of literary criticism fails me in describing Mrs. Gallant: I must resort to calling her a cool customer – never a tough customer, but a cool one.

The three novels – *Green Water, Green Sky* (1959), *A Fairly Good Time* (1970), and *The Pegnitz Junction* (1973) – are all stories about women who love unworthy men, but who are themselves in some way difficult to love. Is this the fashionable theme of the difficulty of making communication? No, nothing quite so simple. What these women are is not wholly their own fault, but we feel that they might, with a little more self-knowledge and resolution, have managed things better. In the earliest novel Florence is in a sense her mother's creation, and her mother is a fool; Flor might, with a very little more luck and good sense, have escaped her toils. But Flor is a clock that never strikes twelve; she is too indolent to escape, and she is a victim of her own beauty, which can be a terrible betrayer of the weak. In the second novel Shirley is another woman marked by her mother, who is the sort of woman who, when her hopeful daughter sends her a bluebell to stir a happy memory, sends her a cold reply, complaining that the flower is "sadly macerated . . . next time you send a specimen press it between two sheets of clean paper and please don't forget the leaf." It is no wonder that Shirley is on the lookout for love and cannot resist even the least probable facsimile. In the third short novel Christine is engaged to a theological student but cannot resist a week in Paris with the reasonable Herbert, and his awful child, Little Bert. What sort of a girl seeks romance with a man who insists on lugging the child of his broken marriage along with them? Christine is precisely that sort of girl, and what she gets is a man without faith but full of remorseless principle, and a mockery of love which is little more than grudging submission.

Mrs. Gallant does not use these highly coloured expressions about her characters; she makes her reader use them, and that is her art. She deploys, displays, exhibits, and leaves the judgements up to us, but there is never any doubt as to what our judgement must be. I cannot say what a woman reader might make of Flor, Shirley, and Christine, but I find them all charming, pitiable, and painfully recognizable. They are women who never have any of those strokes of luck which illuminate the lives of even very unlikely people.

The world in which they move is the world of the wretched who have no suspicion that they are wretched. They are never serious, though they are often solemn; they are never thoughtful, never aware of anything in life greater than the fulfilment of their small desires. And of course they are unhappy — not deeply unhappy, for nothing about them is deep, but unappeasably and crankily wistful. They are unhappy in the mode summed up by

Santayana: "Happiness is impossible, and even inconceivable, to a mind without scope and without pause, a mind driven by craving, pleasure or fear." Appalling as such a world sounds, it is made by Mavis Gallant to yield some splendid comedy. In *A Fairly Good Time* Shirley has lost her first young, adventurous husband, and has lucklessly got herself married to and estranged from Philippe Perigny, a French journalist and television know-all who also functions as "Bobby Crown," a jazz columnist; he is an intellectual of the kind that flourishes in the lower branches of the media, and his serious pursuit is the analysis of such nursery rhymes as "Goosey, Goosey Gander," which he is convinced contains arcane references to Churchill, to the African Problem, and the whole great mystery of Fathers Supplanted By Sons. We see Philippe against the background of his French bourgeois family – his mother who lives in dread of cancer (caused by eating meat and restaurant food) and who is a great self-doser and indigestion crank, and Sister Colette who is a hairdresser and liver hobbyist. Mrs. Gallant is brilliant in her portraits of the French middle class; rarely have we met such a rabble of overbearing, malignant mothers, such tyrannical fathers, loutish inlaws, and odious children. Are we surprised that Shirley seeks love from a Greek who has no love for anyone but his handsome self? Poor Shirley is a tender-hearted victim, a giver and a loser and, alas, a slut.

How different she is from the elegant, beautiful Flor of the first novel, whom we follow from adolescence through adulthood, marriage, and eventual madness. The narrative method in this book is simple only in effect; it is complex in structure, for we see Flor through the eyes of her cousin George, when he is seven years old and again when he is eighteen; we see her as her silly, shallow mother Bonnie sees her, and we see her as she appears to Wishart, a phoney and a sponger, who plays the role in Bonnie's life of "the chosen minstrel, the symbolic male, who would never cause 'trouble.'" Wishart is a fine creation, a man who lives off women not because he serves as a lover, but because he can be depended upon never to offer anything but bitchy wit and a masculine shell. To Wishart, Flor is simply a nuisance, a source of expense, needing money that might far better be spent upon himself. The nearest thing to a lover in Flor's life is Bob Harris, whom she marries; but he will not do for Bonnie, because he is a Jew, collects art that will rise in price, and counts how many Christmas cards he sends. No one is ever near to Flor, though she declares that she loves her mother. The novel is an exploration of the fashionable theme of unrelatedness but it goes deeper than a merely fashionable writer could take it. We are not told about Flor's want of feeling offered or accepted; we are allowed to infer it from what people of widely different sensibility tell us. "You see how pointless it is to fix any blame," says Doris Fischer, an American girl who seems for a time to have reached something real in Flor; her remark might serve as an epigraph for the book.

In *The Pegnitz Junction* Christine and Herbert are, or think themselves to be, lovers, but they are far apart. They must end their Paris holiday on a day when the planes are on strike, and as they endure their twelve-hour journey back to Germany by train, they are lost in reverie, whenever Little Bert ceases his demands for stories and diversions. Reverie about each other? Not at all. Herbert is thinking about his divorced wife; Christine fantasizes about the houses she sees out of the window, and about people she sees from the train. Not only are this couple wanting in communication and sympathy – they lack any real will to achieve these things. Living through her dismal adventure with Herbert, Christine is intellectually faithful to her theological student, and is reading Bonhoeffer on the sly. What brings this unlikely couple together? What supplies the resolution to make a journey to Paris to share a bed? Little Bert is likely to intrude during the night, and take a good, considering look at Christine's naked flesh, but this seems to be part of the affair. There is a human need at the root of their miserable adventure, but it is not of the sort that overcomes the grotesque nature of their situation. They are strangers of the worst kind – strangers caught in a pretence of intimacy.

Mavis Gallant is a Canadian by birth; much of her education and some of her earliest experience as a writer took place in this country. She has lived much of her life in Paris, and her chief reputation has been made in the United States. Is it absurd, then, to suggest that there is something Canadian about her writing? Is this coolness of spirit, this clarity of vision, this refusal to be drawn into the same air as that which is breathed by her characters, in any way characteristic of this country or its literary attitude? It would be absurd to press for an answer, but the question is not wholly frivolous. The edged tools with which she works so deftly are the same as those with which a number of other Canadian writers seek to achieve their effects, and their failure to do what she does springs from a want of native endowment rather than a difference in aim. Artistic control of a rare order is one of her secrets, but it is only one among many.

Control and economy of means have distinguished many of the finest women writers. When they have the gift for it they achieve effects rarely found among men, and never among male writers of the highest order. Jane Austen provides a pattern; anyone who has examined her work seriously is aware of the spareness and austerity of her method. She has, in the highest degree, the art of implying more than she says, without ever appearing to be pinched or withholding. She seems to work through an infinity of detail, but what emerges is much more than the sum of the detail. These words might be applied to Mavis Gallant, making allowance for a difference of aim and of time. Her novels are short but they are not, like some economical novels, dense in texture. On the contrary, they are perspicuous, but we should be greatly mistaken if we supposed that for that reason they could be read in a hurry. They yield up their secrets slowly, and we must be watchful, for the shades are minutely distinguished and we must never suppose we have seized the author's meaning before she has finished expressing it. The form is modern but the quality of the art is classic.

Classicism observes from without, romanticism from within. Mavis Gallant observes from without, not clinically but with calm, not from above, but at a sufficient distance to provide a full view and a perspective. The classic attitude is not wanting in pity, but it is aware that pity can do extremely little for its subject, and may become self-indulgence in the one who feels it. Mavis Gallant permits herself no self-indulgence as a writer, and invites none from her reader. But it would be a very great mistake to suppose that the classic attitude, functioning under such controls, is wanting in life. On the contrary, the controls enhance and intensify the life, and it is such intensified life that we feel in these novels. And the strongest intensification of life is that which they evoke in the reader. It is not often that one can say that a writer's work enlarges and cleanses one's understanding of life, but we may say so honestly of the art of Mavis Gallant.

Canadian Fiction Magazine, No. 28 (1978)